AFTER SOCIALISM

New Directions in Anthropology
General Editor: Jacqueline Waldren

AFTER SOCIALISM

Land Reform and Social Change in Eastern Europe

Edited by

Ray Abrahams

Berghahn Books
Providence • Oxford

First published in 1996 by

Berghahn Books

Editorial offices:
165 Taber Avenue, Providence, RI 02906, USA
Bush House, Merewood Avenue, Oxford, OX3 8EF, UK

© 1996 Ray Abrahams

Library of Congress Cataloging-in-Publication Data

After socialism : land reform and rural social change in Eastern
    Europe / edited by Ray Abrahams.
        p.   cm.
    Includes bibliographical references.
    ISBN 1-57181-910-X (alk. paper)
    1. Land reform--Europe, Eastern--Congresses. 2. Europe, Eastern-
    -Rural conditions--Congresses. 3. Agriculture--Economic aspects-
    -Europe, Eastern--Congresses. I. Abrahams, Ray, 1934-   .
    HD1333.E852A36   1996
    333.3'147--dc20   96-38
                                                             CIP

British Library Cataloguing in Publication Data

A catalogue record for this book is available from
the British Library.

Printed in Great Britain on acid-free paper
by Biddles Ltd, Guildford and King's Lynn

CONTENTS

Contents

LIST OF TABLES

LIST OF FIGURES

ACKNOWLEDGMENTS

A book like this is very much a collaborative effort. I am very grateful to the Economic and Social Research Council for the provision of a grant to hold the workshop on which the book is based. I am also grateful to Churchill College for help in administering the grant, and to the staff of the Møller Centre at the College for their help in hosting the workshop. Secretarial and administrative staff in the College and in the Department of Social Anthropology in Cambridge have also provided valuable help in the production of the manuscript. Lastly I thank all the participants for their ready cooperation and help in making this book possible. It would be impossible to find a more positive and cheerful group of colleagues. Deema Kaneff in Cambridge and Nigel Swain in Liverpool were also particularly helpful in the editing process. I hope that in my role as editor I have been able to do sufficient justice to both their and others' efforts.

Ray Abrahams
Churchill College, Cambridge
1996

ix

INTRODUCTION

Some Thoughts on Recent Land Reforms in Eastern Europe

Ray Abrahams

*T*his volume presents the results of a workshop on the Privatisation of Agriculture in Eastern Europe which I convened, with the support of the Economic and Social Research Council, at the Møller Centre, Churchill College, Cambridge from 22 to 24 September, 1993. Eight of the nine participants, including myself, are academic sociologists or anthropologists with active research interests in this field in the countries dealt with in their contributions. The ninth, Dr Kuddo, whose academic training is in economics and demography, has substantial practical experience in the formulation and implementation of national economic policy in addition to more personal interests in the rural areas of his country. Like him, Drs Kocik and Kovacs are also citizens of the countries they discuss. In choosing the participants, I aimed to bring together a small effective working group whose expertise covered a reasonably wide geographical range, while at the same time allowing some overlap of regional research experience. The workshop itself had several functions. It enabled the participants to come together for three days of focused discussion with others whose research interests were similar to their own. Ideas were exchanged, valuable new contacts were made and

1

old ones reinforced. In addition it was intended that participation would lead to the preparation and publication of a set of papers which were presented in preliminary form at the workshop.

The present volume of papers dealing with Albania, Bulgaria, Estonia, the Czech Republic and Slovakia, Hungary and Poland sets out to fulfil this aim. The main purpose of this introductory chapter is to offer some general thoughts about the subject matter of the papers. At the same time, I have also thought it useful to present some of the findings of my own Estonian research both as a complement to Dr Kuddo's discussion and to illustrate some of my arguments and comments.

The papers focus on a variety of aspects of recent agrarian developments following the dramatic shift from Soviet and other official forms of eastern European Communism in the late 1980s and early 1990s. Given the common origins of most of these systems, and the shared experience of Communism in them all, it is not surprising that several themes recur in current attempts to transform them. I will return to some of these themes shortly, but it is perhaps also worth remembering that land reform and policy-based rural transformations have a longer history and a wider distribution than such a relatively narrow focus may suggest.

Of course, socialism and/or reactions to it have figured prominently in many past and present instances of land reform in other areas of the world such as South-East Asia, Latin America, and southern Africa. Yet the existence of agrarian laws aimed at land allocations to army veterans and to the poor in republican Rome, and the history of comprehensive land consolidation and enclosure legislation in Britain and Scandinavia, testify that the significance of land as a focus of reform cannot simply be reduced to its inclusion in a specifically socialist or anti-socialist political package. Rather it tends to have important social, physical and economic attributes that both transcend such packages and, at the same time, render its inclusion in them very likely.

This point is perhaps less obvious in Britain, with its mercantile tradition and its long history of urban settlement and industry, than it is elsewhere. Under a wide variety of regimes, however, land is the most fundamental productive resource, apart from their own bodies, which human beings have at their disposal. As such, it is not surprising that it has been a source of bitter and often violent conflict among those who seek to control its use and possession, as well as an important subject of practical and academic interest to social and political scientists, economists and lawyers.

As a 'gift of nature' which outlives its users, but which can be rendered more productive by their efforts, land readily becomes the focus of arguments about the most effective ways to utilise it and about the rights of individuals and groups to own and dispose of it. Despite possibilities of reclamation and improvement, it remains a relatively inflexible factor of production, and there is commonly not enough of it to satisfy the ambitions of all sections of society. Also, as the location on which humans live, work, find their sustenance, and reproduce themselves, it is commonly endowed with highly charged moral and symbolic value. Professor Hann's discussion of the work of Malinowski in the first part of his chapter is an apt reminder of some of the more general and persistent issues in this field.

My research in Estonia has drawn my attention sharply to some aspects of this point. I was initially attracted to work there when I learned in the late 1980s that family farming was beginning to develop once again after several decades of collective and state farm agriculture following the country's incorporation into the Soviet Union. After a couple of brief visits, I carried out field research on this process in the summers of 1991 and 1992. At the same time, as my work progressed, I began to learn that certain basic features of the current situation had a history which went back well beyond the Soviet period.

One such feature is the tension between large-scale and small-scale agricultural enterprises. This dates at least from the special mixture of German baronial estates and peasant smallholdings, whose gradual demise began in the nineteenth century with the emancipation of the peasant serf population and the beginnings of free family farming. This last was in turn temporarily disrupted by attempts at collectivisation in the wake of the Russian Revolution, followed by the further establishment of family farming in the 1920s and 1930s. The Second World War and the see-saw of Russian and German occupations culminated, of course, in the Russian takeover and the eventual collectivisation of agriculture after the brutal deportations of 1949. Today, after the dismantling of that system, there remains considerable uncertainty whether the future of Estonian agriculture lies in family farms or in large-scale cooperatives and agricultural companies. In the course of all these movements back and forth, remarkably similar arguments were advanced from different sides about the relative efficiency of larger and smaller forms of agricultural production units, with feudal lords and Bolshevik revolutionaries alike supporting the idea of large-scale integrated farms. One may compare here too the claims of Count Vigyázó, discussed in Professor Hann's chapter, that his Hungarian estate constituted an integrated whole which it would be folly to break up and divide among the peasantry.

A second and related continuity in the Estonian situation is closely linked to a further theme developed here and elsewhere by Professor

Hann.[1] This is the issue of the 'meanings' of land. The situation is again one where change is clearly taking place, but where it can also be sensibly portrayed as taking the form of a shift of emphasis between component elements which recur persistently over the last century and a half. In this case the two main elements involved are the idea of land as a productive resource for a community and/or society, and of land as private property owned by individuals or groups. Complexly interlocking with this is the further distinction between land as a fundamental element in a symbolic system of moral and social values and land as a commodity. Part of the linear change involved in this situation has been the classic shift, as part of European and ultimately world-wide developments, towards the definition of the human person as an individual right-bearing actor, and of society as simply a collection of such individuals. Of course, there are and have been many sticking points in this process, and there are signs that a variety of attempts are beginning to be made in Estonia and elsewhere to resist it at the ballot box and in other contexts, and to establish a different equilibrium in which jural *responsibilities* and the rights of 'society' and 'community' in one form or another will be given more weight.[2] Professor Juhan Kahk has interestingly documented some of this process of change among villagers from the days of feudal serfdom to the establishment of land-owning farming (and for that matter non-farming) families.[3] This in turn has led on to contemporary demands for the restitution of pre-collectivised holdings to their former owners or their heirs.

Such demands have met resistance from a number of quarters. There are some, including many new private farmers, who consider that the wholesale restitution of small parcels of land to people, who may not wish or are unable to farm it, is a recipe for agricultural disaster. Others, for a variety of reasons ranging from personal gain to a concern for social welfare, are keen to preserve at least some features of the state and collective farm system. Much of this resistance can again only be properly understood as part of a set of persistent comparabilities in the agrarian history of the country, and many villagers themselves have been aware of these. During the Soviet period, similarities between feudal estates and collective farms were often noted, and the nick-name 'red baron' was often used for state and collective farm leaders, just as the term 'grey baron' was used

1. Cf. Hann (1993).
2. One may note in this context the development in the United States and parts of Europe of an interest in so-called 'communitarianist' theory, as well as a series of election results in eastern Europe including those of March 1995 in Estonia.
3. See Kahk's historical contribution to Abrahams and Kahk (1994).

for the first large peasant landowners after the dismantling of feudalism – the grey was due to the colour of their clothing – clearly evoking their similarity to the old German barons even though they were Estonians. Of course, as Dr Swain remarked at the workshop with regard to comparable uses of the term 'green baron' in Hungary, there has been an element of name-calling and political point scoring in such usage which cannot be adduced simply as evidence of structural persistence. Such continuities do seem genuinely to exist, however, and the tensions and tendencies they represent also seem to be among the main features of the longer term historical map of agriculture in Estonia and elsewhere in eastern Europe.

Legal Options

All the countries under review in the present volume have recently emerged from a lengthy period of Communist rule, and most of them have experienced similar patterns of collective and state farming during this period. In most of the countries concerned, family farming was officially abolished after the Second World War and peasant holdings were subsumed on Soviet lines into a complex system of eventually quite large-scale collective and state farms. This was done with relatively little regard to regional differences though, as I shall discuss, agricultural production on such farms was also typically, and at times substantially, supplemented by farm workers and their families on small private plots. As Professor Kocik describes, the main exception to this general pattern was, of course, Poland. There too, a collective and state sector was established under Communism as the officially favoured form of agricultural production. It was in practice relatively small, however, with the state taking ownership of only twenty-four percent of land, while large numbers of family farms continued in operation there under an overarching state regime of 'repressive tolerance'. As such, the process of dismantling the Polish collective and state sector, and of redistributing the land and other capital resources which were included within it, has not involved as large a proportion of land and rural population as in many other countries.

At the same time, it is important to note that all the countries under consideration here came under Communist control at much the same time – around the end of the Second World War – and much later than Russia itself. This is significant because the time-span of roughly fifty years since then clearly falls within the bounds of living, and often enough bitter, memory for a considerable number of people. Moreover, even when those who were most directly affected have died, the events concerned still mean a great deal to their immediate descendants and others who were very close to them. This was particularly noticeable in Estonia, where many thousands of people were labelled as *kulaks* under Soviet rule and deported to Siberia on the orders of an occupying alien regime, and where fear was the main driving force in the recruitment into the collective farms of many of those left behind.

The relatively short history of Communist control in these countries – though it seemed long enough to many who experienced it – has understandably led many governments to try to return to something like the pre-Communist *status quo*. As Dr Swain notes in his paper, this involves a variety of legislative options. In some cases the direct *restitution* of previous land holdings, perhaps coupled with payments of compensation for other property lost in the processes of collectivisation and nationalisation, has been the aim. In other cases, various forms of what he calls *indirect restitution*, which I would prefer to call compensation, have been espoused. Different forms of such compensation for lost land holdings are possible. Alternative pieces of land *in natura* or, as in Hungary, vouchers to enable one to purchase other land, may be provided, or former owners may be simply given money. In some cases, however, he notes that the legal question is, at least in theory, not so much one of restitution or compensation, as of the *regeneration* and *reactivation* of ownership rights technically held by individuals in cooperative resources. In such cases, the rights in question, and especially those of free disposal, had never been formally abolished, but it was impracticable to attempt to exercise them.

The decision to follow one or other legislative line depends in part, as Dr Swain notes, on such earlier differences, though it is not always easy to draw hard and fast lines between different cases on the ground, especially when formal rights may have little practical significance. Such decisions also turn, of course, on a variety of political factors, and these include the relative strength of different interest groups and parties, both inside and external to the country, at the time when legislation was enacted. Thus it seems clear that Polish legislators have not felt under sufficiently strong pressure to make them grasp the nettle of providing redress for the 'legalised expropriation' of villagers' land when it was 'sold' to the state farms. More generally, one may note that the political struggles which have led to the adoption of particular bodies of legislation are little guarantee that the economically most effective or even the morally most satisfying solution to local problems of transition will be found.

The Estonian Legislative Experience

Here again, the Estonian situation may be enlightening. The first moves to explore the possibility of a return to family farming, beyond the level of the private plots on the collective and state farms, were made during the last years of the Soviet regime when a few people were leased land on an *ad-hoc* basis by the farms in different parts of the country. Reputedly the first of these was M.S., who in 1987 was granted twenty hectares of land around a farm house he had bought some years before. He was initially granted this land on a short lease from the local collective farm with the blessing of Party regional headquarters, and the initial agreement was that he should give the farm the amount of produce the land was thought likely to produce under collective use. He was then given the land for a longer period and this arrangement was eventually overtaken by the Farm Law (*Taluseadus*) of 1989. This law was the Estonian Soviet Socialist Republic's first nationwide step away from collectivisation towards the re-creation of family farms, and its provisions have to be understood in the context of Soviet rule which continued formally until Independence in 1991.

Before discussing these provisions, it will be useful first to say a little about the occupation of former farmhouses, on which the law was mainly focused. Some collective and state farm workers were accommodated in centrally situated flats and houses, and many former farmhouses were destroyed or left to go to rack and ruin under Soviet rule. There were, however, still substantial numbers of the now much smaller local population, who were living in such houses, or in new ones built on former farmhouse sites, in the late 1980s. Often the house still belonged to members of the original farming family who lived on the site, but sometimes the property was bought either from the previous owners or from the state or collective farm itself, which acquired it when original owners died out or disappeared, perhaps in Siberia. Sometimes such property was also willed to distant kin or neighbours by its former occupants.

The central feature of the 1989 Farm Law was that it now made it possible for the owners of such houses and house sites to apply for land which previously had been attached to them. The language, as well as the content, of the law is of some interest in this context, in comparison with that of later legislation. Paragraph 8 is headed '*Talu taastamine*' (the re-establishment of a farm), and it refers to the rights of a farm's 'previous owner', as at 23 July 1940, or his heirs, to embark on this process provided that the farm buildings, and with them the rights in question, have not legally passed into

7

the hands of others. Notably lacking, however, is a key expression which figures prominently in many of the more recent laws and regulations. This is the phrase '*õigusvastaselt võõrandatud vara*' (illegally alienated property), which is typically combined with the word '*tagastamine*' (return or restoration). The reference is of course to property which owners lost under Soviet domination, and these later laws clearly challenge Soviet rule in general, and the property system in particular, in a much more direct way.

A great deal of new legislation concerning land and other property was passed in the three years 1991 to 1993. Again, the legislative process in these years has to be seen at least in part as a struggle between divergent political viewpoints, as Dr Kuddo clearly indicates, rather than simply a coherent and rational attempt at problem solving and reform, based on uniformly agreed principles. This probably accounts in part for some discrepancies between the various laws, though a further factor in this context has been the haste with which new legislation has been produced. In this last context, both the pre-and post-independence governments have been faced with an irresolvable dilemma which is familiar throughout eastern Europe at this time. The longer it takes to bring new legislation into force, the more uncertainty remains about the future. At the same time, the rapid introduction of large numbers of new laws whose implications in themselves, and for each other, are by no means always clear, is also the source of considerable anxiety and doubt.

It would not be sensible to attempt even an outline account here of all the many Estonian laws and regulatory decrees of this period concerning the ownership and management of land and other property as these relate to agriculture. There are over twenty of them, and they run into many thousands of words. Moreover many of them are already superseded by new legislation. Major laws were passed on property in general, on land and agricultural reform, and on the evaluation of land. In addition, many regulations and decrees were published on the implementation, interpretation, and occasional modification of these laws. Most recently, in June 1993, a new Law of Rights to Material Things (*Asjaõigusseadus*) was promulgated, and this was followed by a further law defining its mode of implementation and its implications for existing legislation *(Asjaõiguse rakendamise seadus)*.

In these circumstances, I simply draw attention here to some of the major acts involved and to some of their most salient features. In June 1991, the Estonian government passed a law setting out the basic principles of property reform (*Eesti Vabariigi Omandireformi Aluste Seadus*) and this was followed in October of that year by the Land Reform Law (*Maareformi*

Seadus). The Property Reform Law set out the main basis on which property, including land and buildings in both urban and rural areas, was to be returned to its rightful owners. If, for various specified reasons, the actual return of the property in question was not practicable, alternative property or compensation in lieu thereof was to be paid. The law laid down the definitions of such rightful owners and their heirs, and a timetable for such people to apply for restitution of their property. The Land Reform Law further pursued these issues with regard to land in particular, though it recognised the rights of those allocated land under the *Taluseadus* to remain on it. It also extended the range of potential claimants to include the brothers and sisters of a deceased owner and, if they were dead, their own descendants. Some paragraphs of this law were revised in 1993.

In March 1992, an Agricultural Reform Law (*Põllumajandusreformi Seadus*) was passed, and this set out the procedures and timetable for the compulsory winding up of collective and state farms. On each such farm, a Reform Commission was to be established, containing representatives of different local and state interests, and each commission had to develop a plan for the future distribution and organisation of the farm's land and other property and resources.

The new Law of Rights to Material Things constitutes the most radical shift to date from Soviet ideology, since it firmly re-establishes private property as the norm, and sets out the fundamental rights and obligations this entails. The chairman of the State Law Commission, Jüri Adams, highlighted its significance by describing it in Parliament as 'the end of socialism in Estonia'. It supersedes, in varying degrees, all previous legislation, and it provides the legal basis for future capitalist development in the country.

Land Reform in Practice

As one might expect when research has been based on local fieldwork and case study, a recurring theme in several of the papers in this volume is that of a gap between the new laws and reality. In Bulgaria and in Albania, as Dr Kaneff and Dr de Waal show, we find that some communities resist or even ignore the laws in question, which appear to fail to satisfy their perceived needs, and this is partly to be expected when legislation represents specific outcomes of debates between parties with diverse interests and ideologies. It is also predictable that rearguard actions will be taken by those with most to lose from the new legislation.

9

I was able to witness such a local conflict for myself on the western Estonian island of Saaremaa in 1991 and 1992. The Director of the local state farm, and some of his supporters, stonewalled against the implementation of the 1989 Farm Law, and their struggle was continued in the 1992 meetings of the local Land Reform Commission, whose remit was to decide the future of the state farm in accordance with the Agricultural Reform Law. The conflict, which was exacerbated by a history of personal animosities between some of those involved, was waged chiefly between the supporters of family farming and those who wished to avoid dismantling the state farm altogether, and hoped to transform large parts of it by creating a new limited company and a cooperative. The creation of such units is quite legal, providing there is local agreement to do so, and it appears that such arrangements have in fact predominated in the former collective and state farm areas despite official government support for family farming.

In the case I witnessed, arguments in favour of new large-scale units included familiar claims that they would be more efficient agricultural producers, and that they would cater more for the work and welfare needs of those who could not hope or did not wish to farm, and who would have shares in the new ventures. Counter-arguments disputed the claims of efficiency and accused those running the state farm of simply wishing to maintain control. In the end, arguments about the need for a community-wide approach, rather than one focused on the needs of family farmers, swayed some waverers on the commission, and the company and cooperative were founded. Subsequent reports suggest, however, that these new enterprises have been much less helpful to the poor and needy of the area than had been hoped, and many of these are said to have been ultimately driven to surrender their shares in payment for tractor and other services from the two units.

It is perhaps worth noting in this context that the slowness and complexity of large-scale land reform is not simply a modern eastern European problem, since there is ample evidence of difficulties and delays in ancient Rome and eighteenth and nineteenth century Sweden and Finland in addition to some parts of contemporary Africa.[4] Nonetheless, the situation is of course particularly difficult where restitution or compensation is involved. Claims have to be verified, and conflicting claims

4. For political and technical problems of early land reforms in republican Rome under Tiberius Gracchus see Brunt (1971:80-3). For Finland see Abrahams (1991:31). The process of recent land reform and registration has also been slow and ineffective in parts of countries such as Kenya. See Haugerud (1989:63, 80-1 and passim).

adjudicated. After fifty years of collective and state farming there may be many claimants to inheritance, as Dr Kuddo notes, and different families may contest each other's claims when property has been transferred between them. The boundaries of holdings also have to be determined and then registered. In Estonia and many other eastern European countries, the situation threatens to be one in which mainly the lawyers, and in some cases local officials, will benefit, and in which families suffer long periods of uncertainty as they try to amass the complex documentation necessary for successfully asserting a claim. Some of the difficulties of establishing such claims have recently been interestingly brought out in a paper on Transylvania by Katherine Verdery (1994). There, conflicting claims are compounded by problems of inadequate and inconsistent mapping and by changes to the landscape wrought by decades of human activity and even errant river courses. As Verdery notes, such conditions seriously challenge the idea of a land holding, and of land itself more generally, as a solid fixed resource whose extent and location can be fairly readily ascertained by simple investigative procedures.

Some of these problems have been interestingly by-passed by the voucher system, in the case of Hungary, where the high technology of lap-top computers has also been brought to bear on the problem of boundary marking and plot allocation. Yet even here, as Dr Swain reveals, the auction procedure itself is extremely complex and resembles one of the longer forms of 'patience' where the player keeps dealing out and re-assembling a pack of cards until eventually, with luck, a desired formation is reached. Moreover, the procedure has been a developing one which now takes forms apparently not anticipated by the law. Also, the process is still slow and expensive, as Dr Swain remarks, with nationally prescribed deadlines postponed and missed on more than one occasion.

Land Reform and Rural Transformation

A problem which emerges in a number of the cases dealt with in this book is that current reforms focus narrowly on land and other property, and that this fails to take full account of the complex multi-functional character of the institutional system undergoing transformation.

This point is well made by Professor Kocik in his discussion of the Polish situation, and it is particularly cogently argued in Dr Kovacs' paper on Hungary. To some extent the problem is, of course, part of the more general issue of disillusionment with and hostility to the economic inefficiencies and other failings of the Communist system, and the attempts to rectify these by the apotheosis of market forces as the dominant determinant of action. Dr Pine's paper nicely brings out how a wide range of benefits, which the former system offered, have only come to be appreciated in retrospect by many people, as the dazzling promises of capitalism have failed to materialise for them. Guaranteed employment was an important element of the former system. Another was the welfare functions of the former agricultural and other institutions, which have tended to fall by the wayside in the process of reform. Similar tendencies are visible in the resistance of Estonian and some other governments to the provision of direct or indirect subsidy to farmers.[5] Here, as is often said of converts to religion, the new believers are more doctrinaire than many of their teachers in their espousal of the market principle, since most Western capitalist countries in fact provide substantial subsidies for agricultural production by their farmers.

In addition, even at the level simply of agricultural organisation in itself, the transformation of the collective system into one of family farms and modern agricultural cooperatives and companies can easily leave a vacuum with regard to marketing and distribution. In Estonia, some farmers are dissatisfied with the remnants of the previous marketing system of milk and meat *kombinaat*, and are attempting at least in the short term to market produce for themselves through small-scale retail outlets, and no doubt other solutions may be found elsewhere. The problem remains, however, as emerges in a number of chapters, that in this and other contexts a sharp political and ideological polarisation between supporters of large-scale (collective or cooperative) and small-scale organisation, mainly in the form of family farming, threatens to destroy the possibility of fruitful cooperation between them.

Private Plots and Socialist Agriculture

One widespread example of such symbiosis in the socialist period was the allocation of private plots to members and staff of the collective or state farms. These plots had a long history in the Soviet Union and other Communist states, and they provide interesting evidence of the complex reality of what was superficially a monolithic system. Their significance varied

---

5. A small amount of low-interest credit has very recently (from 1995) been made available to farmers in Estonia to help compensate for seasonal fluctuations in their income and expenditure.

from time to time and place to place, but they were certainly important in Estonia, as in several other countries, in more recent years and they have considerable relevance to contemporary developments there.

At first sight such plots might appear to contradict the main principles of the socialist system. Moreover it is true that, in the last years of the system, it was difficult to keep them under tight control and to maintain an equilibrium between them and the needs of the system under whose umbrella they operated. They helped in an important way to keep people ready for the re-emergence of private farming and, as their hectarage increased during the late 1980s, they diverted labour and commitment away from the collective sector.

Nonetheless they were also part of the system. They helped to make the collective farm life bearable – somewhat comparably in Estonia to the 'pay land' holdings of the old feudal serfs – and they contributed substantially for many years to official production figures of state and collective farms. Until reforms began, such workers' plots were normally only 0.6 hectares per person, sometimes with extra hay land and pasture, but they then began to be increased in many places. Even on smaller plots, families commonly kept themselves in potatoes and other vegetables, and some fruit, and they often kept some livestock. Sometimes, the productivity of a family's private plots has equalled or exceeded that of the smaller new independent farms, especially when the family contained several individual plot holders and could exploit collective farm machinery, marketing facilities and other services. For several years, most of the milk and some of the meat produced at home was sold to and through the farms and counted in the farms' production figures. The value of their contribution was acknowledged even by those in favour of the Soviet system and, in a publication on the state and collective farms of Võru region, in south-east Estonia, one such supporter quotes figures for 1984 of 30.8 percent of total milk and 22.7 percent of total meat production in the area coming from what he calls the 'individual sector'.

The private plots also helped at first to maintain some political support for the old system. The creation of new farms under the 1989 Farm Law and later legislation posed a threat to some plot holders, as former owners claimed back land on which the plots were situated, and plot holders were tempted to ally with state or collective farm leaders in their localised attempts to resist this. Moreover, some plot-holding families who decided to take up independent farming prior to the dismantling of the collective and state farms, still hoped in 1991 to keep one or two members working there for as long as possible, if only to retain access to machinery and other services.

Rural Society and Family Farming

As several chapters show, a return to family farming seems to have been an important element in official visions of transformed rural society in post-socialist eastern Europe. Especially in nations like Estonia, whose identity is closely linked to the people's peasant origins, such farming is commonly perceived as both culturally and economically desirable. The ideal of a rural family, working their own land together, making their own decisions on the basis of their intimate knowledge of their farm and the environment, and collaborating with their neighbours only when and if they wish to, is a morally attractive one for many people, in contrast to the bureaucratic, centralised command structure of a large collective or state farm. It is also often argued that such family units are effective economically, if only because their members are committed to the place and are free to enjoy and benefit from the product of their own labour. On the other hand, I need scarcely note that the supporters of larger scale farming enterprises have not simply been confined to socialist 'red barons' in Estonia or their equivalents elsewhere. At the height of Estonia's family farming period in the 1930s, for example, members of the anti-Communist Päts government were pointing to Denmark's and other large-scale farming systems as the only way forward in the modern world.

It would take me well beyond the remit of the present volume, and indeed beyond my own area of expertise, to discuss this issue in its many complex ramifications. Suffice it to say that, in global terms, family farming has been a remarkably widespread and persistent agricultural productive system, and that writers such as Warriner (1964) have argued cogently for its efficiency in certain contexts, such as livestock management. At the same time, it is also true that such a system often enough persists at great cost to its members in both health and labour, and that many farming families typically fall into poverty and debt while others have the fortune to keep going and perhaps even prosper. Coupled with this, it is also true that many farming family members give up farming for a life in the cities where a better material standard of living has often been attainable for less work and risk. Moreover, even where family farms persist in substantial numbers in a European country such as

Poland, this is only understandable in terms of a complex symbiosis between town and country, and between industry and agriculture, in which the farm has served as a base from which at least some family members travel regularly to work in the urban and/or the industrial sector. Different aspects of this well-known point are interestingly illustrated in Dr Swain's and Dr Pine's chapters, and Dr Pine pays particular attention to the regionally varying implications for women of factory closures and the shift in the previous equilibrium between their involvement in farm and village on the one hand and the urban industrial sector on the other.

The impact of current transitions upon different categories of rural women in different eastern European societies is an important and so far little explored issue. I have discussed some aspects of this elsewhere for rural Estonia (1994a), and there are clearly both some 'winners' and some 'losers' in the situation there. Among the former are some of the women who run farms for themselves or participate with their husbands in managing a relatively successful new farm. Most obvious among the losers are widows on deteriorating pensions and younger rural women who have lost clerical and other jobs in the collective sector, without having any clear alternative at their disposal. This pattern seems very likely to be repeated elsewhere in the region.

It is clear that official visions of family farm based agriculture have been only partly realised, and there is more at issue here than the delays, noted earlier, in the processing of land restitution claims. Such a journey 'back to the future' faces many other problems. Firstly, one should note that smaller family farms of the kind abolished under eastern European socialism have often disappeared elsewhere – in countries like Sweden or Finland for example – under capitalism. Also, the contemporary rural areas are often demographically quite different from their pre-socialist state, though there is considerable variation on this. It is true, as Dr de Waal shows, that in at least some areas of Albania, there are substantial numbers of young people still living in the villages, and even in Estonia some thirty percent of the total population and approximately half of the Estonians themselves – as opposed to Russians – live in the rural areas. Nonetheless, the general pattern in these countries is that many people have migrated to the towns in recent decades, and in a number of the cases discussed here, there is a relatively high proportion of older people in the village populations. In some cases, villagers are not even especially eager to claim back their former land, and certainly many who make such claims have neither the wish nor the capacity to take up family farming. In Estonia, for example, there were about 140,000 farms in 1939. By 1994 the number of new farms had reached 10,153, according to the Estonian Statistical Office (1994), and the number of claims was over 200,000 according to some estimates. Yet it is unlikely that more than a small percentage of those claiming land will actually farm. Many people prefer to obtain a title to land than to let it lapse, while some hope younger family members will farm later, or that something can be gained from later sale or rental of the land. Not surprisingly this situation led to much anxiety among some new farmers who received land under the 1989 Farm Law on the basis of their current ownership of a former farm house rather than their previous ownership of land itself. These new farmers at first feared that they might lose their holdings to such claimants, but although their rights have been protected, there remain a number of at times damaging uncertainties about issues of compensation and, in some cases, about the legitimacy of their title to a farm house.

Moreover, even those Estonians who have successfully negotiated the land restitution maze and now try to farm often encounter difficulties. Machinery is scarce, and much of that used on the old collective and state farms is too large for effective use on a small holding. Reliable labour to supplement that of family members is, at least at present, hard to come by. Moreover, there is already competition between farmers. In 1991-1992 conflicts were beginning to emerge in some parts of the country between longer established and other more successful farmers and some of the smaller newcomers. These centred partly on the allocation by the Farmers' Union of overseas aid funds to farmers. The more successful farmers, who described their holdings as 'production farms' *(tootmistalud)*, claimed that the money was being frittered away in donations to many new land holders. They argued that some of these newcomers were not genuinely committed to farming, and that many of them in any case had holdings which would not support viable agriculture under modern conditions. The 'production farmers' also complained that communication with the Union's bureaucracy had to be conducted through local branches which were dominated by such smaller but more numerous newcomers. These in turn argued that more established farmers had received their share of aid, and it was now others' turn. Although the argument with the Union was partially resolved, the 'production farmers' formed local independent unions in a number of areas, arguing that a single Union had served its initial purpose but could no longer represent the interests of all farmers. Such conflict, which relates to that noted earlier between land viewed as property and land seen as a basis for effective agricultural production, seems set to develop further.

Meanwhile, the majority of Estonian collective and state farms have been, for the present at least, largely if not wholly converted into new cooperatives and joint stock companies, as in the Saaremaa example given earlier. These institutions also, of course, have their hazards. Many have been at least initially dependent on material and advisory aid from abroad, and there is a risk that those who run them may be tempted to go in for share accumulation, as I have described for Saaremaa above, and for asset stripping as has already happened in a few earlier conversions. It is too early to judge the future of such ventures in most of the countries concerned, and to assess whether the largely negative reports about their leaders' true agendas are in fact justified. Also, as Dr Kovacs makes clear in her discussion of Hungary, there are many different sorts of new cooperative and limited company whose future depends on a wide range of factors, in addition to their leadership, including both their constitution and their special niche in the wider economy.

Ideals and Strategies

Given the presence of such demographic, technical and bureaucratic difficulties throughout most of eastern Europe – though they vary in their detail from one country to another as the present papers show – it is not wholly surprising if the response to the ideological summons to re-establish family farming is less enthusiastic than most governments appear to have anticipated. There is, however, a further issue which some of the papers raise and which arose particularly clearly during the discussion of Dr Kaneff's Bulgarian material at our workshop. The point was made that not only governments but also academics may be caught up in the ideological atmosphere of the moment, and may assume too readily that eastern European socialism was, in its entirety, always and everywhere a bitterly resented imposition upon villagers. This assumption has become increasingly questionable, perhaps most obviously in the light of recent election results in several countries.

Even in a country such as Estonia, where socialism was never the predominant grassroots ideology, there were of course committed socialists with a genuine concern for the poor. There was also a long history of substantial rural poverty which helped to foster socialist sentiment among some villagers, though many poorer families mainly hoped to gain or keep and then expand their own small holdings. For many people, what really blackened socialist ideas was their connection with the threat and ultimate realisation of the takeover of the country by its immensely powerful and aggressively acquisitive neighbour, who did not wait long before insisting on their violent implementation.

A conversation I had with a former leading south-eastern Estonian Communist, whom I will call A.M., partly brings this out. Unlike several others I encountered, he was keen to remark that he still thought there was much of value in socialist ideas and ideals. His own father had been an impoverished smallholder who, he claimed, found life much easier on one of the first small collective farms. Yet when I asked about the massive deportations of so-called *kulaks* and other 'enemies of the people' in 1949, he spoke with some bitterness about the way in which Estonia had been so cruelly deprived of its best farmers, one of whom was his own mother's brother.

I should add that other evidence suggests that very many people in Estonia disliked even the first small-scale collectives, though the anxieties and attitudes of some were mitigated by the hope that they would not last long. The situation in Bulgaria, at least in the area which Dr Kaneff studied, seems to have been rather different. There, early forms of socialist cooperative and collective seem to have been more generally welcomed by many villagers whose pitifully small holdings offered little promise of a better life, and it is mainly the later large-scale Soviet models of collective and state farms which were more disliked and resented. Such villagers do not seem to hark back ideologically to a 'merrie' Bulgaria of small-scale family farmers, each with their own at least potentially prosperous farm. They seem more inclined to try, if anything, to return to the small-scale 'cooperative' structures of the early socialist period.

My discussion of this issue is quite tentative, if only because it is a subject which demands more study than it has so far received, and such study is not easy. It is a commonplace that the genuinely scholarly history of eastern European socialism, and of the regimes which immediately preceded it, could not easily flourish in the conflict-ridden and often enough heavily oppressive atmosphere of the day. Such study is now beginning, at least in some countries, but even now it is hard to piece together the evidence which would permit a nuanced and well-balanced picture to emerge. There are likely to be fewer lies than before, but the 'silences' of authors and informants may still be difficult to detect and fill, and many people have been keen, at least initially, to move with the times and simply denounce anything to do with socialism. In addition, the question of motivations in such matters is notoriously hard to disentangle at the best of times. While I have no reason to doubt the sincerity of the Estonian Party official A.M., whom I have just quoted, the kinds of events which I outlined earlier, concerning the 'transformation' of a state farm in Saaremaa, clearly suggest that there, as in all political discourse, concern for others can all too easily serve as a rhetoric to disguise self-interest.

At the same time one should also question the extent to which the 'altruistic' and the 'selfish' are inevitably in conflict with each other. In my own varied research experience in rural areas of Tanzania, Finland and Estonia (Abrahams 1967, 1981, 1991 and 1994b) I have been interested to find many situations in which mutual aid and individual interests are by no means incompatible. This was especially noticeable in Finland where, despite a strong self-image of farmers as uncompromising individualists, there was nonetheless a great deal of collaboration and even some joint ownership of major machinery among them. Similarly, machine cooperatives, and other less formal systems of working collaboration among farmers, were common in pre-socialist Estonia and are being resuscitated again in the post-socialist era. The crucial issue in such situations seems to be that people often show genuine concern for each other's needs and problems and are happy to help each other when they are free, rather than forced, to do so. Such willing cooperation is also, of course, often reinforced by internalised moral norms and by local social sanctions whereby reciprocity may be withheld from 'free-loaders' or others who exploit the system. It seems very likely that current eastern European conditions of machinery and other shortages and, in places like Bulgaria, the small size of land holdings also favour the persistence and development of forms of cooperation and mutual aid in many rural communities as, potentially at least, a rational solution to villagers' problems rather than as some irrational adherence to outworn ideals. Yet it is also clear, as I have said, that this potential may be damagingly exploited by politically and economically ambitious individuals.

Rural Leaders

The poet Robert Frost once said that he favoured a 'semi-revolution', and added that the trouble with a total revolution was that the same people ended up on top. This is a recurrent theme in eastern Europe, where 'red barons' and *nomenklatura* have often seemed to do especially well both as new farmers and as the leaders of new cooperatives and companies. It is often assumed that this is simply an undesirable feature of the current situation, but it is in fact a complex matter.

Such men – they seem mainly to be men – were of course relatively well placed to influence the process of transitional decision making, and to hive off valuable resources for themselves by arrangements ranging from the formally legal through the dubious to the more obviously criminal. They were, however, also often relatively well educated, especially in the later years of the Communist period, and this too has no doubt helped them. At the same time one must recognise that many of them have acquired administrative skills, and effective networks of connections, which are valuable for contemporary farmers and for company managers alike, and that many of them were manipulators rather than ideological adherents of the old system. Some of those whom I met in Estonia were more clearly businessmen than Communists, keen to defend their state or collective farm against depredations by the state and competition from new private farmers, if they had not decided to take on that role for themselves.

I should also add that by no means were all new farmers drawn from the new 'baronial' class. Some had simply been collective farm workers waiting for an opportunity to get into farming, and others had been drivers, sailors, builders, or school teachers. It seems significant, however, that whatever their previous employment may have been, many of those who have taken up farming in Estonia have rural origins and come from farming families themselves. This has provided them with valuable previous experience and a 'feel for farming', and it is worth noting here that such characteristics do not appear to be equally widespread in all eastern European countries and especially those, like Slovakia, with relatively high levels of involvement in and commitment to work in industry. Moreover, what many of the more successful new Estonian farmers have in common, in addition to some educational, social and economic capital, and the foresight to get started early, is a crucial capacity for organisation and hard work, and the determination to persist in the face of what appeared at times to be insuperable difficulties. These qualities are not acquired simply by holding office in a state farm or other socialist enterprise, and they are vital for success under contemporary conditions of uncertainty and change.

The Future of Rural Society

It is hard enough to understand the present without trying to forecast the future, and I do not make any serious attempt to do this here. What the present chapters show, however, is that rural life in eastern Europe is full of uncertainties, and it is clear that many of these lie largely out of the control of villagers themselves, and in some cases that of their governments. It is also clear that while many villagers in such countries have been glad to see the back of Russian domination and of Communism generally, they have also begun to miss some of the security and support which the old system provided. Such people are sharply aware that current legislation and agricultural policy are often the result of political in-fighting among parties and other, often enough urban-based, interest groups. Of course some policies, such as those regarding subsidies, are also strongly influenced by pressure from external aid donors, while the viability of agriculture, as the most obvious and for many the only possible main source of rural livelihood, more generally tends to depend on outside markets and involvement in a global economy of food and other supplies.

At the same time, it is clear that agriculture faces difficulties in western Europe also, where subsidies are also under scrutiny, and some of the pressures on the farmers of the West – such as those arising from 'green' and comparable legislation and protest – have yet to hit their eastern counterparts. Some solutions being thought of in the West to problems of this sort – such as farmers 'managing the countryside' as a viable and profitable tourist attraction – do not seem realistic to those trying to wrestle with the harsh economic realities and scarcities facing most eastern European countries. It can only be hoped in these circumstances that eastern European governments and rural communities will manage to find at least some solutions of their own to the problems they face. At least as far as Estonian villagers themselves are concerned, I have not found a great shortage of determination and adaptability, which some more pessimistic commentators have expected as a characteristic legacy of the Communist period. Many individuals and families are ready to try new ventures and to seek new market niches – nutria farming, roof-tile manufacture, and various forms of trading and tourist provision are among examples I encountered – in addition to combining waged work and farming where this was possible.

Such efforts, and indeed agriculture itself, do not seem likely to succeed, however, without some state provision of a genuinely facilitating environment. Nor do the weaker members of rural communities, the old and unemployed, appear able to cope without help in a situation not of their own making. More generally, it has often seemed to me a paradox that while many western Europeans have been cursing 1980s orthodox monetarist capitalism as the source of many of the ills of their society, eastern Europeans have often been quite impatient to adopt it. If rural society has a future anywhere, and the same may be true of European society more generally, it may well be that a viable middle ground between the two extremes of socialism and radical capitalism has to be found, however discredited this idea had become by the beginning of the present decade.

REFERENCES

Abrahams, R. *The Political Organization of Unyamwezi*. Cambridge, 1967.

_____, *The Nyamwezi Today*. Cambridge, 1981.

_____, *A Place of Their Own*. Cambridge, 1991.

_____, 1994a 'Women and Rural Development in Contemporary Estonia', *Rural History*, Vol. 5, No. 2, (1994): 217-26.

_____, 1994b 'The Re-generation of Family Farming in Estonia', *Sociologia Ruralis*, Vol. XXXIV, No. 4, (1994): 354-68.

Abrahams, R. and Kahk, J. *Barons and Farmers: Continuity and Transformation in Rural Estonia (1816-1994)*. Göteborg, 1994.

Brunt, P. *Social Conflicts in the Roman Republic*. London, 1971.

Hann, C. 'From Production to Property: Decollectivization and the Family-Land Relationship in Contemporary Hungary', *Man*, Vol. 28, No. 2, (1993): 299-320.

Haugerud, A. 'Land Tenure and Agrarian Change in Kenya', Africa, Vol. 59, No. 1, (1989): 61-90.

Estonian Statistical Office *Agriculture, Forestry and Fishing 1993*. Tallinn, 1994.

Verdery, K. 'The Elasticity of Land: Problems of Property Restitution in Transylavania', *Slavic Review*, Vol. 53, No. 4, (1994): 1071-109.

Warriner, E. *Economics of Peasant Farming*. London, 1964.

1. LAND TENURE AND CITIZENSHIP IN TÁZLÁR

Chris Hann

There is no more jejune and fruitless distinction in primitive sociology than that between individualism and Communism … Almost to spite the anthropological theorists, the Trobriander insists on having his own plot associated with his personal name. This old opposition is a vicious and unintelligent short-cut, because throughout this discussion the real problem before us was not the either-or of individualism and Communism but the relation of collective and personal claims. (Malinowski 1966: 380)

Introduction

*I*n this chapter I argue that Bronislaw Malinowski's approach to land tenure, though hardly the best known component of his oeuvre and apparently applicable only to certain types of preindustrial society, can offer valuable insight into the contemporary transformation of rural Eastern Europe. Malinowski was himself an Eastern European intellectual, and the full importance of his Polish origins for his later anthropology is still being uncovered (Ellen et al. 1988, Thornton and Skalnik 1993). His intellectual individualism gave him a powerful aversion to anything smacking of Communism, an aversion he appears to share

23

with the Eastern European peasants who have had collectivisation and other radical changes (including now decollectivisation) imposed upon them. I shall argue, however, that Malinowski's rejection of the 'either-or of Communism or individualism' should be extended beyond the range of societies he had in mind. It is important to look behind the competing political rhetorics of our age and examine instead the realities of changing collective and personal claims before, during and after the socialist period. My investigation in this chapter will be restricted to the village of Tázlár, which I shall attempt to situate in wider regional, national and east-central European contexts. Though I do not claim this village to be an archetype in the way that Malinowski implicitly claimed general relevance for his Trobriand studies, I do think that the Tázlár materials demonstrate many points of wider significance. First, however, I will outline the main tensions in the Malinowskian approach to land tenure: tensions between broader and narrower definitions of the subject, and between Malinowski's ostensible rejection of the individualism-Communism dichotomy and his militant personal antipathy toward the latter in the European conditions of his day.

Malinowski lays out his position in the final two chapters of the first volume of *Coral Gardens and Their Magic* (1935). These are the culmination of his ethnographic writings about the Trobriand Islanders and also, as Edmund Leach points out in his Introduction to the second edition, 'a most brilliant demonstration of what Malinowski meant by functional integration' (1966: xii). Malinowski argues that a full appreciation of land tenure requires detailed understanding of the entirety of what the next generation of anthropologists was to call the 'social structure'. He specifies a restricted definition of land tenure as 'the body of rules which govern the practice of cultivation and apportionment of produce' (1966: 376). However, it is essential to locate these practices in a wider context of economic activities, legal titles and also 'mythological foundations'. Here Malinowski has in mind primarily the local myths of original emergence on which sub-clan titles are based. In the matrilineal but patrilocal society of the Trobriands the sub-clans' legal titles do not correspond to the groups that make 'effective economic use' of the land.

> There is thus a permanent split – or perhaps better, there is a double facet to ownership. In its productive aspect it is vested in the men of a local community, their spouses and their children. Such an agglomeration of families constitutes also to a large extent the group of consumers. At the same time, the men and women of the same sub-clans retain jointly the legal claims to

their matrilineal patrimony – if this compound term may be coined. And this unity is embodied in the institution of the *urigubu*. (1966: 378)

Land tenure, in Malinowski's hands, turns out to be far removed from the dry, arcane topic that generations of colonial lawyer-anthropologists made it out to be. Since land was the key resource in preindustrial societies, the study of land tenure must be extended to embrace the full complexity of the social arrangements for meeting the claims and entitlements of citizens.

Malinowski's central polemical purpose in *Coral Gardens* is to transcend the dichotomy between Communism and individualism. This recurrent theme in nineteenth-century anthropology had received its fullest treatment in L. H. Morgan's *Ancient Society* (1877), which in turn became the basis for Engels' *The Origin of the Family, Private Property and the State* (1884). For these writers, the story of human evolution was a story that began with 'primitive Communism' and proceeded through the divisions of different kinds of 'class society' as the encroachments of private property grew ever greater. Morgan, like the orthodox Marxist tradition to which he contributed so much, was convinced that such 'individualist' trends in contemporary society must be reversed. In contrast, Malinowski's 'functionalist' anthropology left no room for evolutionist arguments of any kind. He did not believe that it was possible to obtain reliable information about the origins of human societies, and in place of speculation and conjecture he sought instead to trace the most detailed links possible between different social institutions synchronically, i.e., as they could be observed during fieldwork. It is entirely consistent on his part to argue that, instead of a general evolution from communal to individual, the Trobrianders in fact demonstrated a subtle blending of the two. Thus the sub-clan can be represented, according to Malinowski, by an individual, and although almost all work is done by cooperative groups (notably the 'gardening team'), 'individual titles exist and the land is subdivided, as it were, almost in deference to the desire for individual distinctions' (1966: 378). Hence his rejection of the 'vicious' opposition of individualism and Communism.

This rejection is, however, incomplete: it applies to primitive society only. In the final paragraph of the book Malinowski associates both Communism and fascism with 'the advent of the machine', and the publications of his final years reveal him as a nostalgic, rather romantic European liberal, committed to the superiority of capitalist individualism over the rival collectivist ideologies of his age (Mucha 1988). It seems

now to be widely accepted among Melanesianists that these values viti-
ate the overall analysis of Trobriand social relations. Malinowski persistently describes Melanesians in terms more appropriate to Western
individuals and fails to see, for example, that a district headman's relation
to other villagers cannot be adequately explained in terms of Western
concepts of the person. The exclusion of history is also a major weakness
that later anthropologists have struggled in various ways to overcome.
Yet in spite of these weaknesses, critics have continued to find Malinowski's materials stimulating (often for purposes quite different from
those he himself envisaged). In the context of decollectivisation in Eastern Europe, his invitation to consider 'the relation of collective and personal claims' remains a valuable starting point, as is his insistent advice
to explore land tenure in the broader sense, 'beyond the legal point of
view'. Let me now turn to open up such an enquiry, diachronically
rather than synchronically, in the Hungarian village of Tázlár.

Tázlár before Socialism

Tázlár is not on the face of it the most promising setting in which to
bring Malinowski back to Central Europe. This settlement was largely
abandoned for several centuries after the Ottoman conquest of the Great
Hungarian Plain. It was resettled only in the final decades of the nineteenth century when rapid rates of population growth in neighbouring
regions led to land shortages, prompting the conquest of this 'internal
frontier' (Hann 1979, 1980). Hungary at this time was experiencing the
uneven effects of capitalism. Budapest, a mere eighty miles away, was
expanding rapidly to become a major European metropolis, but industrial progress was slow and, until the radical Land Reform of 1945, large
areas of the countryside were dominated by repressive and inefficient
large estates. Most of the lands of Tázlár were gradually split up and sold
off by their absentee owners, who initially comprised members of the
'feudal' aristocracy and gentry, but later included others such as Jewish
businessmen and traders. In some parts of the region the land was sold
through auctions, but most plots in Tázlár were sold following adver-
tisement through banks and paid for through a mortgage. They were
very close to being parcels of pure private property: no confusions of title
or doctrine of original emergence here!

 The history of this process of resettlement and the formation of a new
community can be illuminated with the help of statistical and other doc-

umentary sources. The population grew from a few hundred in 1880 to over three thousand in the generation before 1950, before falling back to the present figure of around two thousand (further data concerning population and the area under cultivation in the inter-war period are presented in Hann 1980: 6). Of course, one needs to exercise caution in interpreting historical source materials. I am more aware today than I was at the time of my original fieldwork of the diverse backgrounds and motivations of those who settled in Tázlár.[1] Probably most immigrants aspired to establish 'autonomous' family farms, i.e., to own their own land as private property and to farm it using exclusively familial labour. Some bought large areas and relied on extensive methods of farming. Many later arrivals had only small acreages, on which they sought from the beginning to make a living from intensive gardening and viticulture. In all categories, the immigrants generally built their farms on their plots. Consequently there was very little consolidation of a nuclear centre. It should also be stressed that the quality of the soils varies very considerably across the territory of Tázlár. Some sections, particularly the fields known as 'Church Hill', thought to be the site of a medieval settlement and close to what has grown into the centre of the modern village, had fertile dark soils that obtained a high Gold Crown valuation from the state's land surveyors. However, the soils of many of the peripheral parcels were of low value and a grave disappointment to immigrants from other regions.

It was not long before this settlement too experienced 'land hunger'. Poor peasants demanded more land after the First World War, as is illustrated in a document drawn up by a Budapest lawyer in 1924 on behalf of Count Vigyázó, at the time one of the largest landowners in the country. The Count wished to oppose proposals to redistribute some of his lands in line with the Land Reform legislation of the time. His lawyer addressed the following text to the National Committee supervising the implementation of these reforms:[2]

To make the relevant problem and the correctness of my point of view understood I must direct the attention of the Honoured Tribunal to the soil

---

1. I owe this greater awareness in large part to Antal Juhász, Professor of Ethnography at the University of Szeged, whose current research is concerned with migration patterns in the Danube-Tisza region in the period in which Tázlár was repopulated. See Juhász (1990).

2. This document was discovered in the County Archive in Kecskemét by Mr Pál Szabadi, to whom I am most grateful for allowing me to cite it here. For further discussion of social and economic conditions and 'land hunger' in Hungary and the wider region during this period see Warriner (1939) and Jackson (1974).

conditions in the area in question, to the distinctive features of the situation in the vicinity of Tázlár.

This is an incredibly barren world. One only has to leave the path of the railway to enter a real desert. The rough tracks wind their way between sand dunes as high as houses, even in late autumn the cartwheel sinks down completely into the sand. There is no sign whatsoever of any vegetation on these dunes, and the bleak and desolate spaces can barely support even a few weak thorn-apple bushes and spurge. Even the lightest breeze sets these dunes in motion and when they start to move they threaten to engulf the entire area. After an hour's cart ride in this sandy wilderness one gets the unavoidable impression that one is exploring not Hungary but some wild African landscape.

Those who know the area of Kötöny *puszta* [then part of Tázlár, now attached to a neighbouring community] will assure you that these descriptions of mine are not too strong or exaggerated ... The very best fields of this area would, in other regions, be classified as land unsuitable for the purposes of the Land Reform measures ...

The lawyer proceeded to argue that it was in the public interest not to inflict any of this appalling land onto the poor claimants, but to respect the integrity of the Count's property. His estate was primarily forest, which the Hungarian state at the time was trying to encourage everywhere. The lawyer argued that trees were especially important in this area to prevent further widespread movement of the sand dunes. As for the areas of pasture and ploughland owned by the Count, these were secondary to the estate but nevertheless essential to the functioning and financing of his forests. The lawyer strenuously rejected allegations from the government's inspector that the estate had kept too many animals on too small an area, and had, in effect, pursued a policy of ruthless short-term exploitation *(rablógazdálkodás)*. On the contrary, argued the lawyer, even more animals were needed to help fertilise this dreadful soil! Therefore, the text concludes, Count Vigyázó should be left to manage the heritage of his family in his own way, since there was no doubt that 'his private interest coincided with the public'. To allocate sections of the estate to small peasants would be to split up key sections of forest, an 'absurd result'. Finally, the lawyer attempted to deal with another element in the package before the tribunal by casting doubt on whether the claimants from this very poor village really did possess the animals to warrant the proposed increase – at the Count's expense – in the area of collective pasture.[3]

3. Throughout this period some land was communally administered as pasture. All residents were able to gain access to this land through payment of the appropriate fees.

The outcome of this case is unclear but there is no record, either in the archives or in popular memory, of the Count's estate having been broken up. The area in question was not settled and farmed by peasants. After the Count's death it apparently passed to the Hungarian Academy of Sciences, before being taken over by the Forestry Commission in the socialist period. It is still known as the Vigyázó forest.

It may be useful to think of the economic developments of the pre-socialist period in Tázlár as a kind of involution (Geertz 1963). Ever greater numbers of people sought to intensify their agricultural activities, but the supply of land was limited and there was no technological break-through and very little capital accumulation. One consequence was that many people had to work ever harder in order to maintain the same low standard of living. At the same time (in contrast to Geertz's perhaps sanitised Indonesian presentation) social differentiation became even more marked. The very top layer consisted of rich and powerful landowners like Count Vigyázó, who probably never even visited their properties.[4] Much more numerous was the category of middle and rich peasants, people who relied on the labour of other, poorer though not necessarily landless families to operate their farms. The links between households took various forms, among the most common of which was the institution known as *cselédség*. The *cseléd* was generally a young boy from a poor family, who would join a more prosperous household and work for it in the fields as well as in the home right up to the time of his military service. In addition to a small money payment, his parents would receive occasional gifts in kind, and the relationship frequently became a long-term 'patron-client' bond. The patterns of economic cooperation were no doubt less intricate than those identified by Mali-nowski in the Trobriands. Even so, with some women in richer families not participating in field work, and some men in poorer families com-muting long distances to seek supplementary income, the overall picture was clearly much more complex than the ideal type of autonomous fam-ily farming to which most peasants aspired, and which had impelled them to migrate to Tázlár in the first place.

There is much further evidence of desperately poor living conditions in this community during the inter-war decades (see Hann 1980). It is doubtful whether any further distribution of poor quality sandy soils

---

4. It is alleged in the contemporary village that large tracts of the worst quality land were regularly bought and sold in the pre-socialist period by commissioned army officers, who were required to prove that they held estates above a certain size to qualify for membership at the Budapest Casino.

would have made much difference. The inhabitants of this region were in effect excluded from Hungary's stymied semi-feudal society during this period, as the sociographical works of the young Ferenc Erdei show very clearly (see Hann 1995). Even the more prosperous residents of a village like Tázlár were 'peasants', and a great gulf separated them from the citizens of the capital. I find the concept of citizenship to be a useful one here. Residents of Tázlár had many economic rights: the market in land remained very active throughout the pre-socialist period, though for most people, opportunities to participate effectively in the national economy were severely restricted. In the political sphere it seems clear that by the inter-war decades a certain very undemocratic style of citizenship was well established: Hungarian nationalist tendencies were so strong that the large Slovak and Swabian German groups in this region were obliged to give up not only their languages but even their surnames (usually replaced by a similar sounding Hungarian name). For the residents of villages like Tázlár, however, the civic and social dimensions of citizenship were barely developed at all.[5]

Tázlár under Socialism

This period can be sub-divided into two roughly equal parts. In 1949 the Communist Party succeeded in eliminating all its competitors and the whole country was thrown into a phase of high Stalinism. The same year saw the foundation in Tázlár of the first socialist cooperative farm, called the *Red Csepel*. This seems to have taken over most of the lands redistributed to poor peasants in Tázlár in the course of the 1945 Land Reform: these had not provided a sufficiently strong base for viable family farming. During the next few years further cooperatives were founded and here as everywhere else in the country the more prosperous peasants were subjected to land appropriation. In many cases they were brought to financial ruin in circumstances of grave personal harassment and humiliation. At least one peasant alleged to be a *kulak*, i.e., to belong to

5. The term 'citizenship' of course derives most directly from 'city' which itself derives ultimately from Latin *civitas* (the state). The word has a long history in Western philosophy, but Malinowski found it useful for elucidating the broader understanding of property rights in the Trobriand Islands, as did Gluckman (1965) for the Barotse. The classic sociological work outlining the various dimensions of citizenship remains Marshall (1977). The concept has generated renewed interest of late: for a stimulating introduction to recent debates see Andrews (1991), and for innovative anthropological usage see Minnich (1992).

the class of exploiters, was driven to suicide. As the acreage required to qualify as a *kulak* was determined nationally and did not take into account local ecological conditions, many of the peasants who suffered from these policies were actually very far from wealthy. Some had barely produced for the market at all. During these years peasants were also instructed to grow crops that were quite unsuited to the sandy soils, and several major investments in orchards by the new cooperatives proved to be ignominious failures. Many families migrated permanently to the cities in the 1950s.

The political pressures were relaxed after the trauma of the 1956 'counter-revolution', when all existing cooperatives collapsed. Just five years later, virtually all peasants were dragooned into new cooperatives as mass collectivisation was completed nationwide. However, the peasants of Tázlár did not experience this as the decisive moment that it undoubtedly was for many other peasants throughout the socialist world. The type of cooperative formed in this district allowed most families to continue farming their own lands in more or less the traditional way. The requirements of members to contribute to the 'collective sector' of the cooperative were minimal, and in practice those who wanted to were able to evade even these theoretical commitments. The so-called 'specialist cooperative' was favoured in this region of Hungary in order to maintain a high degree of flexibility and avoid the economic losses which would undoubtedly have followed had the conventional (*kolkhoz*) model of cooperative farm been imposed in a region of scattered settlement and small-scale viticulture.

For ideological reasons the authorities and cooperative leaders were obliged to maintain that, in the fullness of time, the specialist cooperative would lose its distinctive characteristics and converge with the standard form of cooperative. The collective sector did expand significantly, mostly through the acquisition of poor quality land that no one wanted to farm privately. In the middle of the 1970s, when I began fieldwork in the village, there was a wave of politically induced pressure to convert some of the best quality lands at Church Hill to collective use. This was implemented despite bitter opposition. Those affected were offered plots elsewhere in compensation, but without legal title. The general tendency of these years was for the cooperative to facilitate high levels of production in the 'private' sector, through the provision of improved services to members in all phases of production and marketing. This was the pattern which I identified as a symbiosis of private and collective, or better, of small-scale and large-scale agricultural activities. It can also be approached in Malinowskian terms as 'functional integration'. Labour-intensive activities were complemented by the capital-intensive activities of the collective sector, which could, for example, supply fodder produced efficiently in the collective sector to enable the family labour force to continue to produce pork for the market without needing to work outside the farmyard.

In general the 1970s and 1980s saw a tremendous expansion of agricultural output. The supportive policies of the government (apart from the above-mentioned hiccough in the mid-1970s) played a vital part in this. The fruitful combination of large-scale and small-scale was also encouraged in this region by significant subsidies that the government paid for output in territories deemed to be of 'unfavourable natural endowment'. The picture was different in villages which had only the standard type of cooperative, though even here other models of integration developed around the various forms of private plot arrangements (Swain 1985). There was also, of course, significant variation within villages. Some peasants in Tázlár were determined to have nothing to do with the new cooperatives; they carried on farming in traditional ways and, if they resented having ten percent of the sale price of their product deducted by the cooperative, they usually had no great difficulty in finding alternative private marketing channels. At the other extreme a few farmers became totally dependent on the cooperative for large quantities of inputs, including additional leasing of land. Most villagers were somewhere in-between. Very few were enamoured of the socialist institution, and for some families the constant accumulation of petty grievances over many years during the 'gradualist' consolidation of the specialist cooperative, left them every bit as bitter as those who experienced comprehensive collectivisation and separation from their family-owned means of production. The Tázlár cooperative was dogged by leadership instability and generally incompetent management. At least some of the various services on offer, however, which included a range of social services to disadvantaged members, particularly the elderly, were taken up by virtually everyone, even those who clung to the self-description 'peasant'. Many villagers preferred to describe themselves as *kistermelok* ('small producers'), while one very anti-Communist man ostentatiously described himself as *magán gazdálkodó* ('private farmer') on his visiting card.[6]

6. Another elderly man vociferously rejects the new entitlements. He lives on an isolated farm to which he was relocated when his original home was appropriated for the consolidation of a large-scale field in the collective sector in 1977. He insists that the food potentially available to him from the canteens in the village centre is likely to be poisoned, and he still maintains this line even now that the canteens are no longer socialist.

The last decade of socialism saw a much more stable cooperative (by now unified, the territory of the cooperative corresponding to that of the village) that was able to carry the programme of symbiosis a good deal further. For example, it was able to utilise generous state supports to finance investments in large-scale vineyards, in which certain tasks could be carried out using modern, mechanised techniques, while others would continue to require the labour inputs of the family. Such vineyards were classified as part of the collective sector, but they were parcelled out on twenty-five year leases to individual members (for further details see Hann 1993b). The leaseholders had to pay an annual fee to the cooperative for its mechanical services, but they had every incentive to tend the vines as if they were private owners in the fullest sense, since they were responsible for harvesting and marketing (again the cooperative was usually able to offer assistance with the latter if required). Through this and other investments the capital value of the land base rose sharply in the later socialist period.

Over the socialist period as a whole it is clear that there were radical changes in production techniques. This was the opposite of involution. The population was now falling (due to lower birth rates and continued out-migration), while output and incomes rose dramatically. Even the most conservative peasants, those who refused any measure of integration into the new cooperatives, became materially better off in the decades of mature socialism. Perhaps the most serious drawbacks of this period were the high social costs of prosperity: many people worked for very long hours in tasks of great drudgery, often in addition to a regular wage-labour job. They were exploiting themselves rather than other people, but in so far as the pursuit of wealth was accompanied by features such as ever higher levels of alcohol abuse, it could be maintained that some of the constraints of the traditional moral community were disintegrating. Yet this 'traditional community' should not be reified: this settlement of scattered farms and diverse immigrants had never had a great deal of social cohesion. It can equally plausibly be argued that there was more cohesion and cultural homogeneity in the socialist period, particularly as more and more families found it advantageous to move to the new centre.

Land ownership did not play a significant role in this conjuncture. In Tázlár, unlike the Trobriands, we cannot speak of a split between the productive and the ownership aspects of land, since legal title normally remained with the original owners. However, when land was required for the consolidation of the collective sector, alternatives were offered for use, but without title. The actual pattern of land attachments thus became very complex. In the later socialist decades the ownership aspect was demoted almost to the point of irrelevance, while all effort was spent on increasing production (cf. Hann 1993a) Certainly size of acreage ceased to be a significant social indicator, for in the new situation hardly anyone was interested in expanding their arable holdings to anywhere near the former *kulak* threshold. Long established vineyards were the most crucial assets in enabling families to take maximum advantage of the new economic opportunities. Some were able to expand and intensify their production to levels at which they once again became dependent on a certain quantity of hired labour to supplement (or even completely to replace) family labour. However, most labour transfers between households were based on direct and indirect reciprocity, and there was almost certainly far less recruitment of non-family labour than had occurred in the pre-socialist period.

Finally, it is important from the point of view of citizenship to note some general social and political trends of the socialist period. The civic rights of individuals were accorded no more respect in the 1950s than were private property rights in land. In the sphere of politics there was generally less opportunity for free expression in the machinery of local government than existed in the agricultural cooperatives. The longest serving council chairman was an unpopular Communist with no local family connections. He was removed from office following corruption charges in the early 1980s, but the council, though it commanded more trust from villagers thereafter, never became an open and democratic organ. No agencies operated effectively in the public sphere, least of all the Communist Party, the only sanctioned political association.

The picture is rather more positive if we look at social improvements of the socialist period. Public investments in roads, parks, cultural and educational facilities etc., were dwarfed by the sum of private investments, but they were significant nonetheless. Bringing these villagers effectively within the scope of a national health care system (through the crucial establishment of a doctor's surgery in the village) and within the scope of an education system that offered all children a thorough eight year's basic schooling, followed in the great majority of cases by secondary education, were major achievements. The guarantee of local employment which almost all men enjoyed throughout the socialist period was not quite equally available to women; but the cooperative itself built up a number of sideline activities that created job opportunities in the village for those rural women who were effectively disqualified from seeking work elsewhere. In general, anyone who sought a job outside the family farm was able to find one without too much trouble. These, then, were among the major benefits of the socialist forms of citizenship. It should again be emphasised that they were experienced much more positively in the later decades of socialist government than they were at the beginning.

The Marshallian tradition in the analysis of Western democracies is to argue that the accumulation of civic and welfare rights compensates citizens for the inequalities of capitalist class structures. In contrast, in this socialist case a radical attack on the old class structure was accompanied by a decline in civic and political rights (though in the Hungarian case these were only feebly developed in the pre-socialist period). This period was then followed by an expansion of entitlements in the social and economic dimensions of citizenship. Some analysts suspected that such a path would necessarily lead to a new structure of class inequality, perhaps resembling the old, but the experiment was brought to a close before any definitive answers could be given. One thing is certain: the legal ownership of land did not have the same social prestige in the socialist period that it had previously enjoyed.

Tázlár after Socialism

Massive changes have taken place in Hungarian agriculture in the last few years. It is possible that at least some of the changes experienced in Tázlár would have taken place in any case, as a consequence of more general trends in agricultural markets throughout Europe, not to mention environmental factors that have also had a substantial negative impact on many villagers. I have argued elsewhere that many significant changes in this village began well before 1989 (Hann 1993b). Nonetheless, the most dramatic changes have been brought about by the change of government and rural policy in Hungary, combined with the loss of markets due to the demise of socialist systems in neighbouring countries.

The process of accelerated change began with the 'naming' of cooperative property (everything except the land itself) in 1990. 'Shares' were distributed to all those deemed to have contributed to the assets of the cooperative, whether through land taken into collective use, produce sold through the cooperative, or labour carried out for wages or salaries. The formula used to determine these allocations was approved at a general meeting of the members: it took into account the size of the original land contribution, the value of produce sold and the value of an employee's work, measured by the income paid to him or her. Because of its complexity, probably few villagers understood the implications of this formula. Some were retrospectively highly critical of the large share allocations made to senior leaders as a direct function of their high salary levels. Most were puzzled by the whole exercise, which left them with pieces of paper that they could not readily convert into any other form of asset. It was theoretically possible to dispose of shares to other members, or to the cooperative itself, but few in fact availed themselves of this possibility. Those who did so made use of their allocation to acquire some machine assets when these were sold off by the cooperative in 1992. The vast majority have held on to their shares, which will pay an annual dividend depending on the farm's performance.

A quite separate exercise, implemented for many Tázlár villagers in the course of 1991, was that set up by the national Compensation legislation. Those who had land or other assets expropriated at any time during the socialist period were able to claim partial compensation – partial because, as Nigel Swain points out in this volume, unlike most neighbouring states, Hungary opted not to aim at restitution of the original lands taken. The vouchers issued after the adjudication of Compensation Law claims can be realised for a variety of ends, including cash. However, the market that has developed for these vouchers in urban locations does not exist in the village. In any case, some people would not, for reasons of principle, consider using their vouchers for anything other than the acquisition of land.

In 1992 it was necessary in Tázlár to undertake a third major distribution of paper assets, this time covering all the cooperative's land that was not already owned by individuals or scheduled for individual ownership through auctions as provided for in the Compensation legislation. By now the cooperative had decided not to continue with collective sector production. The unit for the distribution of these lands was the Gold Crown, the same quality measure that underpinned land distribution under the Compensation legislation. The area involved was considerable, and the formula adopted was the same as that for other cooperative assets two years earlier. Like the property shares distributed earlier, these land shares cannot be alienated outside the community.

The situation in these years was extremely fluid. If Hungary as a whole, because of the decision not to implement full and direct compensation, presents a more complex picture than other countries of the region, the specialist cooperative, with its peculiar blend of family and collective farming, represents the extreme of messiness within Hungary.

In spite of the best efforts of both cooperative officials and the new demo-cratic council to disseminate accurate information, with many families acquiring new types of paper asset annually there was considerable con-fusion among villagers. Many people had the impression that the goal posts were being constantly moved. For example one farmer, whom I reported in an earlier publication (Hann 1993a) as being in conflict with his sons over whether he should use his Compensation vouchers to claim back his patrimony (remote and economically marginal) or some other land that he had been using more recently with a lease from the cooper-ative (nearby and economically attractive), found in 1992 that he would not be able to use his vouchers for either, as neither plot fell in the area scheduled for the auctions. However he was able to regain his original plots from the cooperative immediately, and whether or not he obtains title to the land close to the village will now depend on whether it is claimed by its original owner or a descendant. He was angry again in 1993 because, although he lives in the centre of the village, he did not find out about the first auction until it had already taken place: there was a small parcel of land in the area sold off for which he would have liked to bid because it had been associated in the past with his wife's family.

Many difficult cases have arisen because, once again, legislation passed at the national level cannot possibly provide solutions to all the eventualities of specific communities. The Compensation legislation requires more documentation than most villagers can readily provide, and they are not used to hiring lawyers to conduct the necessary searches. In theory it is possible to make claims for Compensation with-out submitting all the specified documents if satisfactory witnesses can be found to testify to the precise assets confiscated. However Tázlár is located fifty-five kilometres from the county town of Kecskemét where the Compensation office is located, and it has not proved practical for villagers to take up this opportunity. Many matters are referred instead to the local Land Distribution Committee, which is composed for the most part of persons of middle peasant background, and generally upholds the line that wherever possible the claims of the original own-ers should have priority.[7] However this cannot be reasonably upheld in all cases: controversy arises, for example, where land appropriated by the collective sector has later been allocated to another individual, who has

7.   As a consequence of this principle cooperative members in effect have two distinct kinds of Gold Crowns following the 1992 distribution: Gold Crowns issued in relation to one's original land always trump Gold Crowns issued in relation to the other elements of the formula (produce sold or wages/salaries earned).

planted vines on it. Some of the most awkward cases have been those where farmers have not been able to produce all the documentation to submit a claim under the Compensation legislation, but the Gold Crown allocation to them in 1992 by the cooperative has not been sufficient to enable them to obtain title to land they have actually been using for decades (e.g., if they have planted vines a very high Gold Crown valuation will apply, whereas their allocation from the cooperative will reflect the lower valuation of their original arable plots when these were absorbed into the cooperative's collective sector).

Questions of ideology, and even 'mythological foundations' in the sense intended by Malinowski, have entered strongly into the subsequent debates. In spite of all the evidence for integration and symbiosis in the practice of the later socialist period, the individual/collective dichotomy has never been dislodged from common ways of thinking. In the current transformation there are powerful forces that aim to bring the world of practice back into line with the polarities of this ideology. The Independent Smallholders' Party in some ways mimics the mythologies of the high Stalinist period. It has based its entire political strategy on the necessity of treating the property relations of the immediate pre-socialist period as sacred (property relations understood of course in the narrower sense, referring to legal title). It was the most popular political party in Tázlár in the free national elections of 1990, and is well represented on the Land Distribution Committee. In this party's representations of socialism the abuses of the early 1950s are held to exemplify the entire period. Its members dismiss the socialist period as one of neglect or short-term over-exploitation of the environment *(rablógazdálkodás)*, and they deny that the specialist cooperative was a form of cooperative that brought many benefits to its members. Smallholders organised a petition to the cooperative in 1990 for the restitution of the Church Hill lands (the high quality lands drawn into the collective sector in the mid-1970s). When no decision was forthcoming they took direct action to parcel out these fields according to the original private boundaries. The cooperative acquiesced in this 'self-help', which took place not long before it announced its complete withdrawal from collective agricultural activities.

The New Family Farmers

Who are the new landowners and farmers? It is extremely difficult to detect the trends in a village such as Tázlár, because the general prospects in agriculture remain so bleak. In any case the process of auctioneering has been slow to begin, and as of 1993 no new pattern of ownership exists to be analysed. It is easier to illustrate why I am sceptical of some of the grander theories being debated by sociologists than to propose any general theory of my own.

One general theory suggests that the old élites of the socialist period will successfully convert their power. According to this theory (for general discussion see Hankiss 1990), they will exploit their political advantages in the transition to ensure that ownership of desirable resources passes to them. Such patterns can be observed in many sectors of the Hungarian economy, and Swain has also detected them in agriculture where the so-called 'green barons' are just about the only group able to take advantage of the conditions which the Smallholders' policies are helping to create (1993).

In Tázlár there have been three distinct phases in the leadership of the cooperative, the major socialist institution in the village. In the first phase there were several cooperatives, led by local peasants, none of them especially successful. In the second phase the newly unified cooperative was led by a group of qualified experts who had no family connections in the district: they lasted only a few years. In the third phase the senior leaders have been non-local, but from farming families in the same district. The chairman since 1982 has combined a middle peasant background in the neighbouring village with an agronomist's qualification, and this has been the most stable period in the cooperative's history. There have been various accusations of illicit 'conversions' as assets of the cooperative have gradually been sold off, e.g., the cooperative employees obtained tractors and other machinery at, so it was alleged, knock-down prices in the mid-1980s (see Hann 1993b). It was also alleged that one of the senior officials in charge of arable farming was able to protect and augment his own personal activities during his period of cooperative employment. However, these people, if indeed they did benefit as agricultural activities were scaled down, were not even Party members. One looks in vain in this village for a 'green baron élite' that has lined its own pockets in the final phase of socialism. (Perhaps the only example of a former 'red baron' is the disgraced former council chairman, who was able to buy his council house very cheaply and still lives in the village, though he is outside its moral community). The present leaders of the cooperative and its long-serving chairman have never been Party members. Yet there is a suspicion, as noted above, that the asset distribution process has been so managed as to place these officials in a strong position to realise significant personal aggrandisement in the community in the near future.

Another much debated general theory is Szelényi's model of interrupted embourgeoisement. Devised in the 1980s when socialist rule was still firmly in place, this suggested that many of those prospering in Hungary's flourishing 'second economy' were the direct descendants of those who had embarked upon an embourgeoisement in the pre-socialist period. Somehow, in spite of their inability to pass on land and property in the traditional peasant manner, the *kulaks* had passed on their 'cultural capital'. Hungary was in consequence experiencing the apotheosis of its bourgeois revolution in the conditions of mature socialism.

This is an ambitious theory, but it is rather hard to verify with the statistical materials available. It is likewise difficult to specify the mechanisms and the values underpinning this cultural devolution. Kovách has criticised Szelényi for borrowing somewhat superficially from Bourdieu. Rather than take over the concept of cultural capital and assume its uniform transmission, one needs to examine in more detail the values and *habitus* of different rural groups (Kovách 1988). For example, there were some groups of high prestige in the pre-socialist period whose values, such as a reluctance to allow their women to engage in field work, inhibited the family's ability to resume embourgeoisement: success in the small-scale farm economy of the 1970s and 1980s required full mobilisation of household labour, that of women included (Szent-Györgyi 1993).

It is in this group that one can see generational differences most clearly. In Tázlár as in so many villages the children and grandchildren of *kulaks* have for the most part moved away: they have invested in urban housing, and in education, and although some may become owners of land once again through the Compensation laws, they are not going to re-enter farming. As for those who have stayed in the village, few if any can see a future in the land at the moment. Those with resources to invest are putting them into tourist-related activities or other local services, but are not attracted to investing in the land. They explain this reluctance readily enough: why should they, as individuals, take on the huge risks of farming, in conditions where the authorities no longer provide any technical assistance or a guaranteed market for the produce? Why should they, as individuals, pay high insurance premiums to enjoy basic health care, an entitlement that had previously been automatic (and remains so for those engaged in wage-labour)? Moreover, for many younger people, in contrast to their parents and grandparents, the land has become more like an impersonal commodity. This commodification is exemplified by the large-scale vineyards, which have physically obliterated the distinguishing features of the landscape. The scale of the technology is revolutionary and alienating, and when people talk now about buying and selling parcels of these fields they do so without sentiment, without reference to the precise location of their rows within the whole. In contrast, an elderly farmer of middle peasant background is struggling to have one of these large investments bulldozed so that he can regain full legal ownership rights and resume small-scale mixed farming on soil that he regards as his patrimony, land the whole community still labels with his family name.

There is potentially a third group that seems not yet to be the focus of any general sociological theory, though I doubt that its presence is confined to Tázlár. It consists of ordinary cooperative members with a poor peasant background, who as a result of the recent asset distributions may receive an opportunity to acquire better quality land than that previously owned by their families. Some of these people, who have been working with machines and with animals and have retained more of the practical farming skills that have been lost in families that have invested more in education, may be better placed in terms of their *human capital* to make a success of family farming – even in the current bleak conditions. It is likely that they will lease land from owners who belong to the other groups: thus the 'productive aspect' will again diverge from legal ownership, and the Malinowskian invitation to probe beyond the latter will remain compelling.

These three groups and scenarios are of course ideal types and the realities will be more complex. My own guess is that new farmers will emerge from all three groups in roughly comparable numbers, just to spite the sociological theorists! Owing to the breakdown of the old class distinctions, in which land ownership played such an important part, these are not clearly bounded groups at all. Some men of poor peasant origin have married into families with a good land base and can now claim their compensation vouchers *and* their share entitlements. Nevertheless these groups and the conflicts between them do have some recognition from the villagers themselves.

In the discussions that take place among villagers, the legitimating claims of different groups are seldom based on legal title alone. The more powerful claims are those based on work, though on very different types of work, and the age factor is at least as important as social class. For most elderly villagers, it is the sweat of their forefathers that justifies their single-minded attempts to regain ownership rights over their 'patrimony', i.e., the plots associated with their family names (including 'matrilineal patrimony'). They are scornful of arguments that such principles may not be economically rational in a radically new situation. In fact, though upholding the principle of private property, they are contemptuous of the principles of market economy, and of all those who prosper through 'turning money' *(penzt forgatni)* rather than through honest labour. Some younger members of the cooperative emphasise the manual work they have put in over many years in justifying their claim to a generous share of the resources now being distributed. Least persuasive in the eyes of most villagers are the claims of the leaders of the cooperative that depend upon recognition of the productive value of their own white-collar contributions. We can see here the curious congruence of long-standing peasant evaluations of work and the official Marxist ideology of the socialist period.[8]

The first and third groups identified above are the specific creations of the socialist period. In alliance together they can out-manoeuvre the radicals in the second group. The cooperative chairman has followed just such a course throughout the transition. He has astutely presented himself as a leader genuinely concerned with the collective interests of all the residents of the village, while allowing his number two, the chief agronomist, to be perceived in some quarters as the potential green baron, concerned only with his personal aggrandisement. At general meetings of the membership this leadership is augmented by some tame lawyers who can be relied upon to say that only the chairman's proposals are feasible given the constraints of law. Voting is usually decisively influenced by the blocks formed by the cooperative's own work force, who can be relied upon to support the chairman who has given them their jobs (for a detailed account of such a meeting see Hann 1993c).

The very survival of this cooperative, when so many others have disintegrated, may be taken as evidence that many people value the security

8. Older values are also frequently asserted in criticism of the cooperative as it now scales down its agricultural activities and behaves as a more rational market-oriented organisation. When in the autumn of 1992 the leadership decided that, given the market conditions, in the Tázlár environment it made no sense to continue with arable production, this led to negative comments locally and even an article in the county newspaper. How could a distinctively agricultural community abandon its heritage now, when the previous cooperative had basically maintained the territory's bread-producing function throughout the socialist period? Fields that were well tended in the past are now reverting to the kind of landscapes so graphically described in the 1920s by the lawyer quoted above.

and entitlements that it continues to provide.[9] The more doctrinaire smallholders dismiss the communitarian rhetoric used by the cooperative leadership as subterfuge, designed to disguise their long-term private ambitions. A common assumption is that the leaders, whose own links with the land are in other communities, will use their paper assets to obtain some of the most valuable forest land. They will then immediately realise their profits, thereby establishing the pattern for post-socialist *rablógazdálkodás*. The critics also point out that the resources distributed by the cooperative to its members in recent years are in a very real sense not the products of local labour at all, but of the vast resources that the state poured in to agriculture, particularly in the areas designated as having unfavourable endowment. It angers them that the fruits of such public subsidies should now flow into private pockets. Yet, as we have seen, the conversion processes in Tázlár cannot be classified as narrowly red or green: they are genuinely multicoloured, in that large numbers of villagers can be persuaded to feel that they stand to gain something through the formulas applied.

The land itself does remain the focus of strong moral sentiments that appear to transcend group divisions, including to some extent even the generational differences emphasised above. Some villagers are prepared to concede cooperative officials their share of collective property (the assets distributed in 1990), but they regard as unacceptable the allocation according to the same formula of the land itself to non-locals. Land may not be a valuable asset in the present market conditions, but even here in a community of relatively recent settlement where land was parcelled out as a private commodity, there is strong support for the view (endorsed by several of the political parties) that it should not be available for purchase to foreigners. There is little danger that the soils of Tázlár will prove attractive to any outside investors, but people resent what they can hear through the media about developments elsewhere: specifically, I heard strong criticism of decisions to pay compensation to Jews now domiciled in Israel, though it was acknowledged that the likelihood of such people wishing to become landowners again in Hungary was minimal. Perhaps this antagonism toward new outside forces is to be

9. The cooperative did undergo a significant change of name. Previously known as the Peace Agricultural Cooperative, unlike many other socialist organisations it did not need to change the first term. However, when a new Constitution was approved in 1992, it was agreed to drop the word agricultural, in line with its transformed economic profile. Most of the cooperative's income is now obtained through two 'industrial' sidelines, making plastic bags and the upper parts of shoes.

expected now that the socialist state is no longer the easy scapegoat that it was for four decades.

Most villagers are also agreed that even the best soils of Tázlár will not permit profitable arable farming, and that the markets for the labour-intensive products of the vineyards show no sign of recovery. Perhaps, some people argue, with the industrial sector undergoing major restructuring and unable to absorb superfluous rural labour as it did in the 1950s, the country as a whole faces a renewal of stagnation. This can be glossed as a prediction of involution in the classic Geertzian vein. Large numbers of people will struggle to survive through the strategies and simple techniques that were so successful for them in the 1970s and 1980s, but which are now no longer viable in the new climate, following the withdrawal of state subsidy and the large-scale back-up services villagers had come to take for granted.

Some people will, however, buy up comparatively large acreages at the forthcoming auctions, hoping to build up viable farms in the future.[10] This is certainly a gamble, and it will no doubt be many years before we can see whether or not such gambles will pay off. One prediction would be that the various types of valuable issued in recent years (Compensation voucher, property share, land share) will sooner or later merge to form one unitary basis of value. As in the classic work of Bohannan (1959), modern 'multi-purpose' money may break down barriers between the 'spheres of exchange'. Barriers such as the restrictions on the alienation of cooperative shares are unlikely to prove effective. According to this argument, control over 'real' money capital will prove more powerful than the possession of 'political' capital inherited from the socialist period, 'cultural' capital inherited from a middle peasant background in the pre-socialist period, or the 'human' capital of those best equipped to work the land. However, it should be remembered that, even in Bohannan's study of the Tiv, land in fact proved resistant to the logic of commoditisation, and we have noted the reluctance to see it pass to outsiders in Tázlár. Even if land ownership is shaped in future according to more purely commercial criteria, the various other forms of 'capital' will remain of considerable significance. The most pure forms of 'market economy' are still dependent upon 'cultural' capital for their smooth functioning. In the case of Hungary and all the other countries

10. At the time of my most recent visit in September 1993, only one auction had been held in Tázlár. This was a very small one, at which the only large purchase of land had been made by the son of a middle peasant family who was no longer resident in the village and had no immediate prospect of farming it himself.

in the region it seems likely that the kind of personal 'network capital' (Sik 1994) that was so crucial throughout the socialist period will remain so for many years to come. For villagers in a place like Tázlár, to have the right connections in the towns for the disposal of one's product is even more important now that the supports from the cooperative have been drastically cut back.

Therefore the new pattern of legal ownership must be recognised as only one aspect of the newly emerging land tenure system in Malinowski's broader sense. Most of the other aspects will depend directly or indirectly on the policies of the state. State action will determine whether the new owners of land have supporting facilities available to them to assist them in their production and marketing. So far the evidence is extremely discouraging: not only have subsidies for the less well endowed areas been removed, but support for the agricultural sector as a whole has effectively been abandoned in the name of 'market economy'. Together with private property, this is the most pernicious of the mythological slogans that underpin the current reworking of the land tenure system in Tázlár.

State action will also determine whether the many aspects of citizenship that developed in a positive direction under late socialism continue to develop, or wither and atrophy. The initial signs are far from encouraging. In the sphere of politics, the local elections of 1990 were fought with passion and enthusiasm in Tázlár; but there has been no lasting change in the working of the council and the institutions associated with it, and in all essential respects the public sphere remains as it was under socialism. In other respects there has been a clear loss of entitlements. Young people cannot find work, and many villagers have lost their rights to free health care. This is perhaps the clearest instance of the post-socialist state acting to widen the gulf between peripheral villagers and the mainstream of the national society, a gulf that was effectively bridged for the first time in the last decades of socialism.

Conclusion

I close with the example of a family that I have known well since my first fieldwork. Péter and Anna have five children, aged between four and nineteen. Their parents and grandparents were entirely dependent for their livelihoods on the land. Péter comes from a middle peasant family, but is physically disabled and for many years has earned a modest salary through white-collar work at the oil company that operates in the region. They live in a house they built (with generous state assistance, in the form of cheap credits) in the 1970s in the village centre. They supplement their income very significantly by raising pigs in the yard and by utilising inherited vineyards, sharing the wine cellars of Anna's widowed mother who lives next door. There is no realistic prospect that this family will consider an expansion of its farming activities. Given the weak incentives now available it is much more likely that their output will contract. Anna's family has pursued Compensation claims and Péter is pursuing land claims through the cooperative, but there is no expectation that they will actually farm any land they acquire through these routes. Anna worked for some time at the cooperative's shoe plant, and received shares in 1990. She sold these to a relative of her husband, who used them to acquire some machinery in the sell-offs in 1992. None of these 'windfalls' will go far towards enabling this family to maintain the standard of living it attained through much hard work in the small-farm sector in the 1970s and 1980s. Anna has therefore quit her job at the shoe plant, where her remuneration was extremely low. In early summer 1993 she, together with a bus full of middle-aged women from the nearby market town, set off to spend six weeks as temporary agricultural workers on private farms in Germany. Although she knew that the hourly rates she was paid were very low by German standards, she was able to save more in this period than she could accumulate in a year's local work. Her working and living conditions, in terms of accommodation and food, left much to be desired. After the first week she was determined to return home. In the end she stuck it out 'for the sake of the children', and now she hopes to take advantage of similar opportunities in future years. She returned to the village to the news that the apprenticeship scheme her second son had been expecting to join following a vocational secondary education had been cancelled. To escape unemployment, he will now try to follow his brother's example and join the police force, though entry into this previously disparaged career has also become highly competitive.

Malinowski concluded the first volume of *Coral Gardens and Their Magic* by saying that he saw no need 'to apologise for having enlarged upon citizenship side by side with land tenure' (1966: 376). I have sought in this chapter to develop a broad approach to land tenure in twentieth century Tázlár. In understanding the transformations that have occurred it is important not to fall back into the rhetorical dichotomies that were first critically exposed by Malinowski (even if he

was never fully able to transcend them himself). We still need, as Malinowski urged, to go beyond the legal point of view. Adapting his broad
approach to the contemporary East European context it is clear that, following decades of rapid improvement, the majority of villagers have
suffered a significant diminution in their entitlements with the demise
of socialism. Rural people as a whole are the losers. Of course some individuals will in the fullness of time emerge as relative and perhaps
absolute winners, but it is still too early to identify them sociologically.
From the evidence of this village so far they will not be simply the inheritors of the 'cultural capital' of a pre-socialist *kulak* class, nor the beneficiaries of the 'political capital' of a socialist dominant class. Each of
these elements may be important, and indeed they are not mutually
exclusive. Nevertheless, before we can welcome the arrival of a new class
of post-socialist 'family farmers' in place of the 'small producers' characteristic of the socialist period, we can expect to see in Hungary the
revival of something like the old class of 'poor peasants': a rural underclass of second-class citizens. This is now the principal threat to the relative cohesion and functional integration that was built up during the
later years of socialism.

REFERENCES

Andrews, G., ed., *Citizenship*. London, 1991.

Bohannan, P. 'The Impact of Money on an African Subsistence Economy',
    Journal of Economic History, Vol. 19, (1959): 491-503.

Ellen, R. *et al.*, eds, *Malinowski Between Two Worlds; the Polish Roots of an
    Anthropological Tradition*. Cambridge,1988.

Engels, F. *The Origin of the Family, Private Property and the State*. New York,
    1972 (1884).

Geertz, C. *Agricultural Involution; the Processes of Ecological Change in
    Indonesia*, (*Association of Asian Studies Monographs and Papers* 11).
    Berkeley, 1963.

Gluckman, M. *The Ideas in Barotse Jurisprudence*. New Haven, 1965.

Hankiss, E. *East European Alternatives*. Oxford, 1990.

Hann, C. 'A Frontier Community on the Great Plain', *New Hungarian
    Quarterly*, Vol. 20, No. 74, (1979): 116-22.

_____, *Tázlár: a Village in Hungary.* Cambridge, 1980.

_____, 1993a 'From Production to Property: Decollectivisation and the Family-Land Relationship in Contemporary Hungary', *Man*, Vol. 28, No. 3, (1993): 299-320.

_____, 1993b 'Property Relations in the New Eastern Europe: the Case of Specialist Cooperatives in Hungary', in *The Curtain Rises: Rethinking Culture, Ideology and the State in Eastern Europe,* eds M. De Soto and D. G. Anderson, New York, 1993: 99-119.

_____, 1993c 'From Comrades to Lawyers: Continuity and Change in Local Political Culture in Rural Hungary', *Anthropological Journal on European Cultures,* Vol. 2, No. 1, (1993): 75-104.

_____, 'Ferenc Erdei and Antal Vermes: the Struggle for Balance in Rural Hungary', in *East-Central European Communities: the Struggle for Balance in Turbulent Times,* ed. D. Kideckel, Boulder, 1995: 101-14.

Jackson, G. 'Peasant Political Movements in Eastern Europe', in *Rural Protest: Peasant Movements and Social Change,* ed. H. A. Landsberger, London, 1974: 259-316.

Juhász, A., ed., *Migráció és település a Duna-Tisza közén.* Szeged, 1990.

Kovách, I. *Termelök és Vállalkozók; mezögazdasági kistermelök a magyar társadalomban, Rétegzödés-Modell Vizsgálat* (IX), Budapest, 1988.

Malinowski, B. *Coral Gardens and Their Magic; Volume 1: Soil-tilling and Agricultural Rites in the Trobriand Islands,* (1st edn 1935) 2nd edn London, 1966.

Marshall, T. *Class, Citizenship and Social Development.* Chicago, 1977.

Minnich, R. G. 1992 *Homesteaders and Citizens; an Ecology of Person and Self-Realisation among Slovene-speaking Villagers on the Austro-Italian frontier.* Bergen, 1992.

Morgan, L. H. *Ancient Society.* New York, 1877.

Mucha, J. 'Malinowski and the problems of contemporary civilisation', in R. F. Ellen *et al.,* 1988: 149-63.

Sik, E. 'From the Multicoloured to the Black and White Economy: the Hungarian Second Economy and the Transformation', *International Journal of Urban and Regional Research,* Vol. 18, No. 1, (1994): 46-70.

Swain, N. *Collective Farms Which Work?* Cambridge, 1985.

_____, 'The smallholders party versus the green barons: class relations in the restructuring of Hungarian agriculture', paper presented to Working Group Three, Restructuring of Agriculture and Rural Society in Central and Eastern Europe, 15th European Congress of Rural Sociology, 2-6 August 1993, Wagengingen, The Netherlands.

Szelényi, I. *Socialist Entrepreneurs; Embourgeoisement in Rural Hungary.* Cambridge, 1988.

Szent-Györgyi, K. 1993 'Embourgeoisement and the "Cultural Capital" Variable: Rural Enterprise and Concepts of Prestige in North-eastern Hungary', *Man*, Vol. 28, No. 3, (1993): 515-32.

Thornton, R. and Skalnik, P., eds, *The Early Writings of Bronislaw Malinowski*. Cambridge, 1993.

Warriner, D. *Economics of Peasant Farming*. Oxford, 1939.

2. THE TRANSITION IN HUNGARIAN AGRICULTURE 1990-1993

General Tendencies, Background Factors and the Case of the 'Golden Age'

Katalin Kovács

(with the collaboration of Zsuzsanna Bihari and Monika Váradi)

Introduction

*T*his study surveys the main tendencies underlying the social and economic restructuring of Hungarian agriculture between 1990 and 1993. Its arguments are partly based on available statistical and survey data, and documents representing various aspects of the agricultural transition. They are also partly based on empirical evidence gained from the study of twenty-four former cooperatives over the last three years.[1] This

1. The research was funded by the Hungarian Research Fund (OTKA IV.). It was led by K. Kovács and administered by the Centre for Regional Studies, Hungarian Academy of Sciences. We are grateful for data and information received from managers and members of former 'Golden Age' cooperative, the Research and Information Institute for Agricultural Economics (István Kapronczai and Gábor Udovecz), from the Ministry of Agriculture (Miklós Betz, Ferenc Nyújtó), from the

was aimed at an explanation of changes in production and ownership structures as particular responses of former cooperative farms to various challenges and pressures of their political, social and economic environment. Individual responses in the new organisations of production can differ considerably from one case to another, in regard to crisis-management, the re-allocation of assets and landed property, and modes of relations linking former cooperative members to successor units. These relations can hardly be uniform since, in addition to the obvious differentiating effects of external factors, they also reflect the multiplicity of organisational and power structures which were present before the transition. In the first section of this chapter we will discuss general tendencies and the stage of agricultural restructuring reached by 1994. In the second section we will go on to describe the successor units of a producer cooperative which we have given the pseudonym 'Golden Age'. We have chosen this example because the 'fault-lines' along which the cooperative has divided (social and settlement boundaries and differences in productive organisation) are illustrative of the wide variety of alternative patterns available to former agricultural cooperatives in Hungary.

Hungarian Agriculture in Transition

General context: changing conditions of agricultural production

During the 1970s and 1980s collectivised agriculture was usually presented as an efficient, successful, and powerful sector of the Hungarian economy. In fact, collective farms provided some 14 percent of the GDP, and approximately 25 percent of all exports – even as late as 1990.[2] According to census data for the same year, one-fifth of the active pop-

Hungarian National Bank (Katalin Korényi, Mrs Dzur) and from the National Bureau for Compensation (Tamás Sepsey and Ferenc Nagy). We are grateful to Ray Abrahams, Alan Bicker, Chris Hann, Anton J. Jansen, and Nigel Swain for their help in the revision of this article and to Anton Jansen and David Symes for permission to include material from my contribution (in Bihari, Kovács and Varádi) to their recent volume (1994).

2. We use the term 'collective farm' broadly to cover the various large-scale agricultural producers of the socialist era such as state farms, producer cooperatives and so-called specialist cooperatives. The latter, existing in a fruit and vegetable-growing area of the Hungarian Great Plain, represented a genuinely peculiar type of cooperative involving a dual organisation structure of private farming and collective, mainly industrial, activities (Kovács 1993 and Hann 1980).

ulation was employed by the collective sector of so-called 'agricultural' cooperatives and state farms. However, only about half of this workforce was directly involved in agricultural production itself. The rest worked in the industrial, service, and administrative divisions of collective farms.

It is difficult to assess the economic efficiency of collective farms because of the distorting influence of state controlled price setting, state subsidies, export and import regulations, and so on. Nevertheless, it is undeniable that such external regulations gave support to the socialist agricultural system. In other words, collective farms were integral elements of a political and economic system that aimed to ensure the conditions of their functioning, to some extent at least, by the use of direct and indirect (macro-economic) regulations. Thus, the deep crisis of large-scale farming in Hungary can be seen as a consequence of the collapse of this wider political and economic system and also, particularly, that of the mediating institutions of the total food production and distribution system (Fertő *et al.* 1992) of which collective farms were essential constituent parts. Although some market economy institutions and techniques had been (re)installed in 1982, and more obviously since 1990, the four years up to 1994 made it evident that building a new *system* is a difficult enterprise demanding much more time than was expected.

The problem of state subsidies granted to collective farms – in other words, the effects of state-level redistribution – has already been discussed in great detail (Illés 1991; OECD 1993). Less attention has been paid, however, to another equally important condition of the profitable operation of large-scale agricultural producers. This is the practice of redistribution within the collective farms along lines overwhelmingly favouring their administrative centres and agricultural divisions at the expense of sub-units with income from industrial and service activities. The aim of this practice was to ensure the overall profitability of the collective farm as an integral unit.

By the second half of the 1980s state-controlled over-management of collective farms had practically been terminated. Henceforward the character and importance of non-agricultural activities of a particular farm were mainly determined by the combination of two factors: the type and quality of natural resources and the economic-geographical character of the farm's region. Industrial and service activities have been the major source of income on collective farms in the following extended areas: (i) traditional industrial regions and agglomerations of urban centres (the north-eastern mountainous region, Budapest agglomeration); (ii) geographical areas unfavourable to large-scale arable cultivation (sandy regions between the Danube and the Tisza and the north-eastern regions of the Great Plain, south-western hills of Transdanubia); (iii) special wine-producing regions (collective farms of the Balaton region and some other areas scattered throughout the country). (See Figure 2.1)

Figure 2.1 The Share of Agricultural Income in the Sales of Agricultural Enterprises 1991

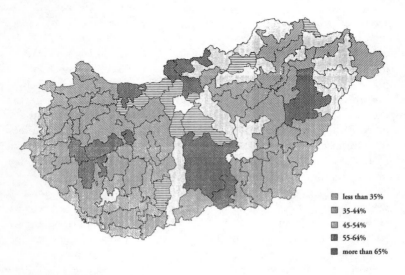

- ▨ less than 35%
- ▨ 35-44%
- ▨ 45-54%
- ▨ 55-64%
- ■ more than 65%

Source: Kovács 1993: 231

It is also important to note that, especially in the first type of area, collective farms pursued industrial activities mainly as sub-contractors of industrial enterprises in urban centres. Under such arrangements, industrial crisis could directly influence the agricultural system since, not surprisingly, these industrial enterprises preferred to see sub-contractors close down and so save their central units, while also cutting back production in the latter. Meanwhile, a considerable number of collective farms were hit by the bankruptcy of industrial firms, and were not paid for their products which had been delivered before the declaration of the bankruptcy. As a result, the production value generated by non-agricultural activities of collective farms decreased significantly between 1988 and 1991 (Table 2.1).

Table 2.1 Changes in the Share of Non-Agricultural Activities in the Value of Output of Collective Farms (1988-1991)

Collective farms		Share of ancillary activities (%)	
		1988	1991
State enterprises		45.5	31.4
Producer cooperatives		38.2	27.2
Partnerships		35.1	41.6
Specialist cooperatives		64.7	64.8
Collective farms	total (%)	40.1	30.3
	billion HUF	145	114

Source: RIAE 1992: 9-10

In summary, two principal factors can be identified as direct determinants in accelerating the crisis of collective farming in Hungary through their fundamental impact on external and internal conditions of profitable operation. The first was *a sharp decline in the amount of state subsidies*, and the second has been the *disintegration or collapse of non-agricultural activities* on many large-scale farms.[3]

Crisis symptoms in Hungarian agriculture

As is well-known, large-scale and small-scale farming in Hungary have constituted a symbiotic system during the last thirty years (Swain 1985); in 1991 the share of small-scale production was 39.8 percent in plant-growing and 52.9 percent in animal husbandry at a time when only about 10 percent of agricultural land was used by small-scale producers (CSO 1993a: 116, 120). The crisis of large-scale farming started in the late 1970s, being one of the reasons for assigning an increasing number of fields of production to small-scale producers. Thus the two sub-systems complemented each other. Undoubtedly, the position of small-scale farming had become increasingly strong until the late 1980s. Since 1989, however, a new, negative tendency has become manifest: contrary to the intentions and expectations of leading political forces, *the entire agricultural system – and not simply the large-scale*

3. The figures from 1989 to 1993 are as follows (in million forints): 1989: 77,163; 1990: 73,144; 1991, 42,039; 1992: 39,120; 1993 (predicted): 47,490. (Source: MF data, 1993).

sector of it – has fallen into a general state of grave crisis. This can be understood as a consequence of the above-noted symbiosis: the sub-systems have not proved to be viable independently. A profound restructuring has been equally important for large- and small-scale agricultural organisations and intermediate (market) institutions. The figures in Table 2.2 clearly demonstrate that 1992 was the year in which the entire agricultural system began to crumble.

Table 2.2 Changes in the Volume of Hungarian Agricultural Production 1988-1992 (1980=100%)

Year	Crops + horticulture products	of which			Live animals + an. products	of which		Total
		vegetable	fruit	wine, grape		live animals	animal products	
	%	%	%	%	%	%	%	%
1988	102.5	98.9	95.6	69.1	102.3	102.4	102	102.4
1989	92.2	80.7	84.3	37.1	99	98.6	100.5	96.1
1990	76.9	78.3	69.1	42.6	92.9	92.7	93.6	87.3
1991	71.1	65.3	40.2	20.6	75.4	75.5	75.3	73.6
1992	44.9	20.4	21.5	19.9	51.6	46.8	68.4	48.8

Source: HNB 1993: 56

Table 2.2 also indicates that the fall in horticultural and livestock production, in which small-scale producers had a considerable share, was more drastic than the overall average of decrease in 1991. The role of collective farms in integrating small-scale production, i.e., providing inputs to production and markets, was fundamental. The cessation of these services has resulted in a sharp drop in small-scale production directed to the market, without generating an alternative source of supply.

The dramatic decline in production in 1992 was also reflected in the foreign trade figures of the following year. In the first six months of 1993 agricultural and food export declined by 32.2 percent (with actual crop exports falling by 72.9 percent!) compared to the same period in 1992.[4] At the same time, although overall agricultural imports also decreased slightly by 0.7 percent, the import of food-industrial products increased by 31.5 percent. (CSO 1993b: 19-20).

4. These figures must be treated with caution because we do not have export volume data, and sale prices and the Rouble/US$ exchange – on a distorted (over-valued) Rouble price in 1990 – influence them. The latter problem does not apply to the 1991-1992 figures.

Predictably, the severity of the decline both in agricultural and ancillary activities resulted in a sharp decrease in employment figures for collective farms. Between 1989 and 1992, manual workers left large-scale farms in proportionately slightly higher numbers than professional and administrative staff (Table 2.3).

Table 2.3 The Number of Active Members and Employees at Collective Farms

Working Groups		1989	1991	1992*	1991/1989 (%)	1992/1989 (%)
Enterprises and partnerships		122,355	110,732	63,930	90.5	52.2
Of which:	manual workers	96,200	84,532	49,376	87.9	51.3
	professionals	26,155	26,200	14,554	100.2	55.6
Agricultural cooperatives		450,397	282,495	197,175	62.7	43.8
Of which:	manual workers	368,125	228,337	157,392	62.0	42.8
	professionals	87,272	54,159	39,783	65.8	48.4

*In organisations providing more than 50 jobs
Source: RIAE 1993: 41

Clearly many interconnected elements have contributed towards the dominance of unfavourable circumstances for agricultural production. The following list includes the most important of them.

(i) A sharp decline in the amount of state subsidies and a disintegration or collapse of non-agricultural activities at many large-scale farms.
(ii) Serious disturbances affecting foreign and domestic channels of the market.
(iii) A severe lag of agricultural prices behind industrial input prices. The price scissors opened rapidly immediately after the liberalisation of the price system: from 109.1 percent in 1989 to 181.5 percent in 1992 (MF 1993). Agricultural producers, although they wanted to, have not succeeded in raising the prices of their products, while domestic consumption declined sharply (40 percent from 1989) and export markets have either been uncertain following the collapse of COMECON in 1990 and/or highly competitive since 1991.
(iv) A series of droughts in 1987-1988, 1990 and 1993, bringing

about a catastrophic cumulative impact by 1993. Credits taken by producers to make up for the serious drop in their incomes make up a considerable share of the total indebtedness of collective farms, even though these credits have received interest subsidies.

(v) These factors resulted in a deep liquidity crisis induced by the accumulation of long-term investment credits taken up in the late 1980s, and short-term credits, which the majority of collective farms had to borrow at a very high rate from 1989. The inflation rate increased from 12 percent to 35 percent between 1988 and 1992, pushing the interest rates far higher (44 percent in 1992) than the possible profit of any agricultural activity. Since that time, collective farms with short-term loans have been caught in a trap of decreasing returns and increasing costs of production. Costs of bank services have been among the most rapidly increasing input prices in the transition period (Kovács 1993).

(vi) Reductions in investments and production expenditure (through cutting back on jobs and technical inputs) have also resulted in a fall in agricultural output.

One outcome of these processes has been a series of bankruptcies and liquidations: one third of all collective farms reported bankruptcy after the relevant law came into effect in March 1992, and some of these (about a third) were liquidated in that year. The proportion of bankrupted and liquidated enterprises was also similar in the case of state farms.

There was also a 35 percent fall in assets on collective farms. The larger part of this loss seems to have been due to liquidity crises, since sales of assets were needed to raise cash or to reach an agreement with creditors. The compulsory transformation of cooperatives, demanded by new legal regulations, accounts for 'only' about 10-15 percent of damage to their assets in 1992. This resulted from the secession of individuals and groups of members who decided to leave the cooperatives.

The above symptoms of decline, aggravated by a severe shortage of capital, are but the natural consequences of the desired transition itself. Needless to say, this fact will scarcely console those having to face the hardships which ensue. Nevertheless, there are some tendencies that might be evaluated as positive steps towards a more effective agricultural system. In the next section we review the stage of agricultural transition reached by 1992 and 1993.

The Restructuring of Agricultural Organisations

The most important indications of fundamental structural changes experienced by agricultural organisations between 1990 and 1993 can be summarised as follows (see also Figures 2.2 and 2.3):

(i) A rapid increase in the number of small and medium-sized companies has taken place at the expense of organisations that employed more than 300 active workers. This development can be attributed to the transformation of former state farms (into public share-holder companies) and the separation or re-establishment of divisions of former cooperatives with agricultural functions. At present, they are usually operating as limited liability companies. The case of the 'Golden Age' presented in the second section of this chapter provides a good example of restructuring in this way.

(ii) Though the case of 'specialist cooperatives' has frequently been cited for its preservation of private farming in the dual organisational structure (see note 1), these cooperatives had very seriously declined (from 67 to 39) by 1992, owing to their vulnerability to industrial crises (cf. Table 2.1 on their production structure).

(iii While in 1990 almost 80 percent of agricultural land had been used by large-scale producers such as state farms and combines (11.7 percent) and producer cooperatives (66.4 percent), their contribution fell below 30 percent by 1993. (State-owned farms: 6.9 percent, producer cooperatives: 21.3 percent).

(iv) About 28 percent of agricultural land in 1993 was used by cooperatives which had adopted a particular alternative form of organisation to that of standard producer cooperatives. This can be termed the *holding cooperative* system. In their operation, holding cooperatives interestingly approximate in some respects to medium-size partnerships working on essentially new, market-oriented principles. Nonetheless, the 'holding' system is essentially a compromise between different principles, and it has the basic shortcoming that it ceases to operate effectively as soon as the delicate balance of a group's founders' interests is disturbed in any way.

Figure 2.2 Restructuring of Agricultural Organisations I: Changes in the Size of Organisations

The Size of Agricultural Organisations (Number of Active Members and Employees) 1990

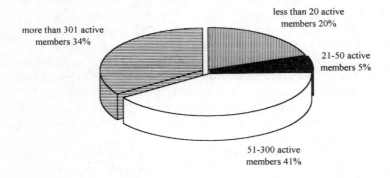

more than 301 active members 34%

less than 20 active members 20%

21-50 active members 5%

51-300 active members 41%

The Size of Agricultural Organisations 1992

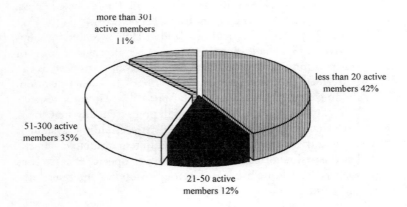

more than 301 active members 11%

less than 20 active members 42%

51-300 active members 35%

21-50 active members 12%

Source: CSO 1993a: 115.

Figure 2.3 Restructuring of Agricultural Organisations II: Changes in Land-Use

Land Use 1990

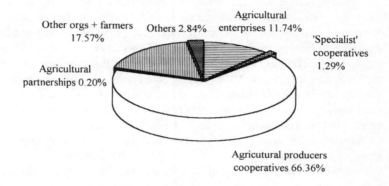

Land Use 1993

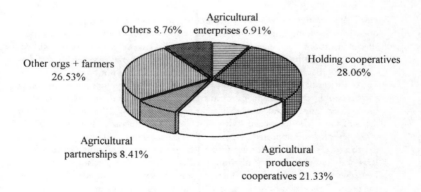

Source: Calculated from data provided by the CSO PD 1990: 46; 1993: 121.

Production in holding cooperatives is usually pursued through limited liability companies (LLCs). LLCs were organised from relatively independent divisions of former cooperatives such as animal farms, plant-growing branches, machinery repair shops, as well as from those of various nonagricultural activities. The managers of LLCs were generally recruited from the ranks of former leaders heading the respective units of cooperatives. Although their autonomy has increased considerably compared to the earlier period, it is still a long way from the degree of autonomy enjoyed by managers of fully independent companies. This can be attributed to two main factors. The LLC is usually not the owner of the assets with which the company operates, and the holding cooperative is usually a majority share holder in the LLC itself. The higher the share of a holding group in the statutory capital of a limited liability company, the smaller is the manager's sphere of autonomy in taking independent economic decisions.

Another factor that poses a fundamental limit to the autonomy of managers is the LLCs' poor access to credit. This is a consequence of their having limited amounts of liquid capital and fixed assets.[5] In this case, once again, we can see the holding unit as the mediator between producers (i.e., LLCs) and creditors (i.e., mainly commercial banks). The holding unit is claimed to be the top representative of the owners' interests as the chief body of the owners' cooperative. In theory, the holding group is not supposed to be directly involved in production. It assumes responsibility, however, for making the best possible use of the owners' property, whether fixed assets or land, and generally it is in charge of the administration of the LLCs.

5.   Until 1994 mortgages could only be imposed on certain groups of assets, most frequently on buildings. Land, however, was excluded from this group of assets and a special institution to manage land-mortgage credits has not yet been re-established. However, an institution for this purpose could hardly operate effectively, considering the fact that hitherto (1994-1995) a new Land Bill had not been accepted and market prices of land were still radically distorted. On the other hand, only asset owners could receive loans from commercial banks. Renters do not have this possibility. These limits considerably reduce the access to working capital and investment loans of those who have been actively involved in production. However, in 1991-1992 new creditors appeared in the market accessible mainly for crop growers; they are the successors of the former integrating organisations of crop production of large-scale farms. These organisations provide loans in exchange for a proportion (generally 40 percent) of the products the applicants wish to produce. The price for the product calculated prior to the agricultural season is considerably lower than the expected produce-exchange price in August, because it must include the interest rates and the creditor's risk as well. Only in recent months have some commercial banks started to provide loans on these grounds as well.

Although holding cooperatives retain a great deal of power, it must be noted that they enjoy significantly less autonomy than former cooperative centres. Crucially, they are not authorised to centralise and redistribute income among producer units, whereas this had been one of the most important functions of socialist cooperative centres. Limited liability companies, even if subsumed under a holding, are economic partnerships with an independent budget that cannot be charged for any service beyond what they receive from the holding at a price settled in advance. We see this as a crucial feature bringing holding cooperatives closer to genuine forms of partnership.

The establishment of this form of organisation could also have some wider social implications. The LLC may well prove to be an adequate form of education through which managers might acquire skills required for managing independent enterprises. Running a profitable business needs open-minded, highly skilled entrepreneurs ready to take risks and a firm stand in negotiations. Otherwise, failure is imminent in today's economy. Thus, the above-mentioned formation seems to be a way of bringing together the rural elite of the future in that it is another way in which social, cultural and entrepreneurial capital is likely to accumulate in a few hands. Thus, the capitalist establishment could become predominant in spite of hostile attitudes – directed against former managers, the 'green barons' of 1990-1992 (see Swain 1993) – displayed by populist political forces and by many of those losing the race of transition. These forces, of course, object to the former managers' having been able to preserve their positions in the new political system.

From the findings set out in this section, we would argue that fundamental structural changes have taken place in Hungarian agriculture since 1990. These structural changes must be considered as steps towards a market economy necessarily accompanied by crisis symptoms analysed in the previous section of this chapter. The structure of agricultural production, both in terms of character and size, is more balanced when compared with the structure prevailing before the transition. Today only one-third of the land is used by organisations that have merely undergone a formal and legal transformation, while functioning according to the policies and principles of the 'pre-transitional' past. These are producer cooperatives, some of the state enterprises and companies. Other organisations have undergone a transformation which has resulted, in addition to the activity of private producers, in the introduction of an alternative, market-oriented model for the agro-economy. These organisations also cultivate about a third of all agricultural land. Finally, the remaining elements such as holding cooperatives and some of the companies are to be found at an intermediate stage of transition in 1994-1995.

Ownership Restructuring

The process of restitution has resulted in severe discrepancies between ownership and the use of agricultural land. The general effects of this process, that is the 'naming' (allocating assets as property shares and land) of collectively-owned assets of cooperatives, are indicated by the figures shown in Figure 2.4.

Active members have received 41.2 percent of collective assets in the form of property shares, while active employees have acquired 0.9 percent. The share of retired members has reached 39.1 percent, while heirs of deceased members and former members (already non-members in December 1991, but having previously worked for the cooperative for at least five years) could altogether claim 18.9 percent. Distinguishing between 'active' beneficiaries (active members and employees) and 'passive' beneficiaries (retired members, former members and heirs of deceased members), we find that the 'active' and 'passive' ratio of assets is 42 percent against 58 percent, respectively, and 29 percent against 71 percent in the case of landed property.

As far as the value of assets and landed property is concerned, retired and former members enjoy a similarly advantageous position with regard to land: an 'average' retired member has received 55 Gold-Crowns' worth of land, while an active member would typically receive 11 Gold Crowns less.[6] On the other hand, the average value of an active member's property share is higher (357,069 HUF) than that of a retired member (277,123 HUF).

The governmental measures concerning land restitution and privatisation of collectively owned and used assets of cooperatives have been strongly criticised by experts and politicians affiliated to the political parties of the opposition in the early 1990s (Juhász and Mohácsi 1993). They argue, rather convincingly in our view, that the modernisation of production has been seriously delayed and disoriented due to the disadvantageous positions of the younger workforce at transformed cooperatives.

6. The Gold Crown is a measurement which reflects the quality of the soil. The average value for one hectare is twenty GC in Hungary.

Figure 2.4 The Allocation of the Assets of Former Agricultural
Cooperatives (1992)

(i) Assets (HUF) Falling to One Person

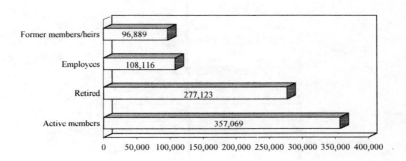

(i) Assets (HUF) Falling to One Person

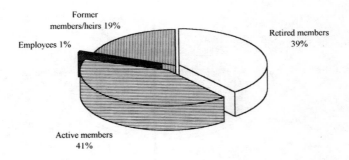

Source: Calculated figures from MA, 1992

Figure 2.5 The Allocation of Collectively Owned Landed Property of
Agricultural Cooperatives (1992)

(i) Landed Property (Gold Crown) Falling to One Person

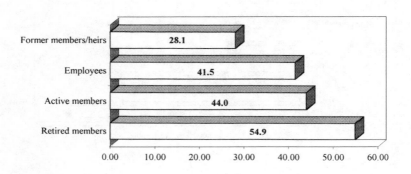

(ii) Landed Property (%) Falling to Owners' Groups

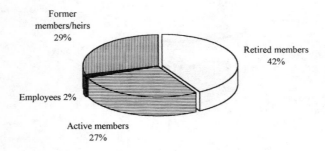

Source: Calculated figures from MA, 1992

The most numerous group of property-share holders is that of retired members (54.4 percent of all members of former cooperatives. [MA 1992]). The majority of this group is constituted by elderly women who, even during their active years, could not take part in making decisions of strategic importance. Not surprisingly, they can hardly be assumed to be capable of taking adequate decisions today. The increasingly intense clash of interests of different generations and resident groups is another negative effect generated by the process of transformation. Elderly people have obviously been demanding the well-deserved allowances they had enjoyed in the past. They are also more interested in receiving dividends. By contrast, active members and employees prefer to keep their jobs and receive higher wages.

This is one of the reasons why the progress and pace of cooperative transformation have not fulfilled the earlier hopes of the government. Leading politicians expected a much more marked tendency towards the separation of collective and individual property.

The deadline for compulsory transformation was 31 December 1992. Some 88 percent of agricultural cooperatives (1,273) had completed the transformation by this date. The remaining 168 cooperatives were closed down. About 10 percent of the members left the cooperatives either individually or in groups. In cases of individual or collective separation, those leaving always took their 'proportionate shares' from the assets and land with them. The share of assets taken from cooperatives was estimated at around 15 percent (15-20 billion HUF in property shares and 105,000 hectares of land. Figures provided by the sources of the Ministry of Agriculture). The importance of such secessions is undeniable. Political and legislative support was essential for members with definite future plans to become independent of cooperatives. They have certainly profited from the opportunity of being able to leave with some private property of their own. Furthermore, they could legally and publicly organise the secession of groups of the membership. Such initiatives would have previously been impossible.

There have probably been many reasons for individual secession. We will discuss two extremes here. First, there are part-time farmers who had been involved in small-scale production for many years, and who decided to continue farming as a full-time activity because they had lost confidence in the collective or hoped to earn more through private enterprise. At the other extreme we find people – mostly the unemployed or those threatened with the prospect of unemployment – not believing in their future in the cooperative. Therefore, they decided to take the opportunity to take their shares from the collective assets, either to make money as quickly as possible or simply to enjoy owning some property. (Some former members took the VCR and the television set of the cooperative, or just a couple of cattle to be slaughtered in order to gain ready cash as quickly as possible.) The 'price' of secession and taking their proportionate part of assets was the loss of membership. Thus, only individuals with no future interest in the cooperative have actually requested their shares.

To summarise the results of ownership restructuring, the profundity of this process, despite its ample inconsistencies, can be compared to that of organisational restructuring. However, land restitution and privatisation of assets belonging to former agricultural cooperatives have resulted in a radical fragmentation of ownership. The average cooperative member has received as little as 1.5 hectares land. By bringing about this enormous discrepancy between land ownership and use, ironically enough, it is the restitution of land that is delaying the development towards a modern capitalist agriculture.

The Transition of 'Golden Age'

This is a pseudonym for a former producer cooperative situated on the southern fringe of the Budapest agglomeration, about thirty kilometres from the capital. The 'Golden Age' cooperative was one of the producer cooperatives in the region (See Figure 2.1) in which the share of income from non-industrial activities substantially exceeded that from agriculture.

Before the transition, the history of 'Golden Age' cooperative had not differed from that of most cooperatives. For our purposes it will be sufficient to highlight the following dates:

1961: Establishment of 'Golden Age' in a small town called 'Nice-Danube' (pseudonym).

1973 : First merger with another cooperative of the same town.

1974: Second merger between the enlarged 'Golden Age' and the cooperative called 'Autonomy' of a village 'Periphery' (both pseudonyms) which, though belonging to the agglomeration of Nice-Danube, was not a neighbouring settlement.

1975: Third merger with the only remaining independent cooperative of Nice-Danube called 'Old-Hero'.

Non-agricultural activities were significant at each of the above stages of development, but had never exceeded 50 percent of the value produced. In 1976, the first year of the greater 'Golden Age', an ambitious plan was formulated by the managers of the cooperative and political leaders of the region: they decided to set up a 'Freezing-House Complex'. Two smaller freezing houses had been constructed outside the micro-region, but the largest building of the 'complex' was built at Nice-Danube itself. A freezing house is at the apex of a vertical system. It requires a constant and ample supply from the production units nearby and, therefore, serious investments had to accompany the construction of the freezing plant in 'Golden Age'. These included new fruit plantations (raspberry, apple, cherry, sour-cherry), new irrigation systems to supply orchards and vegetable production in a territory of 1,700 hectares, and the provision of gas for cheap energy.

These investments were mainly made during the late 1970s and the early 1980s. This was a period during which the character of 'Golden Age' was formed: a huge cooperative with a complete, vertical chain in vegetable and fruit production, a modern beef-cattle ranch and an extensive group of industrial divisions. The latter were largely unconnected with the agricultural sections, and had relatively little to do with one another. They were small, geographically scattered units with a wide range of industrial and service activities. The large investment programme led to the decay of the cooperative, which entered the 1980s with enormous debts running up to almost 400 million HUF. This was one of the reasons why managers were happy to reorganise production according to the guidelines provided by the liberal reforms of the planned economy adopted in 1982. All of the new legal forms of company were established within the cooperative. They were subsumed under, and controlled by, managers of the main divisions of production such as the Agricultural and Industrial Divisions and the Department of Enterprise Promotion, which were all directed by the Centre (of the cooperative). The Agricultural and Industrial Divisions operated as 'sub-centres with semi-independent budgets'. This system implied that, although they did not exist as divisions with entirely independent book-keeping, their overall income and costs of production were registered separately in the unified balance-sheet of the cooperative. Meanwhile, they were neither allowed to dispose of their net income nor determine the magnitude of their share from the so-called 'costs of central administration and management'. Nevertheless, this form of organisation involved two major steps towards greater economic autonomy: both the profitability of main groups of production and the success of the managers' work could be evaluated more precisely.

As many as sixty-four small entrepreneurial groups of up to fourteen active employees operated under the umbrella of 'Golden Age' in 1983-1984. The term 'umbrella' implies a loose connection to the cooperative through special contracts within the organisation. The enterprises provided a fixed monthly payment to the Cooperative Centre in exchange for the working capital or production inputs they generally received from 'Golden Age'. 'Managers of enterprises only needed our rubber-stamp enabling them to buy whatever they intended within a limit settled by a contract' the chairman of 'Golden Age' commented in an interview.

However, serious mistakes and numerous miscalculations were made in the formulation of production plans, forecasts and investments. Efforts to establish a vegetable-growing branch based on small-scale production were unsuccessful because there was no local tradition for it. The selection of the area for a raspberry plantation was mishandled, and the beef-cattle ranch became unprofitable due to falling prices. Agriculture never quite fulfilled the managers' expectations. At the same time, industrial activities sponsored the financial viability of the cooperative as a whole.

By the end of the decade the majority of small industrial enterprises had disappeared, but three small agricultural ventures were established as a new development immediately following the passing of the Company Law of 1988. Two of them were 'one-person' private enterprises: two former members (the former leader of the Department of Integration of Small-Scale Production and an ordinary young member of the cooperative who 'was sitting close to the fire') had been allowed to rent 100 hectares of land. Both of them had failed by 1991. However, the third venture has survived and still operates. It was established by three managers of the agricultural division of 'Golden Age' as a limited liability company called 'Free-Land'. They rented 400 hectares of land and also machinery from the cooperative. The first three years were marked by countless conflicts between the Cooperative Centre and the 'Free-Landers'. One of the founders decided to quit and later established his own private business (Priv-Horticultural LLC, Table 2.5), but the two others continued and by 1993 the group had become one of the most promising competitors for agricultural land in the region. The beef ranch was also re-established as a limited liability company.

The appearance of these agricultural enterprises established by a few top managers can be attributed to both external and internal influences –

on the one hand, a new wave of economic liberalisation during the late 1980s and, on the other, the sharpening conflict between industrial and agricultural sub-divisions of 'Golden Age'. Managers of industrial branches protested more and more loudly against the levies taken from their divisions by the Cooperative Centre for intra-organisational redistribution. Meanwhile, agricultural managers themselves felt the rule of top managers and managers of larger industrial units to be oppressive. They argued that they had never enjoyed the level of autonomy appropriated by industrial managers whether inside the cooperative or outside it.

The following case, recalled by an interviewee, illustrates the prevalent atmosphere of those days. According to him, the Communist Party secretary of the cooperative at the end of 1987 'set an assignment': 'Write an essay with the title: What Would I Do if I Was the Chairman of the Cooperative?' Three people, who later became founders of the 'Free-Land' LLC, actually took the task seriously and proceeded to prepare a comprehensive plan. They proposed dividing the 4,500 hectares of land cultivated by 'Golden Age' into fifteen separate enterprises. To no-one's surprise, the plan was rejected, though they were allowed to set up their own enterprise as a special experiment 'without any organisational work from the ranks of the ordinary majority'.

However, 'Golden Age' was slipping deeper and deeper into a liquidity crisis. The crisis of industry spread and deepened quickly between 1988 and 1990. As a consequence, quite a number of previous sub-contractor industrial enterprises went bankrupt leaving behind debts to be added to the debts of the cooperative. Even industrial units considered to be rather strong lost a considerable part of their markets as some of the largest firms in Budapest cancelled their contracts with 'Golden Age'. Worst of all, in some cases the contractors in Budapest declared bankruptcy without ever paying for products already delivered. The closing down of some industrial enterprises and severe cutbacks in the production of surviving ones resulted in a serious reduction of the workforce employed. 'Golden Age', which had employed 4,000 people less than a decade before, had only 1,527 active employees in 1988, 902 in 1991, and 720 in January 1992. By the end of 1992 the only possible form of successful crisis-management was to 'escape forward' by taking a further step towards autonomy. The independent budget sub-centres were reorganised into a holding cooperative organisation. The last stage of the previous organisational principle (the system of independent budget sub-centres, 1991). The structure of the holding cooperative in 1992 is illustrated in Figure 2.6.

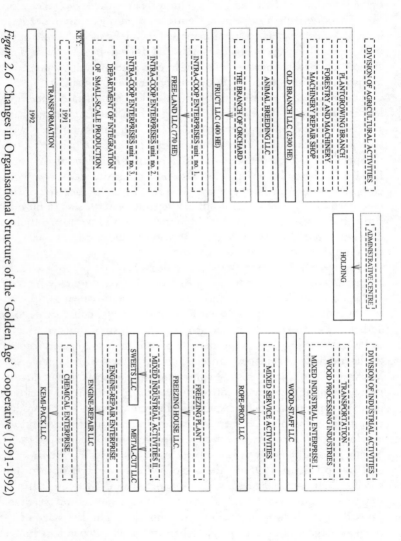

Figure 2.6 Changes in Organisational Structure of the 'Golden Age' Cooperative (1991-1992)

As Figure 2.6 indicates, the number of industrial units had already been reduced considerably by 1990 compared to 1983-1984. The same process was continued in 1991. Those production units, whether agricultural or industrial, which were, according to the managers, potentially capable of profitable operation, were organised into limited liability companies. The cooperative centre, the holding unit, became the 51 percent majority share holder in each limited liability company. To ensure an equal share in servicing debts (25 percent of the value of assets in 1991) each limited liability company was obliged to pay a proportional part. The holding unit was in charge of providing working capital for production units (limited liability companies and the rest of the agricultural branch), since the holding unit was not only the majority share holder in the LLCs but also the owner of the assets they operated with and on which creditors could impose mortgage as security.

The last year of 'Golden Age', 1992, marked the real turning-point. The holding system could not solve the accumulating problems, the most important being the liquidity crisis. The level of indebtedness had risen from 25 percent to 33 percent by the end of the year. 1992 was also the year of the implementation of the Cooperative Transformation Law. Emotions during the months of evaluation and re-allocation of ownership of the assets belonging to the cooperative had reached unprecedented intensity. By the end of 1992 a full secession of production units and individual claimants was decided.

In the interim, however, two interest groups had emerged which openly opposed the first suggestions of top managers for allocating property rights (so-called 'naming') over the assets of the cooperative: a group of retired members who supported the re-establishment of the 'Old-Hero' cooperative, and the majority of residents of Periphery. The latter supported the idea of re-establishing 'Autonomy' as an independent cooperative of villagers of Periphery. The leader of this group, a middle-aged former cooperative member, was the mayor of the newly reorganised local authority in Periphery. Her success in local politics obviously encouraged her and her supporters to recover what had been taken through the use of pressure in 1974, namely, the village cooperative as an economic basis of the community.

Generation was the most important source of solidarity among those favouring the re-establishment of 'Old-Hero'. They accepted the leadership of the last chairman of the independent farm (he was in office until 1975), expecting him to represent their values and point of view. As he stated when citing his supporters' demands: 'They have come up to me saying: "Feri, speak up for us, otherwise they will fleece us."'

An important part of the background to this situation, and the reason why this man in his late seventies became rather unexpectedly involved in local politics in 1990, was a conflict that emerged in 1989-1990 between the united 'opposition' and local representatives of the Communist 'establishment'. An ambitious plan of the cooperative leaders sparked off a scandal which was presented in the local press. In order to ease its liquidity crisis, which was not public knowledge at the time, the senior leaders of 'Golden Age' had decided to sell the most precious lands of the cooperative. These pieces of arable land lying close to the Danube's left bank were to be converted into plots suitable for leisure purposes. They had hoped to gain a profit of 300 million HUF with 150 million HUF of investment.

There were two main arguments against the decision. On the one hand, many local residents were reluctant to accept 'newcomers' – the future owners of the leisure plots – who would over-crowd the area and pollute the environment, as well as limiting public access to the bank of the Danube. On the other hand, in the eyes of elderly inhabitants of Nice-Danube, land was primarily to be used for agricultural production. 'They want to sell up our best pieces of land that used to be our vegetable-gardens', they exclaimed. The last chairman of the 'Old-Hero' cooperative was a prominent representative of this view and he gave an interview to a journalist from a newly launched private newspaper. 'This man saved those plots of land in 1972-1973. At that time he had to run the risk of losing his job as a chairman of the "Old-Hero", since Communist leaders intended to appropriate this land for similar purposes' the journalist explained. 'To gain an equal income from these 24 hectares by agricultural production, we would have to plant and harvest for 100 years' responded the chairman of 'Golden Age'.

As the procedure itself was legally unassailable and the local council approved the plans for a new recreational area, the leaders of the 'Golden Age' won the fight in 1989. However, this public debate provided an opportunity to formulate distinctly different approaches towards land issues. It also marked the beginnings of the involvement of different actors in the subsequently unfolding intra-cooperative debates.

The naming of property rights

In the transformation of the cooperative in 1992 the first task was to allocate property rights through 'naming' the collectively owned assets. Rules governing the distribution of assets in the form of 'property shares' had partly been determined by the Transformation Law (see Swain 1993), and partly by cooperative members (General Assembly of the Cooperative).

Senior managers of 'Golden Age' lost the support of many retired members by trying to assert the interests of the managers during this process. They based their claims on the alleged merits of young and middle-aged managers in accumulating the assets which were to be allocated, and they demanded a share proportionate to their past 'efforts'. Retired members, in turn, argued that their contribution had been equally important. 'We were forced to join the cooperative in 1961. We were extremely poor in those years. We received a pittance in return for the hard work we were doing everyday with our bare hands'.

Meanwhile the 'Autonomy' and 'Old-Hero' groups had formed an alliance against the senior managers, and succeeded in holding a vote of confidence in June 1992. They needed two thirds of the votes to have the three senior managers dismissed, but they only received 56 percent. Despite this failure, the results indicated an equal division of power among confronting groups, and it was primarily this that forced representatives to negotiate and seek compromise instead of choosing confrontation. New principles concerning the allocation of assets were accepted by the General Assembly, increasing considerably the value of property shares to be owned by retired members. In addition, senior managers gave up their original aim of reorganising the holding structure into a public share-holding company. A full separation of production units was agreed, and each seceding unit was to allocate 33 percent of the asset value taken to cover debts to various creditors.

The second task in cooperative transformation was for organisers to assemble as many property shares as possible from the new property share holders in order to cover the value of assets which they needed to take out of the cooperative. The main parties concerned at this stage were managers of LLCs and groups intending to secede from the cooperative. First, the asset entitlement of these groups and individual claimants (28 persons) had to be established. Next, campaigns were launched by managers of the larger units, relying on both fair and false promises, to attract as many 'property share holders' as possible to join with them in their venture. (Tables 2.4 and 2.5 indicate the largest groups of asset holders in 1992 and various aspects of the structure of property shares collected by managers from active and retired members.)

Table 2.4 Owners and Operators of Larger Successor Organisations of the 'Golden Age' Cooperative, December 1992

Successors	The number of owners of LLCs	The number of active members + employees	The number of property share holders	The value of taken assets HUF	The value of taken assets %	The average value of property shares HUF
Freezing House LLC	9	160	348	181,500,000	21.77	521,552
Sweets LLC	3	17	33	11,667,000	1.40	353,545
Engine Repair LLC	28	153	146	65,717,000	7.88	450,116
Wood-Staff LLC	38	43	33	23,315,000	2.80	706,515
Old Branch LLC	30	47	117	70,647,000	8.47	603,821
Fruct LLC	69	64	304	135,435,000	16.24	445,510
Old-Hero Coop	11*	6	175	85,291,000	10.23	487,377
Autonomy Coop	167	1	167	56,584,000	6.79	338,826
Total	355	491	1,323	630,156,000	75.58	476,308

*Statutory Members   *Source:* 'Golden Age' Documents

Table 2.5 Successor Organisations of the 'Golden Age' Cooperative according to Shares of Owner Groups (%)

Successors name	active earners	Retired members	Active members	Employees	Outsiders*	Others	Shares, total
Legal successor coop	3	31.9	23.9	2.6	37.7	3.9	8.7
Non-Agric. Act.s	430	28.5	51.0	4.9	13.5	2.1	35.7
Freezing House LLC	160	39.8	42.0	3.5	12.4	2.2	21.9
Sweets LLC	33	0.0	54.0	5.4	22.7	1.7	0.4
Engine Repair LLC	153	13.7	62.4	4.4	17.0	2.3	8.8
Kemi-Pack LLC	13	21.4	54.5	5.6	18.4	8.5	1.0
Rope-Prod. LLC	3	0.0	79.3	15.3	5.3	0.0	0.4
Metal-Cut LLC	25	10.3	77.6	7.6	4.4	0.0	1.2
Wood-Staff LLC	43	0.0	75.8	9.7	10.3	4.2	1.9
Agricultural Act.s	114	34.0	32.7	3.2	26.4	3.7	26.3
Free-Land LLC	2	0.0	54.0	5.4	38.8	0.0	0.4
Old-Branch LLC	47	18.4	54.7	7.7	13.8	5.4	6.4
Fruct LLC	64	40.0	25.5	1.7	29.6	3.0	18.4
Priv-Horticult. LLC	1	36.3	18.3	1.3	40.0	4.3	1.1
Opponents	7	46.0	20.2	1.5	27.5	4.8	28.4
Old-Hero Coop	6	49.0	23.1	1.4	20.9	6.4	13.0
Autonomy Coop	1	44.1	17.8	1.4	33.2	3.6	15.5
Other							
Wife	n.d.	23.2	29.4	2.9	44.4	0.0	0.9

*Former members/heirs   *Source:* 'Golden Age' Documents

The 'stakes' at this stage of the 'game' could only be clearly assessed by 'professional gamblers'. Two vital issues were (i) the acquisition of assets with which a profitable operation would be possible, and (ii) a considerable reduction in inherited debts immediately following the secession itself. The first of these was difficult to control but the second could be influenced by the managers through the acquisition, and subsequent sale in order to service debts, of as large a share as possible of movable and small fixed assets (for example stocks stored in the Freezing Plant, flats, and leisure plots near the bank of the Danube). There was also some possibility of ensuring that the debts which they agreed to service were ones which could be renegotiated.

Needless to say, former managers, and senior managers in particular, were much better placed in this situation than ordinary members who lacked the information, relevant knowledge, experience in financial matters, and valuable contacts with chief bank officers which allowed the managers to exert considerable influence on the conditions of independent production about to be launched.

It is significant in this context that the transformation of indebted cooperatives was highly dependent upon which of the commercial banks was its most important creditor. The blueprint of business policies had to be approved by the creditor of the indebted cooperative.[7] The banks thus had an important say in the modes and circumstances of transformation at a great number of collective farms.

Senior managers were well aware of their advantages, and they did their best to make use of their skills. They succeeded in dividing 'the alliance of the opposition'. 'Old Hero' and 'Autonomy' openly demanded the Freezing Plant, the most valuable portion of the assets which senior managers were determined to keep under their control. Managers finally attained their objective through a special agreement over the shares of the leaders of 'Old Hero' in the stocks of the Freezing Plant.

Their remaining opponents, the leaders of 'Autonomy', were subsequently fiercely criticised for their inflexibility and ineptitude in reaching a compromise. Their response was to declare both the assessment and the distribution of the assets and debts unfair. Putting their faith in 'justice' and the support of leading political forces, they initiated legal proceedings against the senior managers of 'Golden Age' in 1992, ques-

---

7. In 1992 the degree of indebtedness (debts related to the value of liquid and fixed assets) of cooperatives was 21.2 percent, a high rate but much lower than the scale of indebtedness of state enterprises (30.6 percent) and companies (50.2 percent). (RIAE, 1993: 8-10).

tioning the validity of the value assessments. Unfortunately for them, they failed. It was far too late to restart the whole tedious and troublesome process once again. 'Autonomy' found itself isolated. The full secession of other successor units of 'Golden Age', approved by the creditor banks, was completed by December 1992. The most important independent companies are indicated in Figure 2.7.

Figure 2.7 Successor Organisations of the 'Golden Age' Cooperative, July 1993

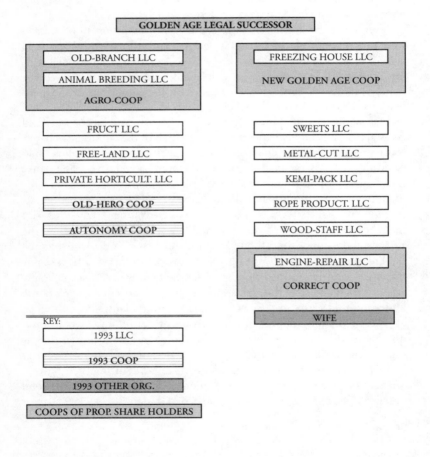

Source: 'Golden Age' Documents

A comparison with Figure 2.6 clearly shows that the structure of production in 1992 fundamentally determined the set of important successors in 1993. However, one important point is not shown by these figures. This is the fact that senior managers of limited liability companies could maintain their positions intact. Some smaller sub-units have disappeared as their enterprises were not financially viable. Two new units were established: the 'Old-Hero' and the 'Autonomy' cooperatives. 'Autonomy' took its share from the legal successor of 'Golden Age' one year later than all other successors. They finally accepted failure at the end of 1993. By this time their share was reduced to 50 percent of its original value, as indicated in Table 2.5. 'Autonomy' was the real 'loser' in the 'game'. Those opting for the 'losers' when investing their property shares have lost accordingly, while those who associated themselves with the 'winners' have so far managed to at least stay in the game. However, to a large extent, most active members and employees have shared mutual interests with the managers. Active members and employees, no matter what position they would have, aimed at keeping their jobs and investing their property shares into successful enterprises. They have accepted the managers regardless of their political past, management style and possible lack of fairness. They considered them to be the most likely to meet their expectations by achieving success in business. People hoped to receive their due share from the profit of these successes. Of course, many of them were disappointed in their expectations.

It is clear from Figure 2.7 that in 1993 a compromise between the owners of the assets (the former members of 'Golden Age') and the managers of LLCs was reached and put into practice. One of the most important indications of this compromise can be identified in the multiplication and modification of holding cooperatives.

Only two out of the six successor cooperatives operating in the summer of 1993 were originally established as cooperatives after their secession in January ('Old Hero' and 'Autonomy'). Although these organisations are ordinary producer cooperatives, their production – though for different reasons – is considerably restrained. 'Autonomy', while distracted by legal and political confrontation, could only cultivate half of the district belonging to its base village, creating only one job opportunity. 'Old-Hero' employed six active members, including a senior manager, and cultivated 300 hectares of land. Nevertheless, the majority of its income came from rents and sales of the assets taken from 'Golden Age'. (Ironically, the editor-journalist, who had played a prominent role in involving the chief organiser of this cooperative in local politics in 1990, was elected as a senior manager of the re-established

'Old-Hero'. Even more ironically, this cooperative took five plots of land, which were the focus of the political debate in 1990, from 'Golden Age'. Four of these were then sold at a very good price in 1993).

The legal successor ('Golden Age') was formed as a residuary body to organise auctions for allocating the assets for which more than one claim has been registered. It was also responsible for the sale of remaining assets. Its active workforce was a chairman and two administrative workers.

However, only six months after the successor units started to produce independently, three holding cooperatives were established on the initiative of managers of successor limited liability companies. As Figure 2.7 illustrates, the 'New Golden Age' cooperative unifies the 348 property share holders in the assets of the Freezing Plant (value 182,000,000 HUF). 'Agro-Coop' was established by 117 owners of the assets of the former agricultural division (plant-growing and beef-ranch branches of production) and 'Correct Coop' is a cooperative of 146 owners of the assets of the largest industrial branch. These organisations are, undoubtedly, among the most important successors of the former 'Golden Age', taking a considerable part of its assets. By organising new owner cooperatives, managers solved the communication problems that were emerging between owners (between 100 and 350 people) and managers. This way they only need to keep in touch with the elected leaders of new cooperatives. The same managers head the Old-Branch LLC and Agro-Coop. This organisation structure allows managers to influence the decisions of the owners more successfully.

At the same time, owners preferred the re-establishment of cooperatives because they wanted to exercise collective control over the decisions taken by the managers. Since the majority of owners hold property shares of relatively little value, they hoped to have their interests better represented as members of a cooperative in which the principle of 'one member, one vote' balances the voting power of share holders.

The re-establishment of collective ownership so soon is evidence of the fact that the discrepancy between fragmented ownership and the use of land or other assets is a serious problem. However, these new holding cooperatives differ considerably from most of the cases discussed in the previous section and in the 1991 history of the former 'Golden Age', in that they do not own limited liability company shares. Under the current arrangement, the limited liability companies are entirely independent organisations; ownership and production are fully separated. The owners' ambition to exercise control over the decisions of managers is frustrated by the extreme fragmentation of rights in the property. For this reason we consider these parallel structures of production and ownership to be short-lived, intermediate phenomena. More or less open plans to initiate a series of reunifications coupled with capital concentration have already been prepared by senior managers. The contracts of investors will usually terminate in 1998. By this time managers hope to accumulate sufficient capital to be able to buy the majority of shares at a reduced price (30-50 percent of their value).

The restructuring of the industrial and agricultural successor organisations of the former 'Golden Age' did not differ greatly one from another up to 1993. Among agricultural producers various types of cooperatives and limited liability company are represented. The managers of one of the most promising successors, the 'Fruct LLC' cultivating 400 hectares of orchard, plan to reorganise it as a public shareholder company. There are also small enterprises among agricultural successor organisations – e.g., 'Free Land' in which the two owner-managers cultivated 700 hectares of land in 1993 – as well as the medium-size enterprises such as 'Fruct' and the 'Old-Branch' LLCs. These three units will probably survive in the future (with further cuts in employment in the latter two organisations).

What does the case of 'Golden Age' exemplify? We have hoped that this 'short story' may have helped to clarify the long and highly complicated process of transition of agricultural organisations in Hungary. This process has been in train for many years, under the strong influence of economic, social and political factors and interests. In the final analysis, economic and social forces, usually underlying far-reaching transformations in the society and economy as a whole, can also be seen at work in this case. It also illustrates that the initial hopes and intentions of creating a market economy, while at the same time avoiding social polarisation, have proved to be illusory: the shift back (or forward?) to a capitalist system seems to be as dramatic and painful for many as was the opposite process forty-five to fifty years ago. Nevertheless, some of the new economic units which are the successors to former producer cooperatives have promising prospects. They are certainly much 'healthier' organisations than their predecessors. These results must be appreciated as signs of improvement, perhaps the initial steps in a positive development that will increasingly prevail in the future.

Conclusion

Considering the outcomes of empirical and statistical evidence, the agricultural transition in Hungary can be characterised as follows:

(i) It is a *gradual* and *moderate* process as opposed to some of the more radical changes taking place in Romania and Bulgaria. In this respect it has been similar to the agricultural restructuring in Slovakia and the Czech Republic.

(ii) It is a *continuous* process following and accelerating changes that have already been initiated in the socialist period. This continuity – in other words, a chance for a more or less *organic* development – is probably the most characteristic feature of Hungarian transformation. This highlights the historical significance of the liberalised, so-called 'socialist market economy' of the late 1980s.

(iii) Finally, despite the lack of political radicalism, the changes taking place since 1990 have been profound and fundamental. Contrary to the original intentions of the Smallholders Party, carrying out the task of shaping and implementing governmental policies concerning agriculture (see Swain 1993), the shift from an agro-economy based on large-scale farms to a fundamentally small-scale, private-farm system has not taken place exclusively in accordance with governmental designs.[8] Agrarian restructuring has also involved the continuation of previous developments. The processes which began during the 1980s have been accelerated and deepened as a response to challenges and pressures of the political, social and economic environment.

Of course, the special circumstances brought about by political transition have also conditioned the process of restructuring. In times of such eagerness to see fundamental changes take place, new forms, new inventions, and new constellations are more likely to develop. Interest groups supported by triumphant political forces stand a better chance of having their plans considered and even carried out. However, the basically democratic political system of Hungary provides no absolute guarantees for the thorough implementation of any party's programme, especially when that may threaten the interests of a considerable number of social groups. The restructuring of Hungarian agriculture is a good example of this phenomenon. We are not claiming that political forces

8. The Independent Smallholders Party (Független Kisgazda Párt) is more or less a single-issue party claiming to represent the interests of small-scale agricultural producers. They stand for full reprivatisation of land. Being the second smallest party of the ruling coalition they were only assigned the Department of Agriculture. However, the Party was split in 1992 and nowadays several competing successors are representing the slightly differing aspects of its original political program.

have not influenced the directions of change whatsoever, but their authority seems to be limited due to the clashing interests of major social groups, directly or indirectly involved in agriculture. Therefore one of the keywords that may help to understand the process of transformation in Hungary is *compromise*.

ABBREVIATIONS

CSO: Central Statistical Office.
HNB: Hungarian National Bank.
LLC: Limited liability company.
MA: Ministry of Agriculture.
MF: Ministry of Finance.
RIAE: Research and Information Institute for Agricultural Economics.

REFERENCES

CSO 1993a: *Magyar Statisztikai Zsebkönyv 1992*, Budapest.

1993b: *KSH Tájékoztató*, September 1993, Budapest.

CSO PD: *KSH, Időszaki adatok*, 1990 and 1993, Budapest.

Fertő, I. *et al.*, 'Characteristics and Crisis Symptoms of the Hungarian Agricultural System', *Acta Oeconomica*, Vol. 44, No. 1-2, (1992): 95-115.

Halmai, P. '*Magyar agrárexport és az EK-társulás*', *Társadalmi Szemle*, Vol. 6, (1993): 3-14.

Hann, C. *Tázlár: a Village in Hungary*. Cambridge, 1980.

HNB *A Magyar Nemzeti Bank 1992, évi jelentése*. Budapest, 1993.

Illés, I. '*Az agrárválságról*', in *Válság és kiút*, ed. F. Csefkó and T. Kovács, Pécs: MTA RKK, 1991, 18-29.

Juhász, P. and Mohácsi, K. '*Az élelmiszergazdaság átalakításának ellentmondásai*', *Közgazdasági Szemle*, Vol. 40, Nos 7-8, (1993): 614-624.

Kovács, Cs. '*A mezőgazdasági termelés szervezeti struktúrája és jövedelmezősége tájlörzetenként*', in *Település, gazdaság, igazgatás a térben*, ed. K. Kovács, Pécs: MTA RKK, 1993, 223-247.

Kovács, K '*Le combinat agricole de Boly. La cooperative "Kossuth", village Boly. La cooperative speciale "Népfront", commune de Jakabszállás*', in *Les*

Katalin Kovács

decollectivisations en Europe Centrale, ed. M. C. Maurel, *Espace Rural*, Vol. 30, No. 12 (1992): 113-139, 169-223.

_____, 'Slow Transition in Hungarian Agriculture', *Anthropological Journal on European Cultures*, Vol. 1, No. 1, (1993): 105-112.

Ministry of Agriculture *Az állami gazdaságok és a mezőgazdasági termelőszövetkezetek eredményesség szerinti sorrendje és főbb mutatói megyék szerint 1988 évben.* Budapest, 1989.

A szövetkezeti átmeneti törvényhez kapcsolódó önkéntes adatlap főbb adatai megyénként. Budapest, 1992.

OECD *Review of Hungarian Agricultural Policies.* July, 1993.

RIAE *A mezőgazdasági, az erdőgazdasági és az elsődleges faipari vállalatok, vállalkozások eredményességi sorrendje és főbb mutatói 1991-ben.* Budapest, 1992.

A mezőgazdasági és erdőgazdasági szervezetek árbevétel nagysága szerinti sorrendje és főbb mutatói. Budapest, 1993.

Swain, N. *Collective Farms which Work?* Cambridge, 1985.

_____, 'The Smallholders Party versus the Green Barons: Class Relations in Restructuring of Hungarian Agriculture', (Paper presented to Working Group Three, Restructuring of Agriculture and Rural Society in Central and Eastern Europe, of XVth European Congress of Rural Sociology, 2-6 August 1993, Wageningen, The Netherlands), 1993.

Symes, D. and Jansen, A., eds, *Agricultural Restructuring and Rural Change in Europe*, Wageningen, 1994.

3. Responses to 'Democratic' Land Reforms in a Bulgarian Village

Deema Kaneff

Introduction

*L*and reform has been an important feature of the changes taking place throughout eastern Europe, and Bulgaria is no exception. The law concerning the restitution of land, asserting the primary role of private farming in agriculture, was introduced in Bulgaria in February 1991, with some subsequent revisions in March 1992.[1] Restitution required the restoration of the land to its pre-1944 owners. This in turn demanded the disestablishment of the state agricultural cooperatives, some of which had been in operation in Bulgaria since the mid to late 1940s.[2]

Of primary concern to this work is the issue of land reform in rural Bulgaria; more specifically, the focus on these changes is centred on a Bulgarian village I call Talpa, located in northern-central Bulgaria.[3] In

---

1. See Wyzan and Sjoberg (1992).
2. See Lampe (1986: 124-7) for a discussion on the beginnings of post Second World War cooperatives in Bulgaria.
3. This work is based on nine months fieldwork completed between December 1992 and August 1993. Previous fieldwork was carried out during 18 months in 1986-

Talpa two private cooperatives have replaced the previous socialist agricultural cooperative. An examination and comparison of the new private organisations reveals two opposing views held by the Talpians – differing attitudes which were rooted, I suggest, in villagers' political-historical location. The village has a strong socialist heritage dating back to the last century and held a privileged position in the socialist state since 1944 because of its relatedness to high-level state officials.[4] Of more general relevance, Talpa has, as in the case of most Bulgarian villages, undergone considerable loss of population since 1944 – the greater proportion of the remaining inhabitants being pensioners.[5] These factors have contributed to the predominantly negative reception with which most Talpians have greeted the present changes with respect to the land. Consideration is thus given to the restoration of villagers' land (or rather processes leading to restitution, since it is by no means completed) and what they chose to do with it, as a means of exploring their views towards current 'democratic' changes of land reform.[6]

1988. In writing the present paper, I am grateful for comments from Ray Abrahams, Katalin Kovács and other participants in the Cambridge 1993 workshop.

4. Talpa was not unique in pursuing such ties on the basis of its political-historical connectedness with high-level officials, but it was more successful than most for reasons discussed in Kaneff (1992).

5. In fact two-thirds of the Talpian population are over sixty years old. Such an aging rural population poses problems for decollectivisation (Pryor 1991: 15) especially since, as in the Hungarian case (Hann, 1993: 310), the younger and more educated are settled in the cities. Given this and considering the deep-seated negative associations made with village life as 'backward', I find it difficult to understand how 'Land reform as well as the transition of the agricultural sector to market mechanisms is likely to attract a considerable number of people from the cities back to the villages' (*Bulgaria's Agriculture* 1991: 102).

6. This work focuses on land which, pre-1989, was considered as cooperative or state owned rather than that falling within the private sector ('auxiliary plots'). I note, however, that while seen as potential sources of 'new family farms', it is usually not emphasised by authors that such a 'private' sector was very much dependent upon the state. For example Keliyan (n.d.: 2) speaks of the work done on the 'auxiliary plots' as 'quite independent' from the state. Yet Wyzan (1987: 24) quite correctly points out that the relationship between the two sectors was 'symbiotic', much more so than in the case of most other East European countries: for the land was not privately owned but leased from the state cooperative (Lampe 1986: 210). Further the State agro-industrial complexes provided pastures for animals and veterinary services (Wyzan 1987: 21) and produce was almost always sold via contracts to the state or cooperative sectors (Wyzan 1987: 24). Presumably such state support is now declining and this places some doubt on the hope placed in the 'auxiliary plots' as the 'future private farms' in Bulgaria (by for example Draganova 1993).

Background

The advent of the socialist state in Bulgaria on 9 September 1944 resulted in land reformations. Over the period of a decade, private own- ership of what were basically small private holdings in 1944-1945 – which averaged between four and five hectares (*Bulgaria's Agriculture* [1991: 4] provides the figure of 4.3 hectares) – gave way to cooperatives and state farms. State farms always remained a relatively small propor- tion of the total worked agricultural land (about eight percent) and were differentiated from cooperatives in that in the latter case land was not state owned but remained – legally if not technically – under private ownership.[7] Indeed owners were paid rent until 1959.[8] In the late 1950s to early 1960s the cooperatives were merged; 3,290 cooperatives (which accounted for ninety percent of the total worked agricultural land) were united into 930.[9] A further merger into 150 to 160 agro-industrial com- plexes (aimed at introducing industrial methods of production to agri- culture) occurred in the early 1970s but were evidently unsuccessful. Reversals of the mergers were carried out in the late 1970s and again in 1986, the latter restoring cooperative sizes to essentially 1960s levels.[10] Final reforms in May 1989 had little opportunity to take effect before the upheaval in November of the same year.

Whatever else may be said about the period of socialist rule, Lampe is correct to point out that it brought about forty-five years of political stability in a century which has otherwise been characterised in Bulgaria by political instability (1986: 226). Since the collapse of the socialist

7. *Bulgaria's Agriculture* (1991: 42). *Social and Economic Development of Bulgaria 1944- 1964*, gives a different figure of four percent (1964: 87). Both figures are for the same period, that is 1958-1960. In either case it is clear that there were far fewer state farms than cooperatives.
8. Wyzan and Sjoberg (1992: 6), and also *Social and Economic Development of Bulgaria 1944-1964* (1964: 118) and Singh (1959: 33). In this respect – that is the legal if not technical ownership of land – the Bulgarian cooperatives held some similarity with those discussed by Hann (1993: 304) for Hungary; and Swain (1993a: 15) for Czechoslovakia, Poland and Hungary, especially with the Czechoslovakian case where land rental was phased out and only labour payments were made. See also Swain (1993b: 10).
9. *Bulgaria's Agriculture* (1991: 42).
10. The cited references do not agree on the number of cooperatives involved in the mergers and their average land areas. The basic trends of unification are not debated however. For further information with respect to the major reforms in Bulgarian agriculture since 1944, see Lampe (1986), Wyzan (1987), Dobrin (1973, especially 56-8, 62-5) and Singh (1959, especially 187-88) on the earlier years.

state, this instability has again become a problem. There have been two elections of the National Assembly since 1989 (and many more changes within the governments), the last in October 1991 being marginally won by the UDF – Union of Democratic Forces – a coalition of nineteen parties bound by only one principle, their anti-communist stance. The agricultural reforms introduced by the first elected socialist government were revised by the UDF, which gave priority to the reprivatisation of land and to this end made the disestablishment of the state agricultural cooperatives compulsory. (The political and ideological reasons for such an action – to the extremist point of not caring about agricultural performance – is alluded to in Wyzan and Sjoberg [1992: 24].) This was viewed as an important precondition to building a new democratic society, founded on the primacy of private property operating within a market economy. By the end of 1992 the UDF had lost its small majority in parliament and an independent government supported by the Bulgarian Socialist Party (BSP), The Movement for Rights and Freedoms (DPC) and some UDF members had assumed control. A UDF president is still in power. With the loss of outright rule by the UDF and the formation of a government representative of a larger variety of viewpoints, policy towards cooperatives in general became less hostile, although agricultural reforms introduced by the UDF remain, in essence, largely unchanged.

In order to carry out the liquidation of the state agricultural cooperatives and to return the land to pre-1944 ownership, two government organisations were formed. Firstly, Land Commissions were created to return the right of ownership, that is, to work out the amount (who has how much) and type (category) of land to be returned to its individual pre-1944 owners. This documentation was to be sent to Sofia where a private firm was concerned with the land division in terms of giving it actual boundaries. The Land Commission, which was located in the nearby district capital, was responsible for Talpa and neighbouring villages. The Commission made use of existing state agricultural cooperative records; for every individual when entering the cooperative in the late 1940s or early 1950s had declared his/her property assets. Although the process of returning the land was under way, many issues remained unresolved; for example, debates at the federal level were concerned with the question of whether the original land plots should be returned to the pre-1944 owners, or whether the same land area should be returned but in more convenient plot sizes (that is, newly consolidated plots where all land of one quality is amassed in one area). The former, it was argued, was impracticable as the already small and unconsolidated farms were now even smaller – given fifty years of inheritance accumulation and the decrease of available land area due to its use for other purposes – thus making present mechanisation techniques impossible.[11] Secondly, Liquidation Councils introduced by the UDF began to function throughout Bulgaria in mid-1992, wherever previously a state agricultural cooperative had operated. Their purpose was to run the state agricultural cooperatives temporarily until they were able to liquidate them by the division of all cooperative wealth to its members by means of shares. The Liquidation Council in Talpa was formed on 18 May 1992 and was comprised initially of four members; assigned by the regional administer, suggested by the UDF and with one restriction, that members of the Bulgarian Socialist Party could not participate. Considering the strong support for the BSP throughout the rural areas of Bulgaria, including Talpa (evident in post-1989 elections), these non-BSP Liquidation Council members were not viewed by the villagers as *their* 'representatives'; instead they were seen as political appointees imposed by the largely city dominated UDF. A further source of irritation to villagers was that they were forced to financially support the activities of the Liquidation Council, since the latter's salaries were paid out of the old state cooperative profits. As government officials, the Liquidation Council members were initially answerable to no-one except the administrator in the regional capital, a situation redressed in the following year when changes to the law were made.[12] This step was taken because of crimes carried out by many of the Liquidation Councils.[13] For such rea-

11. In *Bulgaria's Agriculture,* (41-2) it is noted that in 1944 there were 1.1 million private farms which were fragmented into 12,000,000 plots. Since then the number of inheritors to the land has increased more than twofold (Anastasova n.d.: 3). Milner (1993: 35) quotes the contemporary Bulgarian agricultural minister who points to a present average plot size today of 0.16 hectares.

12. Tensions within the Liquidation Council were not evident, unlike the 'Land Reform Commissions' in Estonia (which appear to hold a similar function to the Liquidation Councils in Bulgaria), where internal tensions have been noted by Abrahams (1994: 357,363).

13. The new law made the Liquidation Councils responsible directly to the Minister of Agriculture and gave villagers a say in the composition of their Liquidation Council membership. In practice however, the apparently more equitable law was not effective according to Talpa village's mayoress. She explained that not only did it come too late, but in other villages where people had chosen to make changes to their Liquidation Council, their choices were not acted upon by higher level authorities. The need for this law casts some doubt upon Draganova's statement (1992: 8) that the presence of the Liquidation Council had not resulted in major conflict in more than one percent of villages. Of course, it depends on how 'conflict' is defined

sons, unsurprisingly, villagers resented the city-UDF initiatives. As one villager told another during a private conversation about the Liquidation Council at the village plaza '... at what other time do you allow some-one into your house, they stay there and live off you?'. The other man added in agreement '... and take all your money'.

From what I have been told – by the mayoress amongst others – most Talpians did not want the state agricultural cooperatives destroyed. State cooperatives had been formed through the largely 'voluntary' pooling of land and other resources (at least in the area in which I worked). Indeed my landlady – a distant relative who was once a Communist Party member but who had, well before 1989, become disillusioned with the Party, and after 1989 had chosen not to be actively involved with any party – informed me that more villagers were forced to accept the liquidation of the state cooperatives now, than the five or six households in Talpa who had not wanted to join the state agricultural cooperatives in the 1940s.[14] However, the destruction of the state agricultural cooperatives and the present transformation to private land ownership was not a voluntary process; the liquidation of state agricultural cooperatives was being enforced throughout Bulgaria. In a neighbouring village to Talpa, the villagers surrounded the state agricultural cooperative and held a one-week strike in protest at its liquidation, but with no success. In a village in the Plovdiv region, clashes between state cooperative members and present authorities cost a human life. Opposition to the Liquidation Councils has gained increasing momentum because of the widespread corruption which has became evident in the activities of many of the Councils throughout Bulgaria, including reports of the cheap selling off of cooperative wealth by members of the Liquidation Council who sold machinery and livestock for the personal attainment of wealth.[15]

(an issue which Draganova does not discuss); but I knew of no villages or townships in the vicinity of Talpa where 'conflict' of some form did not occur. The fact that Draganova's paper was written soon after the formation of the Liquidation Councils and that the figure quoted was taken from 'official data' may also provide some explanation of her seemingly low estimate.

14. Households in the 1940s usually comprised a number of generations, while migration to the cities in the past fifty years has meant that current village households are commonly made up of one or two elderly persons. Thus opposition from five or six households in the 1940s involved a larger number of people than it would today.

15. It was of course difficult to find 'factual' information on this subject, since the all powerful UDF-supported Liquidation Councils were not held accountable to any one within the village, while anti-liquidation information in socialist and agrarian newspapers may have exaggerated the situation. Nevertheless the problem was

Individual Talpians also expressed their opposition to the Liquidation Council; during one period of its year-long functioning, the head of the Council had been pelted with stones after leaving work late at night, while on and off for a six-month period he had received threatening telephone calls. Often in village meetings, I heard anti-Liquidation Council views being expressed. However, unlike the situation in other villages, there was no unified resistance in Talpa to the Liquidation Council. The mayoress explained that at the beginning the village did hold a few meetings but no further action was taken. She said that other demonstration activities, in neighbouring villages, and in the Plovdiv village, had no results and so realistically she felt it was pointless to take any protest action. Nothing would be achieved and 'If you can't achieve something, it's better not to start it'.

Indeed, after the first year of its existence, it was agreed in a public meeting that, given their task 'from above', the Talpian Liquidation Council was acting in a satisfactory manner. The BSP led in this acknowledgement, announcing publicly that it supported the activities of this particular Liquidation Council – for at least their Liquidation Council had managed to preserve the wealth of the state cooperative for its eventual acceptance by the villagers.[16] The head of the Liquidation Council provided an explanation for this by stating that they understood, unlike many other Liquidation Councils, that their task was to destroy the state cooperative as an operating system, that is, to destroy its structure but preserve the wealth of the old cooperative – its buildings and so on – so that it could be divided up between the people. (Many Liquidation Councils destroyed indiscriminately both the structure and the wealth of their cooperatives).

In 1993 the Liquidation Council completed calculating the villagers shares in the state agricultural cooperative. Using records from the state cooperative, each villager's share in the past cooperative was defined in

---

considerable enough to require the government to act in mid-1993 with a new decree (see note 13).

16. Thus the accusation that any resistance in rural areas was led by the BSP and that '… Their main weapons are still the threats and fears which they spread among people' (Draganova 1992, p.7), was unfounded at least in Talpa, in spite of the prominence of the BSP in the village. Indeed, it was leading BSP figures, such as the mayoress, who discouraged resistance from other Talpians. Attributing village protests to BSP inspiration, or to resistance by the rural *nomenklatura* (Wyzan and Sjoberg 1992: 11), accepts unquestioningly Bulgarian government-supported interpretations while disregarding rural Bulgarian views which are both valid and worthy of consideration in their own right.

terms of the total land, machines and animals with which they or more likely their ancestors had entered the cooperative. Length of service (number of labour years) was also given consideration.[17] The pieces of paper received which gave a villager's share in monetary value, represented documentation of the state cooperative's liquidation and served as the blueprint for its destruction. In late August 1993, the villagers were allowed, on the basis of their share papers, to either claim directly from the state cooperative or give all or a proportion of their shares to their newly formed private cooperative(s). I witnessed the beginnings of the actual liquidation of the state cooperative as claims were made on sheep and cows in the state animal farm. The division of the machines and buildings still had not been carried out at the time of my departure in August 1993.

In this transitional period, two private cooperatives had been registered in Talpa and both had their first harvests in the autumn of 1993. The land, which had not yet been transferred to the owners, was temporarily leased to the two cooperatives by the Liquidation Council which still officially controlled the old state cooperative – its lands, machines, buildings – and was divided between the two cooperatives based on the respective number of decacres held by the total membership of each new organisation. No Talpians chose to establish private individual farms, although in a neighbouring village I learnt that one such private farm had been created and existed alongside a huge cooperative to which the vast majority of the other inhabitants of that village belonged. Generally however, my impression of this region was that private individual farming – despite government encouragement – was an impracticable (at least for the present) form of agricultural organisation.

I turn now to look at the two newly formed private cooperatives in Talpa. By comparing their differing forms of organisation and operation, we can see two differently constituted relationships to the land,

17. The division took place as follows: first, government officials from the Ministry of Agriculture came and valued the Talpian cooperative at 22 million leva. A Liquidation Council member explained that when people had originally entered the state cooperative with all their wealth, it was worth 2 million leva in terms of the cows, machines and so on contributed by the members. Two million leva of the total 22 million was thus set aside to be returned in cash to the original investors. The remaining 20 million was separated into two lots – 10 million for labour days and 10 million for given lands. This was returned in shares expressed in monetary value dependent on villagers' proportion of work and land contributions calculated in terms of the total. A separate issue, was the return of ownership rights over the land, which was the concern of the Land Commission.

which in turn represent two rival views to the present 'democratic' changes occurring in the village.

Cooperative 'Progress'

'Progress', which was far the larger of the two cooperatives, was registered in October 1992 with a membership of 474 and land area of 15,400 decares (i.e., 1,540 hectares).

Structure of the cooperative

A president, a governing council of seven and a regulatory council of three are charged with managing the cooperative. All were elderly men, many of whom had grown up in Talpa, moved away from the village in their working lives and had returned as pensioners. The fact that a considerable number of those in the leadership body of the cooperative worked outside the village (which in the past socialist administrative hierarchy was at the bottom of the career ladder) is an indication of their once authoritative and generally successful career paths. They were not tertiary educated although – as is common for many of their generation – they had completed secondary school and also had gained further education at a stage intermediate between the tertiary and secondary levels. Many in the leadership positions had only limited – or no – previous experience in agricultural work; this was the case of the president of the cooperative and another from the regulatory council with whom I was acquainted. Thus the president was trained in mechanics and worked for eleven years in the State Talpa cooperative (not solely within his trained area) until he left the village in 1966 for the regional capital where he worked in a radio assembly plant until his retirement. A leading figure of the governing council worked in internal security for the Department of Foreign Affairs. The latter was an active Communist Party figure who held important public positions before 1989 and indeed returned to Talpa only because, with the political changes in the country, he was forced into retirement – a factor which gains significance when considering the political alliance of members (see below).

Apart from the leadership cadre, the cooperative had a salaried staff of approximately thirty-five workers, including three accountants, a cleaner, six general workers, four mechanics, nine tractor drivers, a veterinary assistant, a brigade leader who held general responsibility for the flock of 385 sheep and a herd of 205 cows, two shepherds and eight working in the cow farm. They were currently seeking a suitably quali- fied agricultural scientist, since the previous incumbent had become involved with the other cooperative. All were salaried positions, except those of the regulatory council who were paid only when they performed a day's work and if payment was approved by a general meeting. A vet- erinary surgeon worked by part-time arrangement, being paid only when he was called out.

A sub-branch of the main (production) cooperative was 'cel coop' which was also headed by the president. This consumer branch of the cooperative, the president explained to me, originated well before 1944, at which time it was involved in village business activities (buying agricultural products such as animal skins) and also giving loans to villagers.[18] During the socialist period it was united under the district state consumer (marketing) cooperative located in the nearby town cen- tre. At a meeting last year the villagers decided to regain control of 'cel coop' and, in paying 75,000 leva (Bulgarian currency unit) to its mother organisation the Regional Consumer Cooperative, bought back owner- ship of the sub-branch. The 'cel coop' was comprised of a tavern and shop. The profits from both went to the cooperative and the two shop assistants working in them received salaries. There were also a bakery, confectionery shop and second tavern which were owned by 'cel coop' and rented out to private individuals. It was hoped 'cel coop' would pro- vide an outlet for selling Talpian grown produce at a lower cost to vil- lagers; for example cooperative 'Progress' hoped in the future to take over the bakery and sell bread made from wheat grown by the cooperative.

Modus operandi

After receiving from the Liquidation Council their *dyalov kapital*, that is, their sum of shares in the past state cooperative expressed in monetary terms, villagers formally entered cooperative 'Progress'. Any profit made by the new private cooperative was to be divided amongst its mem- bers – proportional to their original shares in the cooperative. Salaries of employees were to be paid out of the organisation's turnover. There was also a general cooperative fund where a certain percentage of the annual profit was to be allocated for the benefit of its members and the vil-

18. In fact cooperatives have existed in Bulgaria since early this century, possibly earlier. See Lampe (1986: 30) and Singh (1959: 110). The first Talpian consumer and credit cooperative was established in 1906.

lage – for the sponsoring of village social events and contributions to village institutions such as the school, the library, theatre and so on (activities previously carried out by the state cooperative) and of course reinvestment into the cooperative.

In actual fact, profitable return on shares was not expected because of the two-and-a-half million leva debt inherited by the cooperative from the Liquidation Council. This debt was accumulated by the Liquidation Council in the year it had operated the state cooperative and included; costs for the sowing, ploughing and general working of crops tended by the former cooperative while under Liquidation Council control and taken over and harvested by the new cooperative 'Progress'; the salaries of Liquidation Council members (rumoured to be five times the national average, a rumour fuelled by the members of the Liquidation Council who refused to comment publicly on their pay); and a half million leva debt that the Liquidation Council claimed to have inherited from the past state cooperative. Thus members were told that they could not expect the cooperative to have any profit in its first year and possibly not even for a few years to come. The cooperative mortgaged its expected crops for the season in order to pay off its debts.[19] Indeed not only are members to receive no income from the cooperative, but at one of the first meetings (at a time when membership in the cooperative was strictly speaking not formalised, since villagers at that point did not possess their *dyalov kapital* papers) members proposed to give five hundred leva each in order to buy back the 'cel coop' from state ownership and reestablish it as a Talpian enterprise and as a sub-branch of their cooperative. The fact that most villagers were pensioners and received an average pension of 1,200 leva per month, that is about £30 (although I knew many villagers who received much less e.g., 900 leva/month) was an indication of their level of commitment to the cooperative, since 500 leva amounted to almost one-half of their monthly incomes.

Cooperative 'Progress' provided basic household goods at cost price to its members, who were entitled up to ten decacres i.e., one hectare's worth of animal fodder -including alfalfa, corn, hay, lucerne – in any given combination. They paid for its planting and ploughing and merely collected the fodder at the end of the season. Members were also given access to the use of as much meadow land as they desired. Such an

---

19. Neither cooperative is legally able to obtain mortgages on the basis of the lands of its members, although the president of cooperative 'Progress' told me with respect to his organisation that animals, buildings and machines, as well as produce, may be mortgaged.

arrangement enabled householders to look after animals for meat – usually poultry, pigs and sheep – without having to produce their own animal fodder. As in the socialist past, the new cooperative also intended to sell to its members its harvested crops in processed form – such as sunflower oil (for cooking purposes), wine and a number of other basic household goods. Further, the president promised that various equipment, such as trailers, would be made available at minimal cost to members if they wished.

In both cooperatives, the members were elderly and therefore not in a position to work their own land. However, unlike the other cooperative, their land held little interest to members in 'Progress'. My landlady (a retired school teacher who as already mentioned, had no party membership) said to me and other villagers a number of times, 'I do not want my land; what will I do with it? I cannot work it'. This view was expressed publicly at a cooperative meeting when one of the members said to an invited office holder of the Liquidation Council (who was also a member of the other cooperative), 'I don't want documents, I don't want land. Let them plough it, do what they want with it. I don't want it'. To which the Liquidation Council member replied 'Want it or not, you'll take it'.

Not only did cooperative members express little interest in working their own land, but significantly, they conceived of the land not as their own personal property but spoke of it as 'ours' (i.e., the cooperative's). 'We are the owners of this land' said one member, who until 1989 had been a senior active village Communist Party figure and remained to the present a staunch supporter of the BSP. At another meeting, he said '… the land is not owned by one, it's owned by the cooperatives – big and small'. Thus land was not conceived of as individual property but as part of a cooperative enterprise. Associated with this collective emphasis on the land was also the prominence given to cooperative, over individual, interests. A leading figure of the governing council said to the members at one meeting of the cooperative, that 'Our obligation is to think first of the cooperative', so granting primary importance to the collective needs instead of to individual requirements. At the same meeting the president concluded by saying, 'There's no going back. Now all that remains is for us to follow our cooperative, to give to our cooperative'.

In this context, personal motivation of profit was not acceptable. When at the beginning of the season the Liquidation Council had relinquished the state-held land to the two cooperatives and thus fired all the tractor drivers, cooperative Progress took them on. However salaries and other details for the workers had not at the time been sorted out. After a week of working for the cooperative, when no decision had yet been made about their salaries, the tractor drivers rebelled, wanting to know what they would be paid and when. During this period, the president had proposed an amount but it had been rejected by the tractor drivers as insufficient. Further, the president's action had angered both the tractor drivers and other cooperative members – especially the governing council – since he had acted on his own initiative without consulting anyone in the cooperative. As a sign of protest, some of the tractor drivers walked off the job and joined the dole queues. The president then began collaborating with the governing council and the following week a general meeting was called where the cooperative administration, as a unified body, announced to all members the new proposed salaries. During the frequently heated discussion, the head of the governing council, who was in charge of the proceedings, informed the tractor drivers that 'The ultimatum – "we want so much money" – is not acceptable. Because that's what drove the state cooperative into the situation it was in ... everyone was guaranteed a salary and the people weren't concerned with what happened thereafter'. He continued by pointing out to the tractor drivers that other workers who had also just begun working for the private cooperative, had nevertheless put the interests of the organisation before their own and patiently waited until the management had time to talk to other cooperatives in neighbouring villages, meet with its own governing council and make decisions about appropriate salary levels.

The event provides an insight not only into the emphasis placed upon cooperative above individual interests (in the above case profits), but also reveals a central tension within the cooperative: namely between some members and cooperative workers and their leadership. Such a view was expressed by the tractor drivers during their pay dispute when they showed dissatisfaction with the president. They commented that their president was from the old generation and that he wanted things done as they had been done in socialist times and that this was no longer appropriate. They were referring to the fact that initially the president acted in a dictatorial way by not involving the governing council of the cooperative in the decision-making process. Both a leading figure of the governing council and ordinary cooperative members had expressed similar views at different times. Importantly however, these problems vocalised by members of 'Progress' were issues concerning their dissatisfaction with the methods used by the leadership rather than a fundamental dissatisfaction with cooperative principles.

The concern for cooperative rather than individual profits extended well beyond the issue of tractor drivers' salaries. Since members of this cooperative thought of their land in terms of a unified entity, not as individual plots, wealth obtained from the lands was also not conceived of as personal gain, but once again as '*ours*'. This can be underlined by a comment made by the president at one meeting where he said 'Whatever we save or earn is ours, it's no longer a state cooperative' – thus not only impressing the collective nature of profit but also underlining the difference between it and the past state cooperative in terms of who controls the profits.

Cooperative 'Talpa 1993'

Organised in February 1993, this cooperative had a membership of about thirty (with another twenty whose lands were being worked and had membership rights but were not yet officially accepted as such). Thus the total number of those in the cooperative was about fifty. Land worked was 2,500 decacres i.e., 250 hectares.

Structure of the cooperative

'Talpa 1993' was organised in a similar way to the other cooperative although on a smaller scale; there was a president, a governing council of three and a regulatory council also of three members. The president, who was also the president of the governing council, commented to me however, that in this type of cooperative although the councils had 'functions' there was '… nothing for them to do because our relations are very simple and clear'. These 'simple and clear relations' were due to the fact that there were no salaried positions in this cooperative and that the multitude of functions, from keeping accounts to harvesting, was carried out by three men – one of whom was the president of the cooperative. Together they rented the land from the fifty member land owners. On the odd occasion when needing assistance, the three rentees hired casual help, for example, tractor drivers from the other cooperative were paid on a day-to-day basis for ploughing. This practice, according to the president, saved costs and kept the cooperative small. The size of the cooperative was a consciously designed feature; the owners and rentees wished to keep it small not only for reasons of costs, but also because they believed a smaller cooperative would be more efficient in other ways; ordinary members to whom I spoke noted that fifty people can find agreement over an issue more easily than 450; one of the rentees pointed out that this was an appropriate (optimum) size for a cooperative run by three men. Members see this as an important distinguishing feature between the two cooperatives and say they have no intention of allowing it to become 'big, like the other cooperative'.[20] The feature of size influenced the way Talpians distinguished between the two cooperatives; 'Progress' being referred to as 'the big cooperative', 'Talpa 1993' as 'the small cooperative'.

Apart from size, another distinguishing and important feature of the cooperative as far as the members were concerned, was the nature of its leadership. The rentees who controlled the cooperative were young men in their thirties. The president and the Liquidation Council member were both agricultural engineers (the latter also had a degree in economics) while the third was an agricultural scientist. Thus they were tertiary educated. Unlike the other two, the president had not been employed in the state Talpa cooperative, but had worked in a neighbouring village's state cooperative. Their education and experience were important features to members of cooperative 'Talpa 1993', who boasted of their leaders as young, educated and competent people. The three men did not live in Talpa and only the president had kinship connections with the village.

Modus operandi

The three men paid hard rental, that is, leva per decacre to the member land owners at an agreed sum predetermined at the beginning of the season, and calculated in terms of average market price for the crop to be grown, taken over the past two years. The rentees did not have their own land invested in the cooperative as did the leaders of 'Progress'. Rent was to be paid not only on the basis of land but also on machines and buildings owned by the land owners and used by the rentees, once this equipment had been released by the Liquidation Council for 'purchase'. (To date, the rentees had rented from the Liquidation Council.) Unlike the other cooperative, 'Talpa 1993' kept no livestock but was involved solely in grain production. The president told me that it was possible under the

20. As a means of obtaining further capital via shares and therefore being able to 'buy' more equipment – tractors, buildings and so on – the rentees and members were hoping to increase the cooperative land area to approximately 3,000 decacres, but found it difficult to attract more members.

terms of their cooperative for someone to keep livestock; however it would have to be in line with the rental system advocated by the cooperative, whereby a certain number of animals would be given to a person who would keep all their produce (milk, wool) and pay the owners an annual sum of rent, for example 100 leva per sheep. In the first season of operation, there was no interest shown by the members or outsiders in beginning such a livestock farming method.

All profits or debts were to be carried by the three men who therefore received no salaries; instead they had rights to the remaining profits after rent had been paid to the owners. In order to cover all initial starting expenses (including rental costs to the Liquidation Council) the rentees found it necessary to take out a loan at the beginning of the season of half a million leva. As with the other cooperative, crop production was mortgaged, but of course in this instance repayment was the sole responsibility of the three men.

In their first season of operation there was no cooperative fund set aside as the rentees maintained they were responsible for all costs – insurance of land, hired labour, equipment maintenance and so on. For the following season, members were demanding that a fund be formed; however, agreement needed to be reached as to where this money was to be found – from the owners' or rentees' profit. This I suspect will be a major source of tension between the two interest groups within the cooperative. The president was strongly opposed to such a fund, commenting to me that a cooperative is first and foremost the people '… because everything must be for the people – for them to receive greater rent and for us [meaning the rentees] more profit. In the end you must look at what the people will receive, not some dead money sitting there in the cooperative. The important thing is what the people actually receive'. On the other hand, ordinary members were concerned that having no fund would place them and their land at risk from abuse by the three men.

In general meetings, the president emphasised the flexibility of the cooperative and the freedom it offered its individual members who were entitled to work a proportion or all their own land, to rent from other cooperative members and to sell their produce along with the three rentees or individually. These options were not put to use by the greater majority who chose, rather, to let out their land to the rentees (hardly surprising given the advanced age of most members). The three men were also prepared to sell to their members animal fodder at cost price if it was so required; but unlike the other cooperative there were no limitations upon amount of fodder in terms of land area.

The president also emphasised individual decision making and following their own interests as important features of the cooperative. For example, at one meeting he said to members 'In this cooperative the majority can't oppress the minority, all must make their own decisions'. Prominence was thus given to individual interests above collective needs. Indeed the formation of a cooperative via legal registration enabled access to possible government benefits and held little other significance for the president, who said to me that 'I don't believe in production cooperatives but there is no other way at present'. On another occasion he repeated that 'I personally don't believe in cooperatives' and then continued 'The only production cooperatives that work well are in Israel. Ours really isn't a production cooperative – it produces but someone simply rents the land and works it'. The engineer implied something similar when he told me that they registered the organisation in the courts as a legal body, thereby being entitled to make use of government loans and other privileges given to agriculture '... because we're not that stupid as to dip into our own pockets'. (Note the difference in attitude when compared with the other cooperative, when members did 'dip into their own pockets' to the value of 500 leva each). Such a perspective clearly had implications for members' views on land; land was not seen as part of a collective enterprise, but as the personal property of individuals. It was not 'our' land as in the other cooperative, but 'my' land. Thus the president told the members to 'Work your own land if you want, it's your own property, no one will say a thing', so emphasising the freedom of individuals to pursue their own interests in the cooperative, to make their own decisions about how much of 'their' land, if any, the members wished to include in the cooperative to be worked by the rentees.

The prominence of individualism in this cooperative was connected to the importance placed by members upon land as a personal source of wealth. Several members, in speaking about their cooperative, made it quite clear that the attainment of wealth from their lands was an important motivational factor for joining. For example, both my neighbour and another member told me, on different occasions, that they joined the cooperative because 'I never saw a *stotinka* before from our lands, now I will'.[21] The great importance of land as a source of wealth was also underlined by the above-cited comment made to me by the president when he clearly established the belief that the whole point of a coopera-

21. *Stotinka* is the coinage unit of Bulgarian currency.

tive was defined in terms of the profit to be made by the people – both by the ordinary members and by the rentees.

The importance of the promise of money from their lands was not only a significant driving force in the cooperative, but also a source of tension between the ordinary members and the rentees. With the first harvesting in July/August 1993, it became clear to the members that the three men had made a huge profit even after paying off the half a million leva loan incurred, while the ordinary members had made comparatively little. For example, of the 1,600,000 leva profit on the wheat harvested, the three men pocketed over 100,000 leva each (the actual figures were never disclosed in detail by the three who, as noted earlier, also kept the accounts) while the rental paid on the prearranged sum of 110 leva/ decacre meant that the average plot holder in Talpa – with fifty decacres – would have received 5,500 leva rental.[22] After several days of behind-the-scenes meetings and disagreement with the regulatory council, a general meeting was called where some of the members expressed dissatisfaction that the rents were comparatively low compared with the vast profit made by the rentees. A demand was made for a more equitable sharing of profits, which included offering the three men high salaries, although the members backed down when the rentees reminded them of the contract agreed upon which gave all profit to the three apart from a compulsory rent of 110 leva per decacre. Such a tension between members was rooted in the clash of individual interests; an attitude clearly expressed by my next-door neighbour (and also regulatory council member) who said to another member of the cooperative at the meeting concerning the profit from the wheat, that in the end all must consider their own interests, for after all 'You are dear to me, but I am more dear'. Afterwards when discussing this incident with me, the president said, 'What was our problem here? Some people thought we had become millionaires. Well it's OK for a person to become a millionaire. And it's OK for the rent to rise'. Thus, while both the land owners and the rentees held a common view in placing importance on wealth as a source of motivation and land as a personal source of wealth, it was also a source of tension between them; that is, between what were essentially two competing interest groups within the same cooperative.

The competition between individuals pursuing their own goals, the emphasis on profits and of land as a source of personal wealth, defined

---

22. This was the average village plot size according to a member of the Liquidation Council.

this cooperative much more closely (than the other) with ideals of capitalist enterprise. Indeed the members themselves used the model of a small business – a shop – to describe their cooperative. When one member who supported the rentees explained to the other members at the meeting why the three men were acting properly in taking all the profits, he explained it to them exactly in terms of a small business where the owner of the shop has no concern with how much money the rentee makes so long as s/he pays her/his rent and on time. He told them they were in a similar situation, where they let out their land but had no concern how much profit or loss the rentees made, as long as the rent was paid. The appealing nature of this analogy of the shop was evident in that it was used a number of subsequent times – when the president spoke to me and by members to each other.

A Comparison of the Two Cooperatives

In summarising the characteristics of the two cooperatives we can see a number of ways in which they differ:

(i) *Size*
Cooperative 'Progress' was much larger than 'Talpa 1993' in land area and membership.

(ii) *Structure*
'Progress' was headed by elderly, non-tertiary educated Talpians; 'Talpa 1993' by young, tertiary educated non-villagers. 'Progress' had over forty regular salaried staff, whereas 'Talpa 1993' was a risk-taking business conducted by three rentees who employed casual labour as required.

(iii) *Function*
'Progress' was a consumer and production cooperative whereas 'Talpa 1993' was a production cooperative only.

(iv) *Land and Income*
Land holds communal importance for 'Progress' as opposed to more individual importance in 'Talpa 1993'. Profit in 'Progress' is 'ours', distributed to members according to share holdings with some set aside for communal needs. In 'Talpa 1993', all profits go to the three rentees, after payment of set rent to land owners and without provision for communal needs.

Given the fundamentally differing nature between the two cooperatives, it is hardly surprising that their relations were fraught with friction.
During a private meeting with the president of cooperative 'Talpa 1993',
I asked about the relationship between the two cooperatives. He replied
that as far as the two leadership bodies were concerned, their relationship
was similar to that between a husband and wife; '... they both can't
stand each other yet can't exist without each other'. The response supported my own observations; the smaller cooperative which as such had
less *dyalov kapital* in the State cooperative and which therefore would
receive much less in terms of buildings, machinery and so on, was somewhat dependent on its larger counterpart. On the other hand despite the
greater independence of the better-equipped large cooperative, it in turn
needed the small cooperative, which provided occasional 'specialist'
advice. For the large cooperative had lost both the engineer and agricultural scientist of the State cooperative, both of whom had become
rentees in 'Talpa 1993'; cooperative 'Progress' had not yet found suitable
replacements. The dependency between the two was thus based on the
better material resources of the larger cooperative and the greater agricultural expertise of the workers of the smaller one.

Despite this dependency, a degree of competitiveness also existed
between the two cooperatives. Thus the president of 'Talpa 1993'
explained to me that 'Competition will start between us. At the moment
we [the smaller cooperative] are relaxed because we're doing better. But
they'll catch up and we'll start thinking and try to beat them again'. Such
an element was in his terms 'normal' and desirable. The other president,
however, played down the existence of such competitive relations, saying
that 'I personally am not interested in what they do. Indeed ... I haven't
had much to do with them'. For the former president, competition was a
'normal' and healthy feature, while the latter refused to recognise (to me
at least) that such terms of involvement existed and in so doing refuted
his engagement in any relations of a competitive nature. Yet later on in
the same conversation, the president of 'Progress' explained how he was
allowing the other cooperative to store its sunflowers in the large cooperative's warehouses. The small cooperative he explained, had rushed to sell
their wheat and lost money and now they were using the larger cooperative's example of storing and selling later at a better price. If not a form of
competition, this is a form of one-upmanship; a means of demonstrating
that the small cooperative had something to learn from the larger one.

In a different way ordinary members of both cooperatives were also in
relations of a competitive nature with each other. Thus my landlady and

I would be regularly reminded by our next-door neighbour and member of the 'Talpa 1993' cooperative that she would be receiving money from her land while we would receive nothing from the 'Progress' cooperative. (Such comments were part of her long campaign to convince my land-lady to join the smaller cooperative). Further, whenever a scandal broke out in either organisation, members of the opposing cooperative would comment on it to each other with delight. When, for instance, the issue of the huge profits for the rentees arose in the smaller cooperative, it was commented upon with some satisfaction by members of the larger coop-erative that it would only be a matter of time before relations in the small cooperative broke down further. Members of the small cooperative had a reputation as 'difficult people' (see below) and it did not surprise mem-bers of 'Progress' that 'Talpa 1993' were always arguing and disagreeing with each other. In the same way members of the smaller cooperative, frequently commented about the ineptness of the leadership of 'Progress' and speculated about the organisation's downfall. In this context, the president of 'Talpa 1993' once commented to his fellow members '… you'll see they won't last beyond this year'.

Cooperative meetings provided another occasion where members expressed their mistrust and/or envy of the other organisation. Thus in one meeting of 'Talpa 1993', a member expressed feelings of being threatened by the larger cooperative when he said that '… they think just because we are smaller we are nothing'; and another added 'They say the large fish eats the small'. Someone complained that 'Progress' had '… taken the better land'. Similar complaints about having re-ceived the better blocks of land were made in a meeting of the big co-operative in respect to the smaller one. Additionally my landlady speculated that because the members of 'Talpa 1993' were largely UDF supporters, they would get loans more easily and thus be placed in a position of greater advantage.

Vocalised competitiveness and one-upmanship, combined with more privately expressed feelings of mistrust is an aspect of the fundamentally different, indeed opposing, nature of the two cooperatives. Such a split into two cooperatives is based, I suggest, on the political-historical loca-tion of individuals, as the above comment in respect to the attainment of loans indicates.

Both organisations, at a formal level, claimed they had no political alliances and occasionally at meetings the heads of the cooperatives explicitly distanced themselves from any political affiliations. However, in considering the political views of the membership, it becomes clear that this area is also polarised; the two cooperatives represented opposing political views and this appears vital in understanding the contrasts between them and more particularly their differently constructed relationships to the land.

The larger part of the leadership in 'Progress' were socialists. Thus both the president and governing council members with whom I was acquainted had been members of the Bulgarian Communist Party (BCP) and were presently members of its successor party, the BSP. The ordinary membership of the cooperative were also largely BSP sympathisers, if not members. In fact, one cooperative member I was sitting next to at a cooperative meeting, commented to me, as she looked around the full hall, that she saw only one UDF supporter, the rest of the members present were BSP supporters. A relatively small number of the members claimed alliance with a second party, the National Bulgarian Agrarian Union which held similar views to the BSP and was in fact the second political party in socialist Bulgaria, holding power jointly with the Communist Party before 1989.

The political orientation of the 'Progress' cooperative differed considerably from that of 'Talpa 1993'. None of the rentees had membership in the BCP or in the present BSP. The president and engineer held compatible political views, which corresponded with the other members of the cooperative to whom I spoke; namely an affiliation with the UDF. The president was a founding member of the UDF – the anti-communist coalition – both in a nearby town and also in a neighbouring village to Talpa (such a party has never existed in Talpa which had a reputation amongst neighbouring villages as having 'many communists'). The engineer, while never a member, said he had been a sympathiser of the UDF in the first elections. Both men had become disillusioned with this party – the president currently claimed his outlook as that of a social democrat, the engineer said he had no political interests. The fact that the rentees were, during the socialist period, working in the village (where few young Bulgarians willingly remained) is an indication of their once politically disadvantaged position in socialist society. Indeed, the fact that he had been discriminated against because he was not a BCP member before 1989, was given by the engineer as the reason why he worked in Talpa despite the fact he was not a resident of the village. He said that when he returned to his town after he had finished his degree, because he was not a Party member, '... they told me I couldn't work in the town and must find employment in a village'. Whether this account has some truth to it or not, is less important than the way in which it is used by the engineer to portray himself – as disadvantaged in socialist times because of his lack of Communist Party membership.

Ordinary members of 'Talpa 1993' with whom I became acquainted, also presented themselves in a similar light. When it was observed above that members of cooperative 'Talpa 1993' were often seen by others as 'difficult people to get on with', this was essentially a recognition of their peripheral position within, and perhaps lack of support for, the past socialist state. One such example is that of my neighbour who married into a wealthy family which was opposed to the formation of a state cooperative. Indeed the family had, with its wealth, bought a title – *hadjiya* – which signified their wealth and high status. My neighbour had, according to my landlady, battled long and hard to keep the title but under the Communists she eventually had to remove it from her passport, although now she was certain to have it reinstated. (Interestingly the president of 'Talpa 1993' was a distant relative of this woman and his family thus also held the same title. Both had – with respect to the rest of the village – above average land holdings, the president eighty-six decacres, the woman 120.)[23] Whether because of their resistance to joining the state cooperative or because of her family's wealth and support for the class structure, this family earned the official title of 'people's enemy' during the socialist period. My landlady, in explaining to me our neighbour's isolation, said that she had 'distanced' herself from the people '… and so during the communist times she wasn't at the centre of things and was left behind' (meaning she was disadvantaged in economic, cultural and other ways). In being located in such a manner with respect to the socialist state, her family – unsurprisingly – did not hold prominent public positions during the forty-five years of socialist rule. She was currently a member of the National Bulgarian Agrarian Union, but in the right wing of the faction-ridden party.

My neighbour was one of a number of members in this cooperative who expressed anti-socialist state sentiments. In fact when I questioned

23. The fact that the poorest villagers were most receptive to the formation of cooperatives in the 1940s, while the wealthier were less enthusiastic about these changes, is given support by Singh (1959: 156). Such a wealthy-versus-poor land owner distinction to some extent – but by no means totally – reflects the present split into two cooperatives. In the overlap of political and economic interests, those who felt that their incomes and standard of living had risen during the socialist period supported the old state cooperative; the wealthier were more critical of it and the whole political system it represented to them. Although not elaborating the point, Draganova (1992: 6) also provides support for this when she mentions that some villagers – those with smaller land holdings – do not want their property returned.

the president about how the cooperative had been formed, he replied that 'It happened naturally. Well, we started off initially as an anti-Communist foundation, but almost from the beginning I said there must not be politicisation'. Nevertheless given its clearly anti-Communist stance from its inception, political views did arise in implicit and explicit ways in the course of their meetings, often with the president taking the lead. Thus on several occasions the president boasted to members that a few years earlier he had faced court proceedings as a result of attempting to initiate changes, which were seen as anti-socialist in principle, in the neighbouring village state cooperative where he was working at the time. Much of the image of 'Talpa 1993' was thus constructed in terms of previous opposition to socialist rule; comprising individuals who could be interpreted as 'not being in the centre of things' during socialist times. Their past lack of Communist Party membership was an indication of their previously disadvantaged location within the socialist state. There are two instances – and undoubtedly more of which I am not aware – of members in this cooperative who in the present claimed to have always been anti-socialist, yet had declared the very opposite when I knew them six years ago. Such political opportunism, for example, was evident from the fact that one member of 'Talpa 1993', who had been a school head mistress and a Communist Party member, now claimed to have always been anti-socialist.

Thus the membership of the two cooperatives came from opposing political backgrounds determined by events that occurred well before 1989. For this reason the cooperatives represented not only two differently constituted relations to the land but also acted as a reference point for villagers' location within the socialist past and therefore also provided a commentary upon the villagers' presently constituted relations in the non-socialist state. Perhaps the importance of this past in acting upon present village affairs with respect to the cooperatives is most evident through the names of the organisations; names which epitomise the respective cooperatives' relationship to the past (both the members' view of the socialist past, their location within it and therefore also their position in the non-socialist present, since such political-historical alliances are still shaping contemporary village life).

Indeed the two cooperatives, working on quite different principles, represented (and at the same time reinforced) opposing relationships to the past; one which reflected a continuation with the previous socialist state, one which rejected this past. The very name given to the large cooperative reveals its connectedness and continuity with the past;

'Progress' was the name of the original 'cel coop' started well before 1944 and operated throughout the socialist period. The name has now been adopted by the new cooperative as a whole. Cooperative 'Progress' may be viewed as a continuation of its predecessor, the state agricultural cooperative. As with the state cooperative, 'Progress' was also a large organisation – in terms of land, membership and administrative structure. It was associated – via its membership – with the BSP (which was the renamed BCP); its workers received salaries and thus financial security. Further, land was not a personal source of wealth, and the individual was not given prominence above collective needs. This was exemplified by the fact that cooperative 'Progress' intended to maintain an active role in all areas of village life, not only via the 'cel coop' but also by continuing to contribute funding for social events, making available its mini-bus and driver for funerals, and a whole range of other services once provided by the state cooperative. There was indeed only one factor which distinguished the previous state cooperative from 'Progress'; the latter was an autonomous body and could depend neither on the government nor on other state agricultural organisations for financial or other assistance.[24]

Members of both cooperatives recognised the commonality of 'Progress' with the old state cooperative. One member of 'Talpa 1993' said to me that the only thing that was different between 'Progress' and the previous state cooperative was the name. However, this seemed to be precisely the most attractive feature about the cooperative to some of its members, who clearly lived with the hope that it would again become a state cooperative. Thus an elderly member of the cooperative – and a once-active Communist Party member – speaking to my neighbour from the other cooperative who was trying to convince him to join 'Talpa 1993', explained his reticence to join in terms of the hope that the large cooperative might once again become state run. This is not to suggest that its members hoped to create a replica of the state cooperative; on the contrary, they recognised that some changes were both necessary and desirable. Recall the above-mentioned tension between the president and cooperative workers. Indeed my landlady commented to

24. Even this is also not so different from the earlier socialist period where each village cooperative had greater relative autonomy. It was only in the last twenty years, after the early 1970s merger, that village cooperatives were absorbed under district control. Talpians spoke positively of the initial cooperative formations. On the other hand, I heard a number say that the final merger of the 1970s was financially and in other ways a mistake.

me once with respect to the cooperative's financial problems, that 'We won't be alright until we get younger people, a new leadership' – a sentiment shared by most of this cooperative's members. However, the changes hoped for by members of 'Progress' were ones based on their dissatisfaction with their leadership rather than with anything which threatened their cooperative's principles, for example by granting importance to the private individual ownership of land at the expense of general communal interests.

On the other hand the character of cooperative 'Talpa 1993' – its smallness in land, membership and administrative structure, its UDF roots, the emphasis on the individual over cooperative concerns and land as a means to personal wealth – revealed it to have broken with the socialist past. Again the name of the cooperative may be viewed as exemplary of this. 'Talpa 1993' located the organisation in contemporary terms as an organisation of the present, one without associations with the previous socialist system. Creating a clean break from the socialist past was an important implication of the statement made by members that their cooperative was 'not like the state cooperative'. The desirability of this was frequently emphasised at meetings. For example, at the meeting called to resolve the problem between land owners and rentees when the former became aware of the huge profits the latter were to make after the wheat harvest, some owners suggested that the rentees should be paid salaries as a way of achieving a more equitable distribution of the profit. The president responded by accusing them of wanting a state cooperative and told them that if they turned to the principle of salaries and decided to share the profits more evenly, so denying the three men exclusive rights to them, their cooperative would become in essence a state cooperative and he was not prepared to work under such conditions. He continued: 'If we get paid salaries, we'll become like a state cooperative. I do not want to scare you … but that's how it is', clearly expressing the negative regard in which he held the state cooperatives of the past. Privately, to a different member on another occasion, the president explained that if his position became salaried and wealth were more evenly distributed, he would lose his motivation and it would become '… like the other cooperative'. Considered together, these two comments clearly defined his cooperative in opposition both to the state cooperative of the past and cooperative 'Progress', while at the same time equating the latter two. The attractiveness of 'Talpa 1993' to its members appears to be that it was not linked to the previous state cooperative nor to 'Progress' and therefore, I would add, to the socialist past.

Conclusion

The 'Talpa 1993' Cooperative, in rejecting the socialist period, conformed with the 'democratic' changes initiated by the present Bulgarian government, supporting land as a personal source of wealth owned by the individual to do with as s/he pleases. It is quite clear that the members of the smaller cooperative – 'Talpa 1993' – were working primarily for the purpose of individual profit; they had no intention of providing funds for village communal needs, nor did they place much importance on collective enterprise. Such a stance also had, of course, political significance; it was a statement of support for the present political system and the 'democratic' changes initiated by the government. However, in the village this view was popular with only a small minority which was, notably, led by non-villagers (non-Talpians) residing in a nearby township.

The majority of Talpians were members of the 'Progress' cooperative. Their association with 'Progress' was clearly not primarily for reasons of profit. Indeed many of its members to whom I spoke (as for example my landlady) were certain that 'this cooperative wouldn't give a thing', that is, there was no personal financial gain to be made from membership in the cooperative. In fact the majority of villagers joined with the knowledge that the cooperative had a large debt and that it was uncertain when or even if it would begin to make a profit. Through their membership of 'Progress', members were rejecting lands as an individual source of wealth (and presumably disregarding the economic, social and political advantages that accompany land ownership in a market-capitalist system). Such a regard for their lands represented a particular view held by the majority of villagers – one which displayed an outright rejection of UDF policy encouraging the return to small private farming units and the individual ownership of land. The members of this cooperative did not explicitly express opposition in such a way, but when they said they did not want their land, this is, essentially what they were saying.

My conclusions thus contrast with those of Wyzan and Sjoberg (1992: 24) who write that '... there is little sign in Bulgaria ... of a lack of interest in a return to family farming ...'. Draganova (1993: 13) implies a similar positive picture, when she states that personal interest and independence are currently motivating villagers towards private individual farming. Regional issues may be of importance here; while the above authors' findings may be appropriate for some areas, they hold little relevance to Talpa and from my experience more generally to north-central Bulgaria. Instead, there are good political, demographic and other reasons why a substantial 'return to family farming' is unlikely to happen, at least for the present, in this region.[25]

Further, it was neither inability to adapt to the new conditions, nor lack of education which caused villagers to display preference for past socialist structures (as some believe).[26] Although it is true that a proportion of the villagers' membership in the 'Progress' cooperative can be seen as a passive response by default to the present circumstances, it is equally true that the majority of the villagers' evident support for the past socialist system via membership in 'Progress' was perfectly understandable and rational, given their political and economic interests. For it was in the past system that many of this cooperative's members were politically active and in positions of authority. It follows that villagers' political, and in part associated with this, economic power, has been greatly diminished in the last few years. In a very real way they were now much worse off than ever before; members of the 'Progress' cooperative were not only aware of this, but their actions were rational responses to this fact. Their increasingly disadvantaged position in political terms (as BSP advocates in a state structure which currently promotes an anti-Communist environment) provides some very good reasons why they were opposed to the present changes. Those with no strong political alliances had nevertheless endured much economic hardship since 1989. When their pensions bought so much less than pre-1989 and with an inflation rate of eighty percent meaning that each day they could buy

25. Agreement with my view can be found in Pryor (1991: 23), who notes that private farming as a full time occupation has been unenthusiastically received not only in Bulgaria, but also in Eastern Germany, Czechoslovakia and Hungary. Hann provides a similar conclusion in his work on Hungary (1993, especially 310-13). Similarly, Swain (1993b: 21) finds that in Hungary interest in private farming has remained relatively low, while adding that cooperative farming membership remains high. (In a more recent paper [1995], Draganova is less optimistic about the future of Bulgarian family farming under current political conditions – Ed.)

26. For example Tzvetkov (1992: 34), an activist of the UDF, sets up a contrast between that party – backed by intellectuals, youth and industrial workers – and the BSP - backed up by the elderly, less educated and politically inactive villagers. This is a convenient way to disregard the villagers' own views. Being elderly and 'less educated' does not invalidate these views, while their 'political inactivity' does not altogether fit with my experience and cannot be assumed simply from their preferred membership of cooperatives organised in a similar way to previous state ones. Such comments are, I believe, indicative of the writer's own position as an urban-based UDF activist unsympathetic to the viewpoints of rural Bulgarians.

less, villagers were aware that 'Progress' would provide them with a degree of security that 'Talpa 1993', with its business-like orientation and principles, would not.

In a situation where the new 'democratic' changes were being imposed, legally forced upon the villagers (through compulsory land ownership) membership in 'Progress' provided one form of sanctuary. By taking their land and then placing it in a huge, state cooperative type organisation – and thus revealing a total lack of interest in their property and whether or not it was profitable for the individual – the majority of Talpians were not only rejecting the 'democratic' changes initiated by the government in their present form, but also reaffirming their support for 'the good old totalitarian days', as the socialist past was currently referred to by many of them.

REFERENCES

Abrahams, R. 'The Re-generation of Family Farming in Estonia', *Sociologia Ruralis*, Vol. XXXV, No. 4, (1994): 354-368.

Anastasova, M. 'Start of the Private Agriculture in Republic of Bulgaria' (unpublished manuscript), (n.d.).

Dobrin, B. *Bulgarian Economic Development Since World War II*. New York, 1973.

Draganova, M. 'The Troubles and Conflicts Toward a New Social Order in Rural Areas', Paper presented at the 8th World Congress for Rural Sociology, Pennsylvania State University, 11-16 August, 1992.

_____, 'Auxiliary Plots of Rural Households as a Starting Point Towards Future Family Farming in Bulgaria', Paper for 15th European Congress of Rural Sociology, Agricultural Change, Rural Society and the State, Wageningen, 2-6 August, 1993.

_____, 'Family Farming in Bulgaria: Strengthening its Position and Further Development', Paper presented to workshop on Family Farming in the Contemporary World: East-West Comparisons, Krakow, 29 May-1 June, 1995.

Office for Official Publications of the European Communities, *Bulgaria's Agriculture: Situation, Trends and Prospects*, Commission of the European Communities, Luxembourg, 1991.

Hann, C.M. 'From Production to Property: De-Collectivization and the Family – Land Relationship in Contemporary Hungary', *Man*, Vol. 28, No. 2 (1993): 299-319.

The Institute of Economics, The Bulgarian Academy of Sciences, *Social and Economic Development of Bulgaria 1944-1964*. Sofia, 1964.

Kaneff, D. *Social Constructions of the Past and Their Significance in the Bulgarian Socialist State*. Doctoral Thesis, University of Adelaide, 1992.

Keliyan, M. 'Auxiliary Work in the Household-Run Farm – A Preferred Model of Agricultural Economic Activity in the Period of Changes in Bulgaria', (unpublished manuscript), (n.d.).

Lampe, J.R. *The Bulgarian Economy In the Twentieth Century*. London, 1986.

Milner, M. 'Struggling Economy Threatens to Keep Bulgaria Out in the Cold', The *Guardian*, European Business, 4 September, (1993): 35.

Pryor, F.L. 'When is Collectivization Reversible' in *Studies in Comparative Communism*, Vol. xxiv, No. 1, (1991): 3-24.

Singh, G. *Cooperative Farming in Bulgaria, Indian Farm Mechanization*. New Delhi, 1959.

Swain, N. 1993a 'Agricultural Transformation in Hungary: The Context', Paper presented to workshop on Transitions to Family Farming in Post-Socialist Central Europe, Budapest, 25-28 March, 1993.

_____, 1993b 'The Smallholders Party versus The Green Barons: Class Relations in the Restructuring of Hungarian Agriculture', Paper presented to workshop on Restructuring of Agriculture and Rural Society in Central and Eastern Europe, XVth European Congress of Rural Sociology, Wageningen, 2-6 August, 1993.

Tzvetkov, P.S. 'The Politics of Transition in Bulgaria Back to the Future?' in *Problems of Communism*, Vol. XLI, (1992): 34-43.

Wyzan, M.L. 'Bulgarian Agriculture Since 1979: Sweeping Reform and Mediocre Performance (So Far)', Paper presented at the Eighth International Conference on Soviet and East European Agriculture, Berkeley, 7-10 August, 1987.

Wyzan, M.L. & Sjoberg, O. 'Agricultural Privatization in Bulgaria and Albania: Legal Foundations and Prospects', Working Paper, Institute of East European Economics, Stockholm Working Paper, December, 1992.

4. THE PRIVATISATION AND MARKET TRANSFORMATION OF POLISH AGRICULTURE
New Conflicts and Divisions

Lucjan Kocik

Introduction

*A*lthough some points of tension are beginning to arise, the fall of Communism and the introduction of a market economy in Poland have so far not been marked by widespread major conflicts or divisions within the agricultural population itself. This is due to several factors, of which the most important are the following:

(i) Many years of quiet peasant solidarity and a passive struggle for survival with the Communist system.

(ii) Low levels of specialisation and market orientation, with a large proportion of farm output allocated to the owner's family consumption.

(iii) Relatively low potential for competition and for serious differences in productivity between individual farms.

(iv) The market economy has created neither big farming entrepreneurs nor a village 'proletariat'.

The conflicts and divisions which have emerged in various periods and with varying intensity since the fall of Communism in Poland (1989), have mainly had a macro-structural character and affected the relations between the state and peasant organisations. Conflict between state and peasants revolved around high interest rates for credit and the so-called 'minimum' prices for agricultural produce purchased from farmers.

Conflicts and divisions between peasant organisations themselves have been primarily concerned with current economic and political tactics and longer-term strategic programmes.

The Introduction of Communism into Polish Agriculture

Communism in Poland started with the Land Reform announced in 1944, allocating six million hectares of agricultural land to peasants. As a consequence of the reform, 814,000 new farms were created and another 254,000 farms were enlarged. Through the reform the size of small farms increased only by an average of 1.9 hectares, but landlessness was eliminated. The reform thus produced an increase in the number of dwarf farms based only on the manual work of family members. The reform thus scarcely constituted any full solution of the 'agrarian question', and many problems from that period still exist today.

The next step in agrarian policy was collectivisation. Up to 1956, 10,500 collective farms were organised, but almost all of them were very inefficient. Many of them were dissolved in 1957, and only 1,800 farms continued to exist.

As officially announced, the programme of collectivisation was aimed at applying industrial methods of production to agriculture, the subordination of agriculture to a centrally planned economy, and a radical change in peasant mentality.

Despite the extremely bad experience with collective farms, throughout the post-war period the principal goal of the state agricultural policy remained the transformation of a private peasant agriculture into a collective or state agriculture.[1] In accordance with the ideological doctrine

1. The state farms arose in 1964. They were established on large farms which before the war were privately owned state, latifundial and church landed estates. During 1952-1956, about 33,000 families were settled on state farms in western provinces and in some counties in north-eastern Poland. The socialist sector in Poland in the 1970s owned 25.1 percent of the total agricultural land but utilised only 19 percent, whereas it was the reverse for the private sector (74.9 percent as against 81 percent).

of national economic policy, emphasis had only been placed upon the rapid development of industry, mainly the production of the means of production. The secondary role given to the sector producing consumer goods was one of the main reasons for chronic shortage in this sphere. The permanent lack of basic everyday goods and supplies constituted a kind of socialist crisis. As a consequence of these policies, the agricultural peasant sector has remained far below the levels of investment and development that prevail in industry.

The economic structure of the peasant sector is still very problematic as a result of both the land reform and state agrarian policy. Peasant farmland is widely dispersed and this makes it difficult to organise production effectively. The average area of peasant farms in Poland is about five hectares and has increased only very slowly. Just before Martial Law was imposed in 1981, there were about three million peasant farms in Poland, of which 720,000 were run by farmers of retirement age and another 250,000 by people approaching that age. It is also estimated that almost one third of the farms had no natural successor.

Only one third of peasant families were at that time supported exclusively by their own agricultural production. The remaining two thirds were supported by mixed sources of income, i.e., by farming and non-farming employment. A typical model of such an employment pattern was a man commuting to work, while his wife remained on the farm and carried out the major share of the farm chores. This type of employment pattern was particularly popular among the middle and older generations of villagers.

By limiting the possibilities for developing private peasant family farms, Communism forced peasant families to face the alternatives of either traditional farming or collective farming. The option was offered to a generation who had been brought up to regard soil and the farm as timeless, indestructible and of priceless value, so this generation in the 1950s and 1960s preferred the traditional way. The disparities in living conditions between the rural and the urban population gave rise to the exodus of country people to urban centres and resulted in a 'negative selection' of those who remained in farming (Kocik 1988: 4). Researchers who have studied Polish rural communities unanimously agree that those who reside in villages as farmers remain in agriculture through a process of such negative selection. This process seems to be typical of a Com-

---

Some of the land which the social sector could not utilise at a given time was sometimes leased to private peasants.

munist society where greater wealth does not exist as individual property. There are other forms of stratification in the society, and different ways of locating people on the social ladder. An important indicator of position in this society is an individual's standard of education and a good non-agricultural profession.

'Repressive Tolerance' of Private Family Farms

Private farms in Poland, which covered about 80 percent of all arable land, have always contradicted Communist ideology.[2] Individual farmers, as a 'strange class' within communist society, were not incorporated into state economic planning, and their output was not properly recognised as a portion of the gross national product. They received a small share of investments, and they were basically left to their own resources.

Peasant farms had not been given priority for investment like cooperatives or state farms since they remained beyond the nationalised sector of the economy. Given this situation, state agricultural policy was based mainly on administrative methods of agricultural management. Various efforts were made to limit peasant farming. For example the state did not permit farmers to develop their farms to the extent they wished. The sale of heavy machinery to private farms was forbidden. Only at the end of the 1960s were state farms and 'Agricultural Societies' permitted to sell second-hand tractors to peasants.

Private farming was otherwise unfairly treated in comparison to the collective sector. There were major disparities in the distribution of fertilisers, pesticides and machinery in favour of collectivised farming whose output was nevertheless smaller than that of peasant farms. The goal of state policy was somehow to increase production from the private sector without developing that sector. Such a policy aimed at creating a situation in which peasant farming would quickly reach its 'limits of growth', and hence the peasants would accept collective farming as the only rational option left to them.

The nature of the relations between peasants and the socialist state can be described as 'repressive tolerance'. On the one hand, these relations were based on elements of political and administrative repression of peasant agriculture and attempts to subordinate this sector to the

---

2. I am indebted to K. Gorlach for the concept of 'repressive tolerance'. See also Gorlach, Nowak and Serega (1994).

state-directed economy. On the other hand, some elements of tolerance might be observed, especially in a situation of food shortage when peasant farming was treated as a main source of agricultural produce. Basically, the better the situation of the food market, the more limited were the possibilities of development and investment for individual peasants, and conversely, as the food situation deteriorated, the prospects for private farming became more promising.

The limits of tolerance were mapped out by Communist doctrine in which, despite some official statements, the privileged position of the state and the cooperative sector was quite visible. This was highlighted by the legal limitations set concerning the maximum land holdings to be owned by individual farmers, as well as by the problems of access to the purchase of new farmland.

In practice, family farming was subordinated to local state and bureaucratic agencies which in many cases determined the volume and type of commodity to be produced by particular farmers. These bureaucracies also had the right to decide whether a given farmer could buy a tractor or any other heavy equipment at a state-controlled price. Local state agencies controlled the system of agricultural services and local banks. They also ran the local system of so-called 'cooperative agencies' buying agricultural products from farmers and selling chemicals, pesticides and other supplies to them.

As a result, it might be said that the whole activity of the individual farmer took place within a framework controlled by the state authorities and became a peculiar 'game' within the communist system. This experience stimulated specific strategies among families of individual farmers – a kind of 'game for survival' within the system, which was represented in the first instance by local administrative units. Nevertheless, individual farmers were the only major group who maintained a relatively independent economic basis in the Communist system, and they formed one of the most important social groups challenging Communist power.

Paradoxes, Conflicts and Divisions in the Period of 'Repressive Tolerance'

Paradoxes and divisions have emerged because peasants did not identify with either the functioning of local authorities or the policies of the central government. If peasants undertook any form of group action, it largely had a strained or fictitious character, e.g., making declarations of intention to found an agricultural partnership simply in order to buy tractors at 'state[=lower] prices' or to obtain cheap credit. These were a sort of overture to the Communist authorities who had done their best to stress the economic divisions among the peasantry and to convert potential economic tensions into open class conflict between 'rich' and 'poor' peasants. The results, however, were precisely the opposite to those expected and manifested themselves in a deep mistrust of state policy.

Another important source of conflict was the administrative reform announced in 1973, which set up so called 'communal councils' as basic units of local administration. These were in fact state agencies with a wide range of powers, and they became the instruments of administrative control over private farms.

> The village universe has been divided into two strange and hostile worlds. One, that of farming peasants, convinced of the importance of this mission of producing bread, and at the same time underestimated and looked down upon. And the other world of bureaucratic institutions identified with the state. This line of division, despite the existence of many others, has proved to be decisive. (Halamska 1981)

A clear characteristic and symptom of this situation was the fact that local authorities always preferred if possible to keep to a repressive rather than tolerant course. Their representatives knew that the primary goal of Communism was the dissolution of private farms. In the long run a repressive course was simplest for them, and it enabled them to prove the usefulness of their position in the hierarchy of Communist administration. This is why in periods of more tolerant policies from central government, the local authorities did not fully obey the tolerant decisions (Gorlach 1993: 9). In this situation, the peasants saw the nation as a community in which they were members but without full rights. From this came the extreme sensitivity of rural communities to all manifestations of being treated as 'second-rate' citizens, as those who were called upon to give but were given nothing in return (Ibid.).

The 'survival game' had many facets and aspects, which are still visible to some extent in the attitudes and mentality of peasants. The most important elements of this 'game' together with their social consequences are shown in Table 4.1.

Table 4.1 Sources of Conflicts and Divisions in the F 'Repressive Tolerance'

Policy of the State	Reactions of the Peasants	Social Resul
1. Pressure for collectivisation at all costs.	Struggle to maintain family farms at all costs.	'Surviv the sta...
2. The need to provide food for the cities.	Production oriented towards the state-controlled and centralised market.	Existence of small farms tolerated.
3. Depriving the peasants of their democratic rights.	Closing up the ranks in their own world.	Lack of spontaneous forms of activity. Division of the village into the alien world of the state and the familiar world of peasants.
4. Attempts to break the solidarity of the peasants from within.	Growth of quiet solidarity and low-profile passive resistance actions.	Boycott of central authorities' decisions.
5. Restricting the possibility of land purchase.	Unofficial land trade within extended families.	Discrepancy between the official and the real ownership situation.
6. Restricting farm supplies: economy of shortages.	Pressure for self-sufficiency. Home production of tractors and agricultural machines. 'Psychosis of possession'.	Continuation of the traditional way of life. Irrational investment decisions.
7. Supply privileges for partnerships and various forms of cooperation between farmers.	Informal attempts to secure the allocation of rationed goods. Taking advantage of personal connections.	Corruption, nepotism, fictitious activity.
8. Lack of stability in the policy towards the village and the agriculture.	Attractiveness of non-farming careers for farmers' children. Distrust of all state declarations and plans, even the positive ones.	Negative selection for the farmer's profession. Insubordination of local administration, who usually still support the old repressive measures, regardless of the more tolerant attitude of central authorities.

The Background of New Conflicts and Divisions at the Threshold of the Market Economy

An important element of the restructuring process in Polish agriculture is the transformation of ownership taking place both in socialised forms of production and in cooperative and state institutions providing agricultural services (see Psyk-Piotrowska 1993: 3).

badly understood, socialised agriculture in Poland included: a) state farms, b) cooperative enterprises and other cooperative forms of agricultural production, and c) state or quasi-state institutions providing services for (mainly private) farms. These institutions included among others cooperative banks, dairy cooperatives, and cooperative agricultural societies which all serviced private agriculture and which existed separately from official agricultural cooperatives, as cooperatives (or joint ventures) of the peasants themselves. Yet they too were mostly organised by state initiatives and made to fit into regulations deemed appropriate for an otherwise socialist economy and society. One important element was the agricultural 'circles' which were complemented by the state-owned Machinery Centres. The latter also took over the repair and maintenance of agricultural machines.

The privatisation which has embraced these institutions has also affected the farms of many peasants who cooperated with the system of socialised services. In many cases, these peasants represented attitudes of 'individualistic' socialism, based on favourable relations with managers of state agriculture and the service sector. With this in mind, it is worth considering further aspects of the situation in Polish agriculture.

The problem of actually privatising farming does not arise in Poland. Poland has already passed the stage of transformation to private ownership because of its unsuccessful programme of collective farming in the Stalinist period. So, within the former Soviet Bloc countries, the situation of Polish agriculture was unique. Nevertheless, the present condition of family farming shows the naive character of many statements and declarations. According to these statements, family farms which formed an enclave of free enterprise in the state-controlled Communist economy were expected to become, under improved conditions, the springboard of a capitalist market economy. However, it now becomes apparent that the heritage with which these farms emerge from the Communist economy may cause serious problems in the creation of new economic and social relations in Poland.

An important element of reform implemented in all the ex-Communist countries was the withdrawal of subsidies, which inevitably produced sharp price rises and inflation. This method of reform is greatly increasing the social costs of economic transformation.

Organisational transformations and the process of changing the economic system created a new challenge for Polish farmers. Elimination of state subsidies for the means of production resulted in a sharp rise in the prices of products and consumer goods. As a result, the average Polish family at the beginning of the 1990s began to spend approximately 60 percent of its monthly income on food, while in some poorer sections of society this figure has risen to 80-90 percent. This has limited demand for various food products which has resulted in farmers not being able to market their output. Only those producers who are able to lower their costs sufficiently to offer competitive prices are able to sell all of their agricultural produce. This explains why farmers were calling for the formation of an Agricultural Market Agency, a state office for the purchase of surplus agricultural products.

This issue is closely connected with the prices which farmers can get for their products. Farmers' political and trade organisations demanded the introduction of guaranteed minimum prices for basic agricultural products since poor prices have led to the decline of agricultural production over the last two years, which has also led to a decrease in the growth of exports. The value of exports in 1991 was only 19 percent higher than in 1990. During the same period the value of food imports to Poland increased by 130 percent Gorlach 1992: 3).

It is not surprising therefore that in this process of change, farmers are also severely critical of the new situation and of successive post-Communist governments. For peasants who 'survived' the Communist period, it was very difficult to understand that the role of the state has become limited to financial intervention or to the purchase of surplus agricultural commodities.

There are three main issues concerning the above-mentioned problems. Firstly, there is the influence of external factors. Polish agriculture, like the national economy as a whole, is put to the test by new connections to the European and world economic system. Secondly, some regional differences on a national level have started to emerge more significantly than in the past.[3] Larger and more commercially oriented family farms in northern and western parts of Poland have started to develop and dominate over the small and traditional farms of east, central and southern Poland. Thirdly on a local level, neighbouring farms with different levels of market orientation have now started to compete with each other.

We should also bear in mind that, under the transition to a market economy, some reconstruction processes of the peasantry are occurring spontaneously with a variety of possible consequences. On the one hand,

---

3. The regional differences which are found throughout the country are quite substantial. Many of them are a product of the country's complex history. A major influence in this was the partition of Poland in the late eighteenth century. Particular parts of Poland were for over a hundred years incorporated in the political, economic and social systems of Austria, Prussia and Russia.

one might expect that larger-scale farm owners (not common among Polish peasants) will be forced to transform themselves into businessmen. On the other hand, a possible outcome may be the disappearance of the very large category of small-scale peasants. They are beginning to lose their economic and hence political importance, and are already adding to the number of jobless people (in 1994 almost 15 percent of the labour force). One can then foresee that the social category of 'rural proletariat', typical for the countryside in pre-war Poland, might be restored. These processes will provoke many tensions and conflicts, and some of them have begun to be visible in Polish social life since 1990 (Kwaśniewicz 1993).

A Disappointing 'Reward' for Polish Peasants for Surviving Communism

The most important pressures and constraints faced by peasants were rooted in the real market game and in the redefined role of the state in economy and society. According to Gorlach (1993), the core of this threat lies in the complex of 'oppressive freedom'. Farmers were especially exposed to market constraints because they remained private owners under Communist rule. Therefore, they immediately suffered the harsh reality of economic transition. The experience of paid workers (including state-farm workers) and even that of the intelligentsia was quite different because they stayed protected for a while by the state system of maintaining the level of their wages despite rocketing inflation and interest rates (Ibid.: 40).

The situation described above seems to hold a major historical and political paradox. The peasants, as the only large category of society to be reckoned with, had challenged the Communist system and contributed significantly to its dismantling. Thereafter they suffered the greatest economic losses and found themselves in a situation more difficult than that of other social groups. This was, ironically, the 'economic reward' for the peasants' survival of Communism.

The Character and Range of Socio-Economic Expectations of Peasants

The farmers' solidarity movement was founded in the autumn of 1980 as part of the great national movement challenging the Communist system in Poland. However, it should be stressed that, from the start, the movement was characterised as having both universal and some rather special features. For example, the farmers were the only group which founded a separate 'Solidarity' organisation. This fact seems to confirm the feeling of a specific identity among peasants as a distinct social collectivity with its own class and occupational interests. As Wierzbicki and Rambaud have remarked:

> In contrast to the worker's evolving demands, the farmers' programme never changed, and, moreover, was marked by a greater degree of realism. The agreements between the farmers and the government may be divided into three parts. First, the demands of a 'bourgeois' character, so to speak, in the centre of which we find private ownership of land and formal equality in the eyes of law: then some others that may be termed socialist: and finally those of universal value, i.e., without reference to any specific platform. (Wierzbicki and Rambaud 1982: 216)

The nature and range of the socio-economic expectations of peasants are listed in Table 4.2.

Table 4.2 The Nature and Range of the Socio-Economic Expectations of Peasants

The Nature of the Expectation	The Range of the Expectation
Bourgeois	Guarantees for private property.
	Unlimited inheritance rights.
	Introduction of a free land market.
	Protection of farmers from the abuses of the free market.
Socialist	Farmers' participation in the regulation of prices.
	Farmers' participation in the allocation of low-interest loans and means of production.
	Development of the village cultural infrastructure by the state.
	Equalising the living conditions in the country and in the cities.
	Establishing free trade unions.
Universal	Religious freedom.
	Respect for tradition.
	Limiting propaganda in education and the mass media.

The diverse nature of the above demands and expectations was the reason why, in the period 1980-1981, there existed three farmers' 'Solidarities': The Independent Self-Governing Union for Individual Farmers 'Solidarity'; 'Peasant Solidarity'; and 'Rural Solidarity'. Each of these Solidarity movements concentrated on different parts of the farmers' demands. However, the introduction of martial law (December 1981) resulted in the unification of city workers and peasants in one common Solidarity ethos, which was based on broad values such as freedom, human rights, and democracy.

The Emergence of New Conflicts and Divisions: Peasant Families in the Face of 'Oppressive Freedom'

The period of political and economic reforms which started after the first Solidarity Government was formed could be called 'oppressive freedom'. Let us look more closely at this concept. The term was proposed by Gorlach as a contrast to the idea of 'repressive tolerance', and as a result of the passing of society from a centrally controlled economy and one-party political system to a market economy and political democracy (Gorlach, Nowak and Serega 1994).

A situation of oppressive freedom includes two basic elements. On the one hand, political and administrative pressures on initiatives advocated by individuals and groups are removed. Such pressures are part of a totalitarian system and were removed when this system was abandoned. However its place was taken by a different sort of pressure, namely an economic one in the form of requirements of competition, flexibility and adaptability. This pressure is part of the market system which is increasingly present in different areas of socio-economic life, and of the competition which it includes.

The patterns of reasoning and behaviour established during the period of 'repressive tolerance' conflict with the new socio-economic situation. Survival strategies, methods of adaptation to political and administrative pressures, and the 'game for survival' with the authorities, established under the previous system, are useless in the face of market pressures and the market game.

As a result, the situation of oppressive freedom is really a situation of 'economic compulsion'. Its oppressive character arises partly from the necessity of making decisions and creating a strategy of action in the market game. Apart from difficulties inherent in this process itself, there is additionally a painful conflict between a mentality created during the period of 'repressive tolerance' and the new reality functioning according to completely different rules.

As regards relations between family farms and local administration units, one should stress that all the rules and systems of control have been abolished. Local administrative officers are no longer the decision makers regulating the volume and type of commodity produced in administrative areas. This kind of state regulation of the economy has been replaced by market forces. On a wider level the role of the state has been limited to financial intervention or the purchase of surplus agricultural commodities.

As a result of these changes and factors a specific situation of 'oppressive freedom' has emerged. This is characterised by lack of political pressure and limitations imposed by the administrative system, but also by a situation in which farmers are forced to make their own decisions every single day and adapt to changing economic rules.

During the period of 'repressive tolerance', farms were used to centrally fixed low, but relatively stable, prices of supplies and agricultural produce, and above all to an economy marked by chronic shortages which made the purchase of the means of production extremely difficult, but guaranteed the easy, centrally organised sale of all products of virtually any quality and in any amount.

These problems bring out the need for careful analysis of family farming issues in order to describe and explain the paradox that the most important and largest group of private owners in the Communist economy, in which family farming was treated as a residue of a market economy, has became one of the most important forces calling for state intervention within the market economy game.[4]

Common Ethos – Different Interests

As soon as Communism fell, the common 'evil' and the common struggle disappeared, and the peasants had to collect their disappointing 'reward' for surviving Communism. The common ethos of 'solidarity'

---

4. Ibid. From summer 1989 when the first 'Solidarity' government was formed, farmers organised some spectacular protests to defend their interests. One can point to several road blocks by tractors and machinery, a sit-in strike in the Ministry of Agriculture building, and hunger strikes and protest marches in the streets of Warsaw in 1991, 1992 and 1993.

remained, but interests diverged resulting in a fragmentation of the former movement. Many 'ethos carriers' appeared, however, to have weak
organisational structures (Staniszkis 1992: 45). In this respect, there has
been a clear revival among the peasants of the sense of their separate
identity and separate community with the conviction that 'what is good
for my country may not be good for me'.

The defeat of the common enemy of Communism resulted then in
the division of the previous Solidarity, its goals, and activities as conflicting interests dictated. A number of new movements and groups came
into being or were revived although they had a weak social basis and represented various, frequently very limited group interests. On the other
hand, formal institutions of the Polish state became open to participation
by various groups. This was the reason why conflicts often took place
among the leaders of peasant organisations. This supports Tarrow's
(1989) thesis that political conflicts within and among elites are the way
in which unrepresented groups are encouraged to protest. This was probably the cause of the 'Self-Defence' *(Samoobrona)* movement, which represented primarily the category of heavily indebted farmers, who were
the most immediate victims of the new economic situation. The protests
organised by 'Self-Defence' were also aimed against other peasant organisations recognised as part of the state complex of rural movements and
post-Communist organisations. The populist identity of 'Self-Defence'
was both anti-Communist and anti-Solidarity (cf. Gorlach 1993:41).

The Diversity of Peasant Organisations and Programmes

There are within the rural population some organisations with relatively
strong structures and many members linked to them by their interests.
The most important socio-economic programmes were developed by
four major organisations (Ibid.: 42).

1) The *Polish Peasant Party* (the Former United Peasant Party) stresses
   that in the process of integration with Western Europe, Poland
   should be aware of existing threats and protect its own economic
   interests. The Party supports the active role of the state in the economy, the protection of a domestic market against foreign producers, and trade barriers and quotas. Minimal prices for agricultural
   commodities should be guaranteed by the state in order to protect
   Polish farms facing rapid changes in the market.

2) *Peasant Agreement* (the main Solidarity structure in the peasant political movement). This party shares many views with its above-mentioned post-Communist adversary. It was formed as a political branch of the Self-Governing Independent Trade Union for Individual Farmers 'Solidarity'. According to its programme the domestic market should be protected using all the instruments of such policy – customs tariffs, quotas for imported goods, and so forth. Farmers should be reassured by a programme of minimum prices guaranteed by the state. Moreover, the real weaknesses of many Polish family farms i.e., small acreage, low levels of mechanisation, traditional methods of farming, should be turned to their benefit. Polish farmers should compete on the international market, selling high-quality food produced in a more expensive but more natural way.

3) The *Christian Peasant Party* stresses the necessity of integration with the countries of the European Union. The Polish state should not be overprotective and imports from foreign bodies should be a factor of enforced competition for Polish farmers. State agricultural policy should not protect farms at any price, but should push the privatisation process in the food processing industry. This should help to create new jobs in rural communities but not in agriculture.

4) The Farmers' Trade Union, *Self-Defence* claims that Poland should reach the economic level of Western European countries before starting the integration mechanism. Polish agriculture should be 're-animated' after four years of Solidarity governments, and a new liberal economic policy should be established. 'Self-Defence' introduced the idea of so-called 'payable prices' for agricultural commodities into political discourse. This means essentially that the state should guarantee profit for every farmer in Poland.

As a result of this state of affairs, the rural political sphere is sharply divided into several parts. The former common and universal Solidarity ethos becomes replaced by a variety of populist attitudes towards the state.

Conclusions

In the contemporary situation of rural Poland we can see generally speaking an attempt to transfer behavioural patterns developed at a local level to dealings with the wider society (Gorlach *et al.* 1994: 161). The main focus of demands has become the central government which is seen as 'anti-farmer' by many farmers and as setting the rules of the 'oppressive freedom' game. It is natural therefore that a large percentage of people point to certain general problems which the central authorities ought to solve for the farmers. One result of adopting such a strategy is an inclination to indulge in spectacular protest activities in an attempt to attract widespread attention to the oppression suffered by family-farm owners.

The move from the previous situation of 'repressive tolerance' to the present one of 'oppressive freedom' has brought many constraints on farming families. Old habits and strategies of action are dysfunctional today and some new patterns and strategies are required. This illustrates that political freedom has caused many new problems. As one farmer said in interview, 'under communism there was no freedom but there was cheap credit, but it is over right now' (Ibid.).

The farmer's discourse now seems to be organised around the values recognised as oppositional to the existing reality. Under Communism such a discourse was organised around 'freedom'. A Polish farmer liked to stress that he was his 'own boss' in the static and repressive social order of Communism. Today such a feeling is nothing but ironic reminiscence of the past. Being 'one's own boss' means nothing but taking decisions by oneself, resulting in uncertain consequences in the commercialised reality of developing a capitalist economy.

The freedom or 'credit' dilemma constricts the farmer's space yet again. As is beautifully summed up by K. Gorlach (1993: 47) in a somewhat dolorous statement – many farmers seem to be ready to solve this dilemma simply by selling freedom for credit.

REFERENCES

Gorlach, K. 'Between State and Market: Changing Agriculture in Post-communist Poland', *Program on Central and Eastern Europe Working Paper Series*, No. 29, Cambridge, Mass. 1992.

———, ' Freedom versus Credit', a paper for the conference 'Trials of Transition', Harvard University. December 1993.

Gorlach, K., Nowak, P., Serega, Z. 'Family farms in Post-communist Poland. From "repressive tolerance" to "oppressive freedom"' in *Agricultural*

Restructuring and Rural Change in Europe, ed. D. Symes and A. Jansen, Wageningen, 1994, 153-162.

Halamska, M. '*Społeczne przesłanki powstania NSZZ RI 'Solidarność'*, *Wieś współczesna*, Vol. 11, (1981): 26-33.

Kocik, L. 'Peasants' Private Farms of Consumption Type in Contemporary Poland – Their Economic and Socio-Cultural Background'. A paper for the 7th World Congress for Rural Sociology, Bologna, 1988.

Kwaśniewicz, W. 'The Uncertain Future of Polish Peasants'. Abstract delivered to the XVth European Congress for Rural Sociology, Wageningen, 1993.

Psyk-Piotrowska, E. 'Forms of Decollectivization of Socialized Farms in Poland'. A paper delivered to the XVth European Congress for Rural Sociology, Wageningen, 1993.

Staniszkis, J. *The Ontology of Socialism*. Oxford, 1992.

Tarrow, S. 'Struggle, Politics and Reform: Collective Action, Social Movements and Cycles of Protest, *Western Societies Program Occasional Paper*, no. 21 (2nd ed), Center for International Studies, Cornell University, 1989.

Wierzbicki, Z. and Rambaud, P. 'The Emergence of the First Agricultural Trade Union in Socialist Poland, *Sociologia Ruralis*, Vol. XXII, No. 3-4, (1982): 209-225.

5. Redefining Women's Work in Rural Poland

Frances Pine

Introduction

*O*ne of the ironies of the eastern European socialist states is that what they did accomplish, in terms of social policy underpinned by basic premises of gender, ethnicity and class equality, was rarely recognised at the time and has become valued, and almost reinvented as a positive tradition, only since their demise. In Poland the flaws of the centralised system, its extensive and highly visible levels of corruption, and above all its association, with all of the unfortunate historical precedents this entailed, with Russian imperialism, all served to mask the ways in which actually lived socialism did in fact succeed in making daily life better in some ways for many people. This is particularly germane to the discussion of gender.[1] Poland, like other regimes in the Eastern Bloc, had extremely progressive

1. Versions of this paper were also given at the ESRC Gender Seminar at CREES, the University of Birmingham, and at The ESRC seminar on Post-socialist Transition at Birkbeck College. I am grateful to the participants of both for comments; Ruth Pearson was a particularly astute and generous discussant at the Birkbeck paper. I would also like to thank Keith Hart for detailed comments on a much earlier variation, and Deema Kaneff, Paola Filippucci and Tom Bogdanowicz for careful read-

laws concerning women and the protection of women's rights. During the socialist period, what often caught the attention of Poles and Western observers alike was the fact that these laws were unlikely to be properly implemented, and that most women carried a 'double' or even 'triple' burden, in terms of responsibility for domestic labour and childcare, waged work, and (the triple factor) in the case of rural women agricultural labour as well. Equal participation in the work force, for equal pay, was guaranteed for women, but this often meant in practice participation at the lowest end of the income scale, in the worst jobs with the lowest status. At the same time, the domestic sphere continued to be associated primarily with women, and most women worked both in full-time waged work and in full-time, unwaged and unacknowledged domestic labour and childcare.[2] These issues have been discussed in detail elsewhere, and I shall not go into them further here.[3] The point I wish to stress is that as long as it appeared to be entrenched, the socialist system was popularly judged by its omissions rather than by its achievements. Inside Poland itself, these judgments were formulated in constant reference both to an historical (imagined?) past and a contemporary contrast to the West.

As was (and is) the case in other Slavonic symbolic representations of nation, Poland was historically represented as the mother, 'Matka Polka' (Siemienska 1986; Reading 1992). During the Partition Period, men were portrayed in dominant ideology as active in the public, political sphere, fighting for the nationalist cause, while women were seen as keeping the nation alive in the home, teaching their children Polish culture, language and Catholicism (Siemienska 1986; Reading 1992).[4] Similar trends of symbolic identification of women with home and nation and men with public agency recurred during the Nazi occupation, and again under socialism, projected by an imagery in which women were the core of national identity and the mother who, like

---

ing of the current paper. An earlier version appears in *Cambridge Anthropology*, Vol. 17, No. 3, (1994), 19-22.

2. One of my favourite political cartoons was published on International Women's Day in the underground Solidarity press during Martial Law. It depicts a statue of a woman laden down by a shopping bag in each hand. At the base of the statue is written 'Matka Polska' – 'Mother Poland'. Two male officials are looking at the statue, and one is commenting to the other 'But she is leaning to one side!' The other is responding 'Yes, we are going to increase the burden on the other side to make her balanced.'
3. For more detailed discussion see Scott 1976, Jancar 1978, Rai, Pilkington and Phizacklea 1992.
4. Between 1772-1918 Poland ceased to exist as a nation state and was divided between Austria-Hungary, Prussia and Russia.

Mary, provided and nurtured its inner spiritual strength. These images of women clearly reflect the dominant ideology of each epoch; it seems doubtful that they spoke to the daily experience of peasant or even working-class women. Nevertheless, the imagery was, to at least some extent, incorporated into a more general ideal representation of both femininity and masculinity; like any other dominant ideology, it both distorted and to some extent informed the ideal world view of the dominated classes. Under socialism, the anomalies of class were somewhat circumvented as the symbol of nurturing mother was combined with another representation which was more a part of the peasants' or workers' gender order than that of the intelligentsia. Here women were portrayed, like men, as strong and powerful workers, although their role as mothers continued to be stressed as well. This representation tends to be viewed by women today with the same sort of retroactive ambivalence with which they judge socialism itself: on the one hand the images are taken as symbolic manifestations of the double burden of women, and the denial of their 'natural' femininity, while on the other hand they are seen as attesting to a level of agency and achievement which was possible for women under socialism and which is now being eroded (Einhorn 1993). The new Western-style glossy magazines for women and the endless dubbed television advertisements promoting Omo and Ariel and Pampers reinforce a quite different view of women, one which locates them in the kitchen, the nursery and the bedroom but rarely in the fields or on the factory floor. For many rural and working-class women, these images no more reflect the reality of their lives than did earlier portrayals of the female as icon of the nation.

During the socialist period, the West appeared to extend a promise of a better life for women, regardless of class. It seemed that under capitalism it was possible for women to work part-time or not at all, to reign over kitchens full of modern domestic appliances, and to live a life mirroring the sweetest images depicted in the pages of Western magazines and scenes in Western television serials and films. It is, I think, this idealised view of women's position in the West, and the failure of the new system even to approximate it, which has been in part responsible for many Polish women's disappointment in the new capitalist economy. While the demand economy has provided a range of opportunities and benefits for some women, for many others, particularly rural working-class women, it has merely compounded the load they were already carrying.

Overall, women account for more than 50 per cent of the registered unemployed in Poland, and many more women are among the growing numbers of 'hidden' unemployed. The fact of unemployment and loss of income for women has both practical implications for domestic relations between men and women, and cultural/political implications for representations of women and ideologies of gender. As well as creating unemployment, the process of privatisation and economic restructuring has produced significant changes in the welfare system and social services, many if not most of which have direct bearing on the gendered organisation of kinship and community relations. Severe curtailing of subsidised childcare, cuts in education, increasing privatisation of medical services, and the removal of benefits such as housing, subsidised shops, health and unemployment insurance which were previously associated with state employment all affect the lives of women and men differently, and serve both to reinforce and to transform existing gender ideologies.

Barbara Einhorn's recent discussion of citizenship in post-socialist eastern Europe is relevant here: she argues that 'relegating women to the private sphere in the name of national interest, depriving them of the right to autonomy and self determination through active participation in the public sphere ...' are examples of the contraction of membership in the nation state parallel to restrictions based on race and ethnicity (Ibid.: 259; for a comparative discussion see Morris 1994). What my own research with rural women in Poland reflects is a relegation of some women to the private sphere and simultaneously an increasing number of constraints on the ways in which others are able to participate in the public sphere.

The Public and the Private

Before turning to specific ethnography, it is useful to consider some of the implications privatisation has for newly emergent definitions of public and private. An argument I wish to develop here is that the move towards a free market economy has entailed a conceptual restructuring of boundaries between public and private spheres, which is in itself helping to reshape gendered domains.

The concept of 'private' is an ambiguous one in recent Polish economic history. '*Proces prywytacya*', the process of privatisation, usually refers to the selling off, since 1989, of state-owned assets such as factories, collective farms, transport systems, buildings, land and machinery. This is in itself a highly complex legal and political-social procedure, sometimes involving individual purchase, sometimes new systems of

worker ownership, sometimes foreign investment, and sometimes liquidation. Privatisation of a factory, collective farm or business does not
merely mean a change in management; it also threatens many of the
attached social services such as health care, child care, housing and subsidised shops which the workers came to expect under socialism, and the
loss of which is difficult to bear.

The concept of a *prywatny* (private) sphere was also, however, a significant one in the Polish economy prior to 1989. In terms of the Eastern Bloc, the Polish socialist state was atypical in allowing a significant
amount of legal private enterprise to exist. The most obvious example of
this private sphere, and one highly relevant for the current discussion,
was agriculture.

Polish peasants were both steadfast and successful in their opposition
to collectivisation throughout the socialist period. The result was that,
unlike the rest of the Soviet Bloc, Poland continued to maintain an
extremely high number of private farms (Pine and Bogdanowicz 1982;
Hann 1985; Kolankiewicz and Lewis 1988). Over 85 percent of farm
land was privately owned throughout the socialist period, held mostly
in the form of farms of under 5 hectares. As over 60 percent of the Polish population was rural, and most of these people were involved in
some way in agriculture, there was, even from the beginning of the
socialist regime, a significant tolerance of private ownership and enterprise, which affected the lives and livelihood of a major proportion of
the population.

During the Gierek regime of the 1970s, this tolerance of a private sector increased dramatically. Legal private enterprises were licensed by the
government and their owners were allowed to practise their trade as long
as they paid taxes and worked within a strict quota system. At the same
time, the semi-legal and illegal second economy grew, in which almost
anything could be secured for the right price, often a price set in dollars.
The Gierek regime borrowed vast sums of Western capital from the
United States government and international banks and then, faced with
the insurmountable task of servicing their foreign debt, on the whole
turned a blind eye to second economy dealings, particularly those
involving dollars. Many Poles straddled the boundary between the public and the private sectors, working in both in order to secure a living
income. The conceptual opposition during this period was between
things *prywatny* and things *państwowy* (state or government). While the
boundaries between the two were unclear and the spheres often over-
lapped, there was general popular consensus that things *prywatny* were

superior, both in terms of consumer satisfaction and in moral terms, to things *państwowy*.

The distinction between private and state or public spheres was also significant in a quite different and far more nebulous fashion during the socialist period, in health and social services. This was most apparent in the areas of reproductive rights and general access to health care. During the socialist period, abstinence, the rhythm method and abortion were the most common methods of birth control.[5] Although abortions were carried out within the public, state sphere, the decision-making process surrounding them was on the whole private. In the early 1990s, the Catholic Church and various right-wing nationalist parties fought to make abortion illegal under all but the most extreme circumstances. Women's organisations, the parties linked to the former socialists, and a large proportion of Unia Demokratyczna, the party which emerged from the more progressive branch of Solidarity, were all opposed to the proposed changes as were most of the population (Heinen 1992, CBOS 1993a).

> Abortion is not an affair for the government; it is for a woman and her conscience. I am a Catholic, but the church and the government have no right to decide this. Who will feed these children? Will the government pay for their medicines? Will the government give us school books and clothes? Women are going to continue to have abortions at home, and they will die.

These comments, made to me by a peasant woman with young children, are typical of the responses I heard over and over again, from men and women of all ages, concerning abortion. Strikes and inflation were public issues, about which the government should be concerned. Abortion was a private matter involving a woman and her own conscience, in which neither the state nor the church should interfere.[6] Nevertheless, in 1993 the anti-abortion legislation was passed, effectively removing reproductive rights from the private, domestic sphere and placing them within the context of public legislation and state control.

5. Mechanical contraceptives were in extremely short supply, and when they were available, were often viewed by women as damaging to their health or unreliable.
6. During 1992 and 1993 I interviewed women of all ages and classes in the area around Łódz and in the mountains; I also had many informal conversations with men and women concerning abortion. What was striking was that among all of the people I spoke to, all defined themselves as Catholics, and yet only one woman supported the anti-abortion legislation. The language they used was also remarkably consistent, both women and men continually referred to abortion as a private matter between a woman and her own conscience.

In other matters of health care, rather the reverse process is currently taking place. As hospitals close down partly or completely, and as medical practitioners are increasingly leaving the state sector for private practice, much of the care formerly provided in the public sector is now situated within either the domestic group or the privatised sphere of the public sector. Whether people go to private medical clinics or nurse their kin at home is of course at least partly dependent upon income. This is an important aspect of gendered issues of privatisation, as it highlights the fact that class, regionalism and so forth divide both women and men as categories as much as sex unites each.

Increasingly for women, the public and private spheres are being reversed; work, formerly freely available in the public sphere, is being relegated to the household and family, and increasingly rendered invisible. Health care and social services are being removed from the public sphere and placed under the responsibility of the family, primarily the women. Birth control and reproductive rights, under socialism matters of private decision, have been placed firmly in the realm of state and church control. All of these issues relate directly to the discussion of female citizenship.

Since the demise of the socialist regime, the concepts of public and private have been transformed in various ways. Whereas under socialism *prywatny* activities were popularly opposed to those in the state sector, and in many ways perceived as morally superior, they now are imbued with different sets of meanings. They still tend to be viewed as better than what the state has to offer, but they also often imply a kind of moral bankruptcy associated with the new capitalism. In the same way that people used to speak of doing things privately, they now speak, with conscious irony, of doing things *domowy* (in the house or at home, equivalent to a Western 'do it yourself'). The word private becomes increasingly ambiguous, as it is associated both with the world of the household, the family and the individual, that is with reproduction, and with the development of new economic structures in the 'public' domain, or with production. In terms of gender these are important distinctions, as women's activities are increasingly associated with the domestic and private sphere, while their access to the new privatised, public sector is frequently far more problematic than that of men (CBOS 1994).

In the remainder of this chapter, I shall explore some of implications of the macro-level process of restructuring and privatisation for gender issues in daily life, drawing on material from two very different areas where I have been doing research, the countryside around Lódz in central Poland and in the Podhale region of the south-western Tatra Mountains.[7]

Regional Background

These two areas are interesting to compare because in statistical terms they appear to be very similar. Both have extremely high official rates of unemployment. In both areas the numbers of women account for more than half of the claimants of unemployment benefit. The experience of unemployment, however, is rather different for women in the two areas, and in both it is different again from the experience of men.

The Lódz region – incorporated peasant-workers

The area around Lódz has a long established mixed economy. While peasant farming is important in terms of livelihood to much of the population, the real economic heartbeat of the area is light industry, particularly the textile industry. Lódz has been the centre of the Polish textile trade since the nineteenth century when, as part of the Russian empire, the industry first grew up to provide uniforms for the Czar's army. In the nineteenth century, Kochanowicz argues, 'production moved into factories from family workshops. The Kingdom of Poland became the most industrialised part of the Russian Empire, at least up to the last decade of the century ... Being on the western borders of the Empire, the industry of Lódz could take advantage of the huge Russian and Far Eastern markets and remain protected from neighbouring Western competition' (1989: 121). Light industry continued to grow with the restoration of the Polish nation between the two world wars. During the Nazi occupation most of the large factories, many owned by Jews, were appropriated and Polish forced labour was used, under German management, to provide for the needs of the military once again. With the establishment of the socialist regime in 1947, the factories were nationalised by the state.

7.   I am grateful to the ESRC for funding this research, and to the ESRC (then SSRC) and the British Council for funding earlier research, in 1977-1979, 1981 and 1988-1990, in the mountain region, on which I shall also draw. Some of the data on which this article is based are also drawn from a Polish national survey, *Women 93 (Kobiety '93)*, funded by the ESRC in conjunction with my 1992-1995 project and administered by the *Centrum Badania Opinii Spo-ecznej* (Centre for Research on Public Opinion) in August 1993. For an English translation of the findings see Pine (1995).

From the mid to late nineteenth century onwards, therefore, the textile factories of Lódz itself and its growing number of dormer towns provided employment for many peasant villagers; here, as elsewhere, the textile industry relied heavily on the labour of women.

Until the socialist period, peasant women who worked in factories usually boarded in town, returning to their village homes only on weekends. Those with young children left them in the care of their parents or siblings. Wages were low and working conditions very poor, but for many women there were no alternatives to factory work; in this area inheritance tended to be impartible, and while the labour of wives and daughters was essential to the farming process, they rarely held land in their own right.

Under socialism, working conditions for women improved significantly. Partly because of the repeated failure of agricultural collectivisation programmes, the governments of the 1950s and 1960s invested heavily in industrial and infrastructure development. Old factories were expanded, and new ones built. The male work force had been drastically depleted by the ravages of the war, and during this period there was a deliberate government campaign to integrate women into the workforce. Equally, the policy of full employment meant that in predominantly female occupations, such as the textile industry, more women were able to get and to keep work. In the factories, the government established medical and dental clinics, and all women were given regular checkups. Pensions, sickness benefits and maternity benefit were all linked to state employment, as were subsidised medical care, housing, and often factory shops. Improved communications and transport systems also somewhat eased the daily lives of rural women. For instance, in the village outside Lódz where I conducted research, the government built a railway station in the 1950s. This made an enormous changes in the lives of factory women, who were able to commute to work from the village rather than boarding in town; for those with children this was particularly significant, as it meant that they could live with their children at home and still maintain their jobs.

Although officially factory work was a field of open recruitment, in fact many directors preferred to hire the sisters and daughters of women already in their employ. Bonds between co-workers tended to be strong, and women reminiscing about their working lives frequently stress the pleasure that they derived from the companionship and support of their fellow workers. The work itself was extremely hard and demanding; this area has a high rate of miscarriage, reproductive disorders, and other health problems directly related to hard manual labour and to unhealthy and polluted work places. While they rarely diminish the difficulties of their work or romanticise it in any way, however, all of the factory women to whom I have spoken stress with pride their skills as seam-stresses or weavers, and their physical strength and endurance. What emerges from the women's accounts of their working lives during the socialist regime is a picture of very strong personal identity derived from waged work, from economic autonomy, and from the social relations of the workplace. While these women were certainly critical of the socialist regime, and in many ways of the conditions under which they had to work – Solidarity was particularly active in the Lódz region, and many factories experienced strikes and sit-ins – they also recognised the positive benefits which accompanied state employment, and the marked improvements in working conditions.

Their long history of waged work gave these rural women an established place in the public sphere. It also provided them with a strong position from which to negotiate their relations with their spouses and male kin. All of the married women to whom I spoke said that they controlled the family purse (the phrase they use is *trzyma kasa*, literally hold the till), and most seemed surprised that such a question should even be asked. Most women claimed that they made all daily decisions concerning the domestic budget, such as those concerning food, children's clothes and the like, while an unusual purchase such as a television, a piece of furniture or any other expensive item would be made in conjunction with their spouse. Decisions concerning farm expenditure, however, were nearly always taken by men.

The Lódz region has been one of those hit hardest by the restructuring process. Many of the older factories with outdated machinery have been closed down, while some of the more modern ones have been privatised. Some of the new owners are groups of local entrepreneurs, or workers' cooperatives, but others are Western companies, primarily from Germany and Italy. While lay-offs of workers occur in each type of privatised factory, the most drastic measures of restructuring appear to take place in the foreign-owned firms, and it against these new owners more than any of the others that the local workers express their anger and resentment. The following words were spoken to me by a shop assistant in one of the poorest districts of Lódz: 'See that factory over there [pointing to a mammoth Gothic red brick building, looking like something straight out of Zola or Dickens]? It's closing down, and they say the Germans want to buy it. The Germans come here and buy our factories for next to nothing and fire our workers. They want to EAT us.'

The image of being eaten, or sucked dry, by the West, is a recurring one in this area, and reflects a strong moral judgment on the process of privatisation.[8] The new private foreign owners are depicted in terms totally outside of correct morality; the metaphor of consumption/cannibalism implicitly opposes foreign private ownership to the proper morality of both the nurturing, feeding domestic sphere and the (ideally) nurturing, supportive socialist public sphere. Such local anger is not difficult to understand. Many of the problems which are currently besetting the textile industry stem from the collapse of the Russian market for Polish goods, but others are connected to the conditions set by the European Union for Poland's associate status, which both protect Western textiles from undercutting, and require Poland to import Western goods. It is also true that entire factories, with all of their equipment, were sold to Western firms in the early days of privatisation for ridiculously low prices.

Both men and women, when they become unemployed, are entitled to collect unemployment benefit for a year if they have been working legally for at least the previous three months. When their entitlement to benefit runs out, they can apply for social security benefits. Neither of these payments is really enough to live on.

Some of the unemployed are able to supplement any benefit they receive by working informally, 'on the side'. For men such work may involve manual labour, driving, doing odd jobs for private families or for one or more of the many small business and enterprises which regularly spring up in the region. Women are harder pressed to find such ad hoc work; they may take in sewing for neighbours, but, as several women I spoke to pointed out, in this region all women can sew, and they are unlikely to pay someone else to do it for them. Cleaning and child-minding are also possible sources of occasional income but most people turn to their kin when they need such help rather than pay for it (see also CBOS 1993b, 1993c).

When those who have lost their jobs do manage to find work, it is often through the intervention of kin. If there are vacancies in a factory, the management are likely, as in the past, to employ the sisters and daughters of women already working for them. One factory manager stated this quite explicitly, saying that he really only hired women from families he already knew, as then he could be sure that they would be honest and reliable, would be taught on the job, and would not cause

---

8. Deema Kaneff's comments on this point were very helpful.

trouble either with other workers or with management. One result of this is the development of clusters of unemployed people, who do not have within their networks any negotiable connections with those in work. This suggests that polarisation will increase, as those in work protect their connections for themselves and their kin, while those who lack such connections will find fewer and fewer opportunities open to them (for comparison, see Morris 1992). Middle-aged women particularly have a hard time finding work, even if they have connections through kin. As one woman, recently made redundant, said, 'Even if we still have work, we don't know for how long. The only women who can get work are young attractive women, women who will do a strip tease. No one wants to hire older women.' Newspaper advertisements often ask for 'young, attractive' female applicants. Women also talked about the growing difficulty women with children were experiencing in finding work (see also CBOS 1994). What this all suggests is a deepening division between productive and reproductive spheres in terms of women's labour. Women themselves often represent this division in terms of their maternal role, asking how they can feed and look after their children without waged work. In this sense the process of privatisation is negatively constructed in moral terms; the nurturing mother is, as I have discussed, one of the strongest moral symbols of both women and family (the domestic sphere) and of nation (the public sphere). Privatisation, foreign ownership and female unemployment all tend to be seen as the negation of the proper moral order of both the family and the nation.

When unemployed women do find work, it is often in a small *chałupnictwa* (cottage industry). These are small private enterprises which are springing up throughout the area, particularly in the rural areas. Often located in the basements of private houses, they are run mostly by men who have purchased machinery cheaply from factories which are closing down. Large signs outside the house announce that it is a wholesale-retail establishment, manufacturing tights or shirts, or, most popular in the summer of 1993, computerised embroidery. Women are rarely in a position to open such enterprises, as they are unable to secure the collateral to borrow money to buy the machinery. However, the workers are primarily drawn from the ranks of unemployed women; typically, unless they are kin or the wife of the owner, they are employed for just under three months, and then sacked, so that the owner will not have to pay for their insurance and benefits. Often these enterprises fold after a few months, although some manage to survive longer and to establish a regular market for their product. One man

I know, for instance, borrowed money on the basis of his farm, and bought up sewing machines from a blouse factory. At first he and his wife worked in the basement of their house, while she and her parents also continued to run the farm. As they got more orders, he hired her two sisters to help with the sewing, and his wife did less and less farm work. They continued to expand, and employed more women, kin and then friends from the village. After a year, they had converted one of the outbuildings of the farm into a sweat-shop, and employed about ten regular workers. The man himself managed the enterprise, and personally handled most of the sales and deliveries. In 1994, however, two years after he established his first workshop, this man also was forced to close down his enterprise: overheads, taxes and rising prices of materials proved eventually to be more than he could manage. He and his wife have now returned to farming.

Unemployed women often speak of helping kin in less formal ways. They may say that they sometimes 'help' their brother-in-law or cousin in a small shop, fast food bar, or market stall. What is important about this 'help' is that the women themselves do not define it as work. They may be paid in kind, or receive a 'gift' of cash from time to time, but they perceive it as kinship reciprocity. Here it is clear that for these women work means what they had done previously, and often what their mothers and grandmothers had done before them: waged work in their own trade, sewing and weaving.

A similar situation arises with female agricultural labour. When rural women lose their paid work, they continue to provide a substantial amount of labour on the farm, often rising before dawn to milk cows and tend to livestock, and then working in the fields until dusk. Here again, however, they rarely describe this as their work. Rather, they see themselves as unemployed; farming is men's work, and their farm labour is merely part of what they do as a farmer's wife, sister or daughter. I discussed this at length with Maria who, unmarried and living with her parents and married brother on their farm, had been laid off from her factory work and described herself to me as 'not working'. When I commented that she did a great deal of farm labour, she replied that this was what she did at home, but that she was not a farmer like her father and brother. When I asked whether she could not be both a farmer and a seamstress, she thought for a long time, and said no, she would like to be both, but she could only be one. Hence, she was an unemployed seamstress. Women's waged work in industry was recognised and highly visible; the labour that they provided and continue to provide on the farm, in the household, and in kin-based small enterprises tends to be masked by a rhetoric of women's essential, supportive role within the family, and to be invisible.

The invisible nature of rural women's work outside industry makes the current situation doubly hard. When women become unemployed, they lose not only their jobs and income, but also part of their identity and self esteem. When I asked women what kind of work they would like to do if there was full employment again, nearly all responded that they wanted their old jobs back. One woman stated it quite succinctly: 'I don't want to do any other work. I am a weaver. That is my work. I want to do what I have always done. My mother was a weaver, my aunt was a weaver. That is our work.'

Similarly, when I asked women whether they would be willing to move to another region of Poland, or even abroad, to get work, the vast majority responded negatively. Who would look after their old parents? Who would care for their children? How could they find housing? What would they do? The working lives of these women are firmly located in the region, and each is part of a closely knit network of kinship and friendship obligations which she cannot imagine leaving (see also CBOS 1994: 24-25). There is also no precedent for this type of wage migration here. Until very recently, there has 'always' been work. Further, housing is scarce in Polish cities and is often arranged through close kin, with young couples moving in with elderly grandparents or aunts and uncles, caring for them in old age, and taking over the flat when they die. This limits the possibility of moving to another city, or from the countryside to town. Mobility and choice are by no means a given.

The heritage of more than a century of steady employment in one industry is hard to undo. Many women cannot imagine alternatives to the work they have always done, nor to the place they have always lived. Rather, they cope with unemployment and the crisis of rising prices and worsening conditions by reinforcing networks which were already well established. Women refer constantly to their reliance on their mothers and their sisters for financial and practical help, ranging from childcare and shared meals to economic help of quite significant proportions. These networks, and their significance as the safety net of the socialist welfare state contracts, make the women's unwillingness to consider geographical moves reasonable responses in terms of survival strategies.

As there is a long established pattern of rural urban ties in this region, it is often difficult to distinguish clearly, in practical terms, between rural agricultural workers and industrial workers, or even between rural and urban inhabitants. The coexistence of impartible inheritance with a highly developed industrial sector creates the perfect conditions for the development of a class of peasant-workers, rural inhabitants who engage in waged work but also provide farm labour 'at home'. Equally, former villagers who have moved to town frequently retain strong ties with their natal villages. Often, women who live in town spend all of their free time in these villages. They send their children to their parents or siblings in the countryside for weekends and long vacations, and the children help on the farm, or go to work picking fruit or weeding for neighbours. The women themselves sometimes have their own small allotment where they grow vegetables, and often they also work in the fields. For their labour they are given produce which they either use for their own domestic consumption or sell. While there is no longer a shortage of food in Poland, as there was throughout the latter socialist period, prices are extremely high, and people with established rural kin networks rely heavily on these patterns of mutual support. If they lose their accommodation, unemployed women may move back to their natal village permanently, returning to the family house and 'helping' full-time on the farm. While these women increase the labour force of the farm, they also draw on its resources, which are often already over-stretched.

Listening to the stories and conversations of people living in this region, it is clear that whatever they were expecting from capitalism, it was not this. Women in particular are vocal in their anger against newspaper articles and television programmes which suggest that they should stay at home and look after their families, and lay the blame for delinquency, alcoholism, anti-social teenagers and violence on female employment. This is of course a well-established response to high unemployment; strategies by the state to remove women from regular waged work during times of recession have been well documented in Western sociological literature. The women themselves do not find the arguments convincing, and such debate only fuels their anger about what they see as the government's failure to protect their interests, interests which were at least nominally safeguarded under the socialist regime. In daily conversation, all political events are viewed through the lens of disappointment and anger about economic uncertainty. In the Lódz area, production is moving from the factory to the family workshop, the Soviet empire and with it the great Russian market has collapsed, and industry is suffering enormously from Western competition. A hundred years after the period to which Kochanowicz referred in the quotation I cited at the beginning of this section, we appear to be witnessing a reversal of the historical process he described.

The Podhale – *marginal peasant entrepreneurs*

In the mountains of southern Poland, quite different responses to the new system can be seen, which in many ways represent not an historical reversal, but a marked continuity with the past. The Podhale is part of Galicia which, to quote Kochanowicz again '... remained the most backward [area] in the nineteenth century ... [It] was overpopulated, with almost no industry, so its redundant peasant population had to engage in various non agricultural activities as well as seasonal agricultural employment, even in remote areas. When the occasion arose, people from this region ... started to emigrate to America.' (1989: 121) For the Górale, the people of the Podhale, this very backwardness provided the basis for the development of survival strategies and skills which have continued through the twentieth century.

Originally pastoralists, the Górale became sedentary farmers in the fifteenth and sixteenth centuries. The land in the mountains is uniformly poor, the winters long and harsh, and the growing season short; this is not an area well suited to subsistence agriculture. During the Partition Period this part of Galicia fell under Austro-Hungarian rule, and after emancipation the law of partible inheritance was followed, according all offspring, female and male, equal shares of the parental lands. The second half of the nineteenth century was marked by fragmentation and dwarfing of peasant farms, and by episodes of crop failure and famine. Few families had enough land to be self sufficient, and most relied partly on income derived from specialist activities and petty production within the village, from agricultural day labour and domestic service, and from seasonal or sporadic wage migration to other parts of Poland, to Budapest and Berlin, and most significantly, to Chicago.

The poverty and isolation of the Podhale continued well into the twentieth century, until the first years of socialist rule. Unlike the area around Lódz, with its solid history of industrialisation from the nineteenth century, infrastructure development only began here in the 1950s. The wave of industrialisation which swept Poland at this time extended to the mountains where small local factories were built, roads were constructed and railway stations opened, allowing villagers from even the more remote areas of the Podhale to travel to work in these factories, or in the offices, shops and state institutions of the main towns. Simultaneously, the tourist trade developed in the mountains, drawing skiers in the winter and walkers and climbers in the summer.

By the 1970s the economy of the Podhale had moved from backwardness and stagnation to growth. While many villagers worked, at least for periods of their lives, in the state sector, most were also extensively involved in a range of informal and second economy activities and dealings, including petty commodity production and sale, building, marketing and long-distance trade. Both men and women worked in farming, state waged labour, and in second economy dealings. Although, as I have discussed elsewhere, all of these spheres revolve around a gendering of tasks (see Pine 1992a and b), women's labour was rarely invisible. Women, like men, are valued for their ability to work hard and to deal successfully. Often this means, as it did in the nineteenth century, travelling to other parts of Poland, or even abroad to trade or find work. From the 1970s onwards, when the government eased restrictions on travel to the West, Górale again travelled to the United States, usually Chicago, to live with kin and to work for American dollars. The money they earned was brought home, and usually used to invest in farm machinery, to fund social events such as weddings, and to build large, modern houses. Housebuilding provided work for village men, and when the house was finished, its rooms could be let out to tourists. The tourists provided a market for the villagers' produce and crafts, as well as for women's domestic services. (See Pine 1992a and b; Pine and Bogdanowicz 1982)

When patterns of Górale labour under socialism are compared to those of central Poland, the differences are striking. Both Górale women and men identify themselves first and foremost as peasant farmers, and to a great extent their sense of belonging and personhood comes from this. However, as I have argued elsewhere (see Pine 1994), in order to remain Górale peasant farmers, they have to engage in a range of activities outside farming, and often have to leave the Podhale for a time. What is significant in terms of comparison is that here waged work was only one of a variety of possible ways of making money, even during the socialist period. There was therefore no strong sense of personal identity vested in factory work. Rather, identity was created within the village, in relation to membership in a farming family, kinship, and gender. Neither was there a sense in which the socialist state was viewed as having brought about enormous improvement in working lives. The state was perceived as 'outside' the village, and often viewed with distrust and hostility (see Pine 1992b). Industrial development took place only after 1947, and so there was no long history of past working conditions with which to compare. In addition, many of the political aims of socialism, with their emphasis on centralised authority and collective ownership, were diametrically opposed to established Górale notions of autonomy and individualism.

Since 1989 the mountain population, like the rest of Poland, has felt the effects of factory slow-downs and closures and of cuts in the state sector. However, the repercussions of these changes are more complex than in central Poland. Although many villagers, including a high percentage of women, are claiming unemployment benefit, the kind of poverty which is increasingly visible around Lódz is rarely apparent here. This is at least partly due to the fact that many Górale had long been involved in a range of economic activities; not only does the loss of waged work in the state sector not alter their lives as dramatically as it would have had it been the sole source of income, but many of the types of informal activities which the Górale have long pursued fit very well with the new economy of entrepreneurial capitalism. Most unemployed women knit sweaters or make cheeses, and sell them in the local market, which with the opening of the borders has expanded from a Thursday morning to a daily market; really successful women traders, one or two of whom exist in nearly every village, travel as far afield as Warsaw or Gdansk on a regular basis. These women have been traders for a long time. However, under socialism they were marketing their goods illicitly, and now they are able to trade legally, with the purchase, at some cost, of a government license. Other women make and sell tooled leather slippers, embroidered linens and sundry other commodities. The point about such work is that it is flexible enough to fit in with the needs of the farm and child-care, and to expand and contract with the presence or absence of waged work. In the Podhale, as in the Lódz district, women are more likely to be in control of domestic budgeting; however, many husbands and wives maintain their own separate funds.[9]

As there is a tradition of female entrepreneurs in the mountains, it is not as easy for men to move into classically 'female' spheres of activity. My friend Zośka, for instance, has bought and sold wool and knitted garments, in the market since the 1970s. She also worked for the state until 1990, running the village kiosk. Then the franchise for the kiosk was privatised, and she lacked the money to buy it. It went instead to her brother's son and his wife, who had the necessary collateral from their rather extensive informal economy dealings manufacturing and selling 'folk art'. Zośka now spends all of her free time knitting, and effectively supports herself, her husband, two unmarried sons of whom one is an

---

9. However, if funds are held jointly they are usually under the woman's control.

invalid, and her married daughter, daughter's husband and children. All of the adults work on the farm, and the family gets some income from sale of milk and from the son's invalid pension. Danka, the married daughter, also lost her job at the state-run dairy. She received unemployment benefit for a year, and joined her mother knitting. These women accept that it is their responsibility to bring non-agricultural income into the household: when I asked why Danka's husband did not try to get a job, Zośka explained to me that it was really better for everyone if Danka worked. 'You see how peaceful Adam is at home, looking after the children. When he works he gets money, and when he has money he likes to drink a bit, and then he causes trouble. So we think it's better if he doesn't go to work'.

Wage migration, however, continues to be the most important single source of income in the Podhale. Since 1989, the scope for wage migration has expanded. Many village houses now stand empty, their owners away temporarily in Italy, Greece, France or Germany. Alicja, for example, went off to Athens with a women friend in 1990. They got jobs as cleaners and she sent for her husband, who got a job in construction. They were then joined by Alicja's sister, and later her brother-in-law. The children of both couples remain in the Podhale with their grandmothers. Similarly, Danka, to whom I have already referred, went to Rome in the summer of 1993 to work as an au pair. Her unemployed husband, with considerable help from her mother, looks after their children in the village. Returning migrants bring with them not only foreign money but also consumer goods to sell. Most importantly, however, they bring back contacts which, if they have worked successfully as domestic servants, builders, grape pickers or fieldhands, they can use again year after year, and extend to their close kin as well.

Reflections on 'transition'

For the Górale the decline of the welfare state is producing some of the same problems as it is in the Łódz region. Childcare facilities are being cut, or closed down altogether, which places some strain on household labour resources. Medical care, and the high costs of medicine, are increasingly problematic. The health service available in remote areas was rarely very good under socialism, but the cuts are placing added strain on those who care for the chronically ill or the elderly. Again, it is usually women who take on these responsibilities. In other significant ways, however, the two regions are quite different.

From their position as rather marginal peasants, incorporated into the national political economy neither prior to or under socialism, the Górale developed various survival strategies. Temporary mobility and wage migration are long established paths out of poverty. Trading and dealing are very good things in Górale terms. Unlike central Poland where, in the rural areas at least the term *handlować* (to trade) implies a lack of work ethic and even a level of dishonesty, for the Górale it means skill and cleverness. Women as well as men are respected for their ability to trade, and long distance trade is particularly the sphere of women. As they have never centred their working lives around the state and industry, but rather in opposition to it, Górale women do not lose their identity with their jobs. Because they have always relied upon other types of work, valued in their own terms whether legal or not in the eyes of the state, a lack of formal employment does not leave them without work. In addition, regardless of what else they do, women and men continue to centre their social and personal identity around agricultural work.

These two areas represent two extremes, both historically and in contemporary Poland. In terms of gender issues they provide an interesting comparison because they are both areas in which women's work is central to the economy, but in very different ways. The textile workers were fully incorporated into the state industrial economy and in many ways benefited from it. The system of land tenure located landholding and agriculture with one individual, usually male, and for others in the household work identity was associated with waged labour. Here one can see a clear case of a strong work ethic encompassed by an essential conservatism. The irony of the situation is that it is in the move to capitalism that, for the moment at least, this is the work which is suffering the worst hardship. In the Lódz region, the anger which is directed not only against the West but also against the fly-by-night cowboy capitalists and the new 'mafia', who are believed to control everything from guns and the sex trade to sales in stolen cars, is partly moral outrage against people who are seen as taking, sometimes stealing, what should come only from hard, diligent and formal work.[10] Their conspicuous affluence is a constant affront to unemployed workers, who have worked hard within the state sector all their lives, and now have little or nothing to show for this.

10. The 'mafia' is generally thought to consist of Gypsies, Russians (by which is meant anyone from the former USSR) and ex-*nomenklatura* who continue to exercise extensive power. While powerful underground rings of this nature certainly exist, it is also a clear case of representing of the 'other' as the cause of misfortune.

The inability of many women in the Łódz area to imagine alternatives is tied to their exclusive identity as settled, incorporated workers who also farm. Górale women, on the other hand, already have in place many of the skills and networks necessary to take advantage of the rather peculiar kind of capitalism which is currently developing in Poland. They have a long history of imagining alternatives and pursuing them.

Conclusions

I suggested at the beginning of this chapter that one of the consequences of privatisation and restructuring for women and gender relations in Poland has been a realignment of boundaries between the public and the domestic spheres and new understandings of the concept 'private'. Much of the new writing about women in eastern Europe insists rightly on the importance of an indigenous feminism, and stresses the right of women to make choices about whether or not to engage in waged work, whether to value the maternal role over waged work and so forth. What is very clear, however, from the experiences and stories of women in the Łódz area is that they are to some extent being redefined as invisible in the public sphere, and relocated into the domestic realm very much against their own choice. Here a growing separation between production and reproduction appears to be taking place, a separation which places women on the side of reproduction and thus denies or masks both their role in production and the interdependent relationship between production and reproduction.

While the same processes of factory closures and lack of employment are taking place in the Podhale, their outcome so far has been rather different. Women continue to be identified with both the domestic and the public sphere, as do men. Women and men have a different set of roles and symbolic associations with the two domains, but neither is excluded from one or kept within the confines of the other. Work for Górale men and women means a lot of different things, and to a great extent the process of privatisation is only reflecting, and making legal, the kinds of activities they have long been following. Here, as opposed to the Łódz area, it would be more accurate to say that the interrelationship between production and reproduction is recognised, and that the both men and women play highly visible roles in the public and the private spheres. This brings us back to ideas of morality and proper order. For the peasant workers long integrated into the waged economy, the state and the public sector under socialism represented a moral order of production, which in at least ideal terms provided for and protected areas of reproduction. With privatisation, this interconnection has been disrupted, often to the cost of women. For the marginal Górale, the moral order was historically located in the house, family and community, symbolised by the family farm. The state was viewed as outside this moral order, and if anything as hostile and destructive to it. In this sense, the process of privatisation can be seen as widening rather than disrupting the Górale economy.

It is becoming increasingly clear in rural Poland that farming alone cannot provide subsistence and livelihood for the growing numbers of unemployed. Farming itself is in crisis as cheap Western produce is imported and as simultaneously subsidies are cut and prices received for local produce fall. In 1994 farmers in both the regions I have been discussing were slaughtering their livestock for home consumption because they could not afford to buy feed. One implication of this is that many peasant farmers, particularly those with smaller farms, may turn away from market production and produce only for their own consumption. In order to meet increasing consumption demands, however, outside earnings continue to be necessary. Concurrent with the restructuring of the public sphere, work itself is in the process of being redefined. For many rural women it is flexibility and mobility, not training and experience in a particular trade, which may provide the keys to work in the new economic order.

REFERENCES

Centrum Badania Opinii Społecznej 1993a *Społecznej Przerywania Ciąż*, CBOS, Warsaw.

_____, 1993b *Kobiety o Swoim Życiu Osobistym*, CBOS, Warsaw.

_____, 1993c *Kontakty Rodzinne Dorosłych Polek*, CBOS, Warsaw.

_____, *Pczucie Bezpieczeństwa Kobiet na Rynku Pracy. Ocena Równości Szana Zawodowych Kobiet i Mężczyzn*, CBOS, Warsaw, 1994.

Einhorn, B. *Cinderella Goes to Market: Citizenship, Gender and Women's Movements in East Central Europe*. London, New York, 1993.

Hann, C.M. *A Village without Solidarity: Polish Peasants in Years of Crisis*. New Haven, London, 1985.

Heinen, J. 'Polish Democracy is a Masculine Democracy', *Women's Studies International Forum*, Vol. 15, No.1 (1992): 129-138.

Jancar, B. W. *Women under Communism*. Baltimore, 1978.

Kochanowicz, J. 'The Polish Economy and the Evolution of Dependency', in *The Origins of Backwardness in Eastern Europe: Economics and Politics from the Middle Ages until the Early Twentieth Century*, ed. D. Chirot, Los Angeles, London, 1989.

Kolankiewicz, G. and Lewis, P. *Poland; Politics, Economics and Society*. London, 1988.

Lorence-Kot, B. 'Konspiracja: Probing the Topography of Women's Underground Activities. The Kingdom of Poland in the Second Half of the Nineteenth Century', in *Women in Polish Society*, ed. R. Jaworski and B. Pietrow-Ennker, East European Monographs, Boulder, 1992.

Morris, L. 'The Social Segregation of the Long-Term Unemployed', *Sociological Review*, Vol. 40, (1992): 344-369.

_____, *Dangerous Classes: the underclass and social citizenship*. London, 1994.

Pine, F. 1992a 'Uneven Burdens: Women in Rural Poland' in *Women in the Face of Change: the Soviet Union, Eastern Europe and China*, ed. S. Rai, H. Pilkington and A. Phizacklea, London.

_____, 1992b 'The Cows and the Pigs are His, the Eggs are Mine': Women's Domestic Roles and Entrepreneurial Activity in Rural Poland', in *Socialism: Ideals, Ideologies and Local Practice*, ed. C. Hann, London.

_____, 'Maintenir l'économie domestique: travail, argent, et éthique dans les montagnes polonaises', *Terrain*, Vol. 23, October, *Les Usages de l'Argent*, Paris, (1994): 81-98.

_____, Final report to ESRC on Project R000234 320 'Socio-occupational Status of Women', 1995.

Pine, F. and Bogdanowicz, P. 'Policy, Response and Alternative Strategy: the Process of Change in a Polish Highland Village', *Dialectical Anthropology*, Vol. 6, No, 4, (1982): 67-80.

Rai, S., Pilkington, H., and Phizacklea, A., eds, *Women in the Face of Change: the Soviet Union, Eastern Europe and China*, London, 1992.

Reading, A. *Polish Women, Solidarity and Feminism*. London, 1992.

Scott, H. *Women and Socialism: Experiences from Eastern Europe*. London, 1976

Siemienska, R. 'Women and Social Movements in Poland', *Women and Politics*, Winter, Vol. 6, No. 4, (1986): 5-35.

6. Aspects of the Restitution of Property and Land in Estonia

Arvo Kuddo

Introduction

*T*he purpose of this chapter is to outline some of the main historical and contemporary processes which lie behind the current policies of land and property restitution in Estonia. I argue that in the formulation of these policies insufficient attention was paid to the practical problems which their implementation has predictably encountered. The paper is based partly on my knowledge and experience of these problems as a Minister in the Estonian government and as an officer in the Bank of Estonia. At the same time I have also drawn on my experience as a potential claimant to land and other property in the small village of Puka in southern Estonia.

The half-century of Soviet power in the Baltic countries completely changed their economic structure. It transformed the ownership of private property and land and established significant new social structural and cultural patterns within rural communities. The earlier individual lifestyle and methods of production on private agricultural farms (in the 1930s Estonia had more than 140,000 such farms), were replaced by collective farming and a strongly 'socialised' way of life. Collective and state farms, village soviets and other structures deeply influenced rural households and communities in countries where settlements had been previously dispersed, self-reliant and economically independent.

The Independence Movement and its Legacy

The liberalisation of Soviet society at the end of the 1980s and the activities of the independence movements culminated in the restoration of the sovereignty of the Baltic countries, including the Republic of Estonia in August 1991. In Estonia, as elsewhere, this transition raised in an acute form the question of the future development of the villages – how were rural productive forces and rural society more generally to be best organised in these new conditions? Rural life represents more than just a sector of the economy and a place to live for thousands of people. In Estonia and in many other societies, the rural lifestyle is traditionally considered as the foundation of national identity, of culture, of tradition and even of language. Even today more than three-fifths of Estonian families have contacts of some sort with the rural community: summer cottages, a plot of land close to the city for growing vegetables, fruits and berries, or perhaps the farms owned by parents or grandparents which are still retained for garden crops or for relaxation. Today, about 28 percent of the population of Estonia lives in rural areas; the corresponding figure in the 1930s was more than 70 percent.

If certain historical events and political circumstances are taken into consideration, it is easier to understand the policy of restitution more precisely, as well as the legislative and other processes leading to it. Owing to the desire in the 1980s to accelerate and to achieve the final political goal of a free Estonian society and the restoration of the independent state, the political situation at the end of the decade favoured the development of radical and nationalistic (Estonia- and Estonian-centric) programmes of political and economic transformation. In the first phase (1987-1988) the political movement aiming for independence pursued the concept of 'self-managing Estonia'. However, it was soon replaced by a platform calling for full restoration of an independent Republic of Estonia, politically based and focused on the legitimate citizens of the country. One of the key political issues was the problem of restitution for the suffering caused by fifty years of Soviet occupation.

The political process towards total independence in Estonia was advanced by two quite different structures at that time. One was the Supreme Soviet which was democratically elected for the first time in decades, though it was still partly represented by non-citizens. Within this, the government, elected and appointed at the beginning of 1990, replaced the former Party-controlled governing bodies.

The second and less formal structure was the Estonian Congress. This was a nominally a representative body of the 'citizens' of Estonia at home and abroad and its membership was rather mixed. It contained many national radicals, and it developed a very straightforward platform aiming at the restoration of all political and economic structures of the republic to its pre-war model. Though lacking formal legal power, its declarations and demands were nevertheless a major political force in Estonian society, influencing policy makers and especially the Supreme Soviet in its legislative process. This influence was exerted through the medium of publications and personal connections, and more directly through the fact that some Congress members were also members of the Supreme Soviet itself.

During the Soviet repression, the country and its people suffered a great deal in many different ways, and it was understandable that society and its governing bodies were anxious to compensate for this suffering as much as possible. These feelings were also partly influenced by the post-war migration of non-Estonian citizens who were granted special benefits, such as the procurement of flats and houses. For instance, migrant workers of the former all-Union enterprises, who had entered the country according to the so-called *orgnabor* system (organised admission), were able to get housing free of charge much faster than the local residents. Resentment of this is one reason why the laws and rules on property restitution in Estonia, compared to other countries in transition, are so favourable for the former owners of confiscated and nationalised property or land.

The decisions on restitution and the subsequent approval of the relevant laws were influenced not only by the need to reform the society economically for the short and long-term future, but also by a thirst for justice and the determination to compensate to the full the suffering of the Estonian people. The main laws on restitution – the Law on Property Reform and the Law on Land Reform – were approved by the Supreme Soviet in June 1991 and October 1991 respectively, at the initial phase of fully independent economic policy, and at a time when all the circumstances and conditions necessary for the successful implementation of this policy had not been fully understood.

Estonia under Soviet Rule

It is useful in this context to highlight some of the events in the history of Estonia in the middle of this century. As is well known, in accordance with the secret protocol of the so-called Molotov-Ribbentrop pact, Estonia, with several other countries and regions in this part of Europe, passed under the Soviet sphere of influence. The USSR, as the threatening power, forced Estonia to sign an agreement on 28 September 1939 which resulted in the stationing of 25,000 Red Army soldiers in Estonia. At that time, the Estonian army was 15,000 men strong. On 17 June 1940, after an ultimatum had been presented to the Estonian government the previous day, the country was occupied and later annexed to the Soviet Union. Estonia was given the status of one of the Soviet republics among others.

After the intensive efforts of the Baltic deputies in the Supreme Soviet of the former Soviet Union, the existence of this secret protocol was recognised by that body in 1989. However, neither the Soviet Union nor Russia has ever formally recognised the annexation, or the ensuing consequences of this pact on the history and further development of the Baltic countries. As a result, Estonia has no expectations of external financing for restitutional compensation.

Total repression of the population of Estonia began after the arrival of Soviet troops, and it reached its pre-war peak on 14 June 1941 when at least eight to ten-thousand civilians were deported to Siberia (the final number of deportees has never been established). It should be mentioned that only five percent of the adult males deported in June 1941 survived the ordeal.

In 1940, property, industry, banks and land were confiscated and nationalised on a mass scale with no compensation offered, and this continued until the end of the 1940s. All land was declared state property; all private houses over the size of 220-280 square meters (size varying according to region) were nationalised, partly to provide accommodation for incoming Soviet military forces, which in 1940 totalled more than 125,000, and also for security and party cadres. Most of the private factories and workshops were also nationalised or confiscated. Part of the expropriated land was distributed to small farmers who, in many cases, were afraid to accept such 'gifts', or the land was simply left untilled. Small-scale industries and private farms were not shut down until after the war mainly because of lack of time.

Estonia's total population losses during war time are estimated at about 282,000 or 25 percent of its pre-war population level (Kuddo

1991). In order to evaluate these population losses during the Second World War, the following are taken into account:

(i)   the return of approximately 20,000 Baltic-Germans in 1939-1941 in accordance with an agreement between the Soviet Union and Germany.
(ii) Repression in 1940-1941.
(iii) War losses at the front (both in the Red Army and the German Army).
(iv) Territorial changes in August and November 1944 in which Estonian pre-war territory was reduced by over 2,200 square kilometres, displacing 65,000 people.
(v)   Massive emigration at the end of the war. In 1943 and 1944, in accordance with a special agreement between Germany and Sweden, about 7,000-8,000 Swedes and 72,000-74,000 Estonians left the country because of their fear of a new wave of repression from the incoming Soviet authorities. Mass arrests, in particular those accused of collaboration in one way or another, in fact continued after the Second World War.

After the war, the Soviet authorities began systematically to implement plans to collectivise the villages, and the first collective farms were established in Estonia in 1947. At the same time the operations of private farmers were restricted in many ways. Farmers not belonging to the collective farms were forced to pay increasingly large taxes. They were also restrained from buying new machinery and had to sell their produce at fixed prices lower than the market value.

These measures pushed some reluctant farmers into joining the new farms but recruitment accelerated rapidly after a massive new wave of deportations, on 25-26 March 1949, when at least 20,700 people were forcibly deported to Siberia. At least in theory, the deported farmers were mainly 'public enemies' and *kulaks* who used wage labourers, either on a permanent or temporary basis, or who owned more valuable agricultural machinery or livestock than the average. In many instances, however, the repression of the farmers was not simply based on such criteria. Special plans and orders concerning the number of individuals who had to be deported originated from Moscow and were sent to the authorities at all levels: republic, county and community. In some cases, even subjective factors – such as past quarrels between families or the desire of a local party boss to get some machinery or livestock he needed from another family – were crucial when families were included in the deportation lists.

In total, approximately 50,000 suffered repression during the years 1944-1953. Immigration into Estonia, mainly from Russia, also reached its peak between 1945 and 1950, when it is estimated that over 200,000 individuals entered the country. This was a period of intensive 'russification' of the newly annexed national republics.

Between 1957 and the end of the Soviet period, smaller collective farms were amalgamated into larger units and many of these were converted into state farms. It is these relatively large and complex units which have had to be dismantled under current reform legislation.

Land and Property Reform and Restitution

At the beginning of 1990 the process of restitution and property reforms started in Estonia. However, in 1989 before the basic laws on property and land reforms had been approved, the Supreme Soviet of the Estonian SSR adopted the Law on Farming with the objective of stimulating private farming as an alternative to the still existent collective farming system.

In order to save Estonian agriculture from total economic collapse, the idea of rapid 'farmerisation' of the villages prevailed and portions of collective or state farm land were distributed to rural families who wished to begin farming. Such families were often not the original owners of the land allotted and future relations between them and the former owners still remained to be resolved.

An additional governmental decree on restitution and compensation of property for the repressed was approved in February 1989. At that time the Estonian authorities expected to compensate for the economic losses through the All-Union budget. In 1989-1990 farms were being returned to about 6,000 families (if they wanted to retain them and it was possible without delay) or, in many cases, compensation was given in cash (close to 200 million roubles were paid out). Later, toward the end of 1990, this amount was included by the central Soviet authorities in the Estonian tax contribution to the All-Union budget, thus eliminating this source of compensation.

In 1989 the average monthly wage in Estonia was 270 roubles and in 1990, it was 340 roubles. In some cases compensation payments for destroyed property even exceeded 150,000 roubles which, at that time, was a huge sum. But most of the recipient families were not able to invest the money and during the next few years, massive inflation in 1990-1993 depleted almost all of it.

This early legislation was followed in the newly independent country by a series of further laws – including those on Land Reform and Property Reform (noted above), on Agricultural Reform (1992), and on Compensation and Pricing of Illegally Alienated Property (1993) – aimed at providing a foundation for the ordered transformation of the former system and the re-establishment and restitution of former private property. This is a formidable task given that at the end of 1930s, most land and property was in private ownership.

What are the main characteristics of the restitution programme in Estonia and the main problems and contradictions entailed in it? Firstly, the Law on Property Reform (1991) and the Law on Land Reform (1991) theoretically guarantee full restitution or compensation of confiscated property or land to former owners or their rightful heirs.[1] With the passage of time, however, there is commonly a very large circle of potential heirs. If the former owner (or the next in line) is dead, other relatives of the deceased (parents, husband or wife, children, grandchildren, brothers or sisters, their children, grandchildren, and so on) can apply for the property itself or compensation. Moreover, it is sometimes difficult to discover and confirm the exact relationship of claimant heirs to the deceased. Not all documents have been retained in the archives, and the authorities must find and question other witnesses. All of this tends to make the restitution process complicated, slow and unpredictable. The total number of restitution claims at 31 March 1993 exceeded 220,000, and in many regions it will take at least until the end of this century to check the accuracy of the documents confirming the right to property, the exact form, size and value of the property and land itself.[2]

Another issue is former indebtedness. In rural areas in particular during the 1930s, most of the farms, other productive units, and also private individuals used bank loans to buy necessary equipment, build houses or start businesses. The total sum of internal debts to the banks at the end of the 1930s exceeded 300 million Estonian kroons which, at that time, was

---

1. In some other Central and Eastern European countries a more limited compensation mechanism has been established. In Hungary, for example, the total amount of compensation should not exceed US\$ 40,000 per recipient. In some other countries (for example, eastern Germany) a special inheritance tax for recipients has been established, with varying rates according to closeness of kinship to the former owner.
2. For comparison it can be mentioned that the number of registered restitution claims in Poland was only 75,000. (Poland, 1993).

a huge sum. The individual debts in question have, however, been declared invalid by the Law on Property Reform and the amendment to the Law on Land Reform. This means that, for example, those who agreed on the basis of bank credits to buy or build houses or start businesses just before the Soviet takeover, may now become full owners of these properties without any further obligations. This concession was offered because fully detailed official information on debts of this kind is no longer available (bank deeds and other relevant documents were confiscated in 1940 and transferred to Moscow). Yet at the same time full compensation must be made by the Compensation Fund to bank owners or share holders for such loss, so that such property is in effect compensated for twice.

In most cases, property or land has increased or decreased in value during the last half century (when, for example, central heating has been installed in a house or land has been improved). In principal, as stipulated by the Law on Property Reform, the previous owner must pay for any increase in the value. Similarly if the value has deteriorated, the difference should be compensated to the owners of the property or land. It is though also very difficult to determine these differences in value, and in practice there are very few cases, possibly none, of having to pay the state compensation for appreciated value of an estate or land. As a rule, private houses are simply being returned to their owners in the condition they are today.

There are also very complicated problems concerning the relationship of former owners and new settlers. For example, pre-Soviet private housing is now often occupied by newcomers. For almost fifty years such accommodation was the property of the state which also maintained it and collected rents. Now the new (i.e., former) owner must take over all these responsibilities, and must sign a new rental agreement with the tenants, while some restrictions on the rent ceiling still exist. After a three year period if these families cannot come to an understanding with the new owners about the rental conditions, they have to vacate the premises. For most of these tenant families, there is no possibility of finding or even buying another flat or house.

During half a century, many changes have also occurred in rural communities and in land use. New roads and new infrastructure have been built in the country; new housing and industries have appeared. More generally, it will take an excessively long time to determine the original boundaries of the land between the former farms and household plots. According to even optimistic estimates, it will take at least twenty-five to thirty years to complete this process.

There are many other similar contradictory factors in the laws on restitution and property and land reform. The government under Edgar Savisaar was quite well informed about such problems, but it lacked a majority when attempting to resolve these questions and this was one of the reasons why the government resigned in January 1992.

At the Grass Roots: a Family's Ties to Village Land in South Estonia

Before the Second World War, because of its remoteness from the capital and other main commercial centres, the village of Puka in southern Estonia was a relatively poor rural community. Its remoteness and its poverty, however, probably helped to save some lives there in the 1940s, and not many people were deported from the village.

It is important to mention that at the beginning of the 1920s, many participants of the War of Liberation (1918-1920) in Estonia were granted farms and favourable credits to start farming. My grandfather was not able to participate because he had been disabled in the First World War. But my grandmother's brother fought in the war and was consequently granted a farm not far from Puka. After his death, there were no other heirs and our family today would have the right to reclaim his farm lands.

My grandparents had a small plot of land (0.35 ha.) and worked mainly as waged labourers on other farms in the neighbourhood. With a mortgage, they also built their own house and other accommodation for the family and their four children. As was the case with all debts of this sort, the Soviet authorities cancelled the outstanding balance of the loan in 1940.

In 1947 my grandparents, as poor rural waged labourers, were given a horse and a 10 hectare plot of land annexed from a farm of one of the families who had been deported in 1941. The main motive for such grants was to indicate the Soviet authorities' concern about poor rural families and to encourage more enthusiastic attitudes towards socialism. In 1949, the family had no choice except to join the collective farm and to hand over to it the plot of land they had received in 1947. The family horse, their only calf and all their farm equipment were also transferred to the farm.

In the 1950s, the Puka village collective farm, like many others, was in a lamentable state. For many years my grandmother's salary for a 'twelve-hour day' – which was the prescribed standard unit of work – was 17 kopecks plus a certain amount of grain, which was calculated at the end of the agricultural season as so many 100 grams of grain per working day. Later, as in many other cases, the farm was amalgamated with others and eventually became a state farm.

How was restitution for the former members of the state farm arranged in the village of Puka and especially for my family?

To carry out this process according to the Law on Agricultural Reform, special reform commissions were established at each collective and state farm. Each commission contained representatives from the farm (commonly the chairman or directors, leading managers, and the like), and also from local family farmers, the local authority and the state. The main task of the commission was to determine the value of the property previously held by the collective or state farm; to decide on the actual methods of compensation; to determine whether a farm should be liquidated and decide on structures and arrangements to replace it. A common pattern has been for new share-holding cooperatives and companies to be established on the bases of the former farms, and there are now more than 600 such institutions in Estonia. However, because the deterioration of state and collective farms had continued for some time, and their future (or lack of it) was well known, much of their most valuable equipment, such as tractors, trucks, combines, and other machinery, was often sold off before reforms had properly started at very advantageous prices (at so-called balance-sheet value) to well placed individuals such as farm managerial staff and local administrators.

The members of the reform commission for the Puka state farm decided to create a new cooperative and to issue shares in accordance with a grading system where length of service plus the level of an individual's salary were taken into consideration in order to compensate more highly qualified work with more shares. As a result the former director of the state farm received 57 shares (each equal to 100 kroons in the farm's property). My grandmother, who had worked on the farm for eleven years (she also worked in other places) got six shares. My grandfather had retired in 1957 for health reasons and had died in 1976. His entitlement was valued at seven shares.

According to the Law on the Definition of and Compensation for Unlawfully Acquired Property, one cow was valued as 50 Estonian kroons at the 1940 value. The correlation between the 1940 kroon and the new Estonian kroon (EEK) was established at one to ten (the mid-1993 exchange rate for one US dollar was around 13 kroons (EEK).

Thus, according to the law one cow was valued at the equivalent of 500 EEK or about US$ 38.

Like most others, the Puka farm had almost no money in its bank account after the crucial inflation periods of 1991 and 1992. Consequently, compensation to the former members was paid mainly in kind. As compensation for the horse and calf and some equipment handled over to the collective farm in 1949, our family received two cows and one calf (a horse was deemed equivalent to two cows) from the herd of the state farm. As further compensation, the family was given 300 kg. of grain, 30 kg. of wool and 160 kroons in cash.

Today, all the members of our family live in the cities (including my grandmother who is now eighty-nine) making it impossible to care for livestock, except during the summer in the course of holidays spent at my grandparents' place. As a result, one cow was sold to a local farmer for 700 kroons while the second cow and calf were butchered.

The land originally belonging to my grandmother's brother – in total about 26 hectares – was also returned to the family. However, it had been used for many years by the collective farm. All the buildings on the land were destroyed many years ago in order to enlarge the fields and render them more suitable for the large-scale agricultural technology of collective farming. The holding is located quite far from the village, and no family or farmer wants to rent or use it. My father and his sister also have a claim on another farm of about the same size. But in accordance with the Law on Farming from 1989, this land was given to another family who had also purchased the buildings. This family cannot be dispossessed, but it is still unclear today when, or from what fund, or in what manner compensation for this holding will be made. Similar problems remain all over Estonia.

Conclusion

To summarise, I would argue that although Estonia has attempted to institute a truly just strategy for property restitution, it has also, at the same time, chosen what turns out to be the most complicated way of payment for our suffering in the past. Unfortunately, only the issue of justice was taken into consideration, as against economic, technical and other practical considerations such as those of time.

Under the ensuing conditions of uncertainty, the country's broader privatisation process is also being delayed, and this is often closely tied both to the processes of restitution and to the question of new domestic and foreign investment. Without clear title of ownership to land or other property, investors are unwilling to risk large investments in them. A large portion of Estonian property has thus been kept unnecessarily out of market circulation, and it is expected that land will not be available for sale on a large scale until 1997, with the exception of some land already returned to owners. Land can be sold only according to the decision of the central or local government, and even then only if there are no claims on it, or if it belongs to the state or municipality.

In spite of the fact that a special compensation fund was created in order to meet the claims of owners, it is still not clear from what sources and to what extent such compensation will be paid. As I have discussed, the situation has arisen from the arguments and misunderstandings between Estonian political forces in 1989 and at the beginning of the 1990s. The element of justice and fairness, as against practical and economic thinking, prevailed at that time in our political decisions. The price of these decisions, however just they seemed, will be very costly to the country and its people.

REFERENCES

Kuddo, A. 'Population Losses', in *World War II and Soviet Occupation in Estonia: A Damages Report*, ed. J. Kahk, Tallinn, 1991: 33-41.
Estonian Farm Law. Estonian Soviet Republic, 1989.
Law on Agricultural Reform (*Eesti Vabariigi põllumajandusreformi seadus*). *Riigi Teataja*, No. 10, 1992.
Law on the Definition of and Compensation for Unlawfully Acquired Property (*Õigusvastaselt võõrandatud vara maksumuse määramise ja kompenseerimise seadus*). *Rahva Hääl*, 10 June, 1993.
Law on Land Reform (*Eesti Vabariigi maareformi seadus*). *Riigi Teataja*, No. 34, 1991.
Law on Property Reform (*Eesti Vabariigi omandireformi aluste seadus*). *Riigi Teataja*, No. 21, 1991.
Poland *International Economic Report*. 1992/1993. Warsaw, 1993.

7. Decollectivisation and Total Scarcity in High Albania

Clarissa de Waal

Introduction

*F*or the past half century Albania has been characterised by extremes. Enver Hoxha's dictatorship was the most consistently Stalinist of the socialist regimes in Europe, and together with that of Romania, the most brutal. Centralisation was maximal, politically and economically. Isolation from the outside world, as well as popular ignorance of internal affairs, was achieved by a combination of draconian restrictions on movement and government stranglehold on the dissemination of information.

Thanks to the Communist pro-natalist policy, Albania has the youngest population in Europe (average age 25 years, 37 percent under 15 years), and uniquely in Europe, the larger part of this youthful population is rurally based.

As a result of the former regime's policy of rural population retention, 63.9 percent of the country's population lived in rural areas in 1990 (*Vjetari Statistikor* 1991), while 50 percent of the population during the Communist period worked in agriculture.

Today, Albania's level of poverty ranks it amongst the world's poorest countries with the highest level of unemployment and the lowest GDP per capita income in Europe. The average salary for an urban professional is US$30 a month (1993), while the price of a kilo of bread is now 50 cents.[1]

Small-scale trading and emigration are the commonest strategies for survival. Of Albania's 3.3 million inhabitants, at least 300,000 were estimated to be working (mostly illegally) in Greece in 1993. (Legal emigration requires personal connections in the relevant embassy and/or dollars – US$300 or more for a Greek visa, at least twice this for an Italian one).

In the last months of Communist rule in 1991, the Ministry of Economic Affairs recorded a decline in national income of 62 percent. Industrial production declined by 69 percent, while the workers were being paid 80 percent of their wages despite a supply crisis which prevented large numbers from actually working (Aslund and Sjoberg 1992: 139).

Faced with this economic breakdown, a major priority of the democratic coalition government which came to power in June 1991 (the first multi-party elections since 1920 were held in March 1991) was the privatisation of the economy and complete privatisation of agricultural land. Given that under Communism over 50 percent of the workforce was engaged in agriculture, it made sense to start tackling the economic crisis with the decollectivisation of agricultural land. Twenty percent of arable land was state farmland; 80 percent, cooperative. By the end of May 1993, 92 percent of cooperative land had been privatised (Economic Intelligence Unit, *Country Report* 1993).

While some state farm land has already been privatised, further redistribution and decisions regarding compensation for former owners are still under discussion. This article, therefore, deals exclusively with the privatisation of cooperative land. Before examining this process, it will be useful to summarise agricultural policy during the Communist period in order to clarify the issues involved in decollectivisation.

Collectivisation

From 1946 until 1989 Albanian agricultural policy consistently followed the Stalinist model. Progressively eroding individual rights, the

---

1. An earlier version of this paper appeared in *Cambridge Anthropology*, Vol. 18, No. 1, 1995. For convenience, references to incomes and prices are mainly given in US$ equivalents in the text.

Communist government conducted a continuous campaign to reduce private agricultural activities, attempting in the 1980s to eradicate a free market for agricultural products altogether. Collectivisation began in 1946, gained momentum in the mid-1950s, and by 1959 was completed in the south and west of Albania (Sjoberg 1991: 106). A final drive in the 1960s in the central and northern mountain districts completed the collectivisation of the whole country. By 1967 private agriculture had been eliminated.

A major objective was to become self-sufficient in grain. Up until the 1960s, half of the country's bread-grain needs had been imported. In 1959 persistent shortages had necessitated imports of wheat from the Soviet Union amounting to 48 percent of total consumption (Sjoberg 1991: 93). To achieve this self-sufficiency following the break with the Soviet Union in 1961, the decision was made to increase agricultural production, and to reduce the emphasis on investment in industry. Extension of arable land, retention of the rural population, and reduction of private plots were seen as the keys to fulfilment of this goal.

Arable land doubled between 1950 and 1989 as a result of massive terracing (Chinese style), marsh draining, irrigation works, and desalination projects. Concurrently, however, as a result of the pro-natalist policy, the population tripled, so that land per head actually dropped by 10 percent, leaving only a fifth of a hectare of arable land in 1989 available for cultivation per capita (Sjoberg 1989: 8). The policy of rural population retention practically precluded out-migration. Rural dwellers' movements were severely restricted by the imposition of domestic passports regulating journeys, and the near impossibility of obtaining urban dwelling permits. Rural schools concentrated on vocational training for rural needs such as agronomy, forestry or mining skills, thus influencing the likely geographical future of the pupil, as well as the type of employment.

By the end of the 1960s, cooperative farm workers still had private household plots (state farm workers had already lost theirs), but it was illegal to sell produce in free markets, and no beasts of burden might be owned by individuals. As Schnytzer notes (1992: 46), in virtually all Communist societies a free market has been tolerated in the agricultural produce of private plots; however, in Albania, attempts were made to eradicate even this vestige of capitalism. Hoxha's successor, Ramiz Alia, referring to produce rejected by the village state store due to overproduction or inferior quality, criticised cooperative members who sold such produce – a basket of figs, handful of parsley or a dozen eggs – in town. 'Is this in the interests of socialism, of the people, and of group property? Obviously not, because when the trade sector fails to collect cooperative output, on the one hand the social labour to produce this output is lost, and on the other hand, when the individual goes to market or sells his product to some middleman, he loses time and the private market is stimulated' (quoted in Schnytzer 1992: 46). In 1981 the private market was outlawed in order to 'eradicate petty capitalist' behaviour and to 'erode the psychology of private ownership'. To the same end, plot reduction continued, the ultimate object being its total elimination. By the mid-1980s it was estimated (Luari 1985: 261, cited by Sjoberg 1991), that 16 percent of cooperative families had no land, while 45 percent had less than 500 square metres. The practical object, of course, was to increase workers' labour time on the cooperative.

During the 1970s, Albania was still having to import grain (except for the year 1976) and there were shortages of meat, eggs and milk. In 1978 foreign aid which had been more or less continuous since 1945 (from Yugoslavia, the Soviet Union and China in turn) came to an end. At the beginning of the 1980s families had to hand over their animals to the cooperatives in order to increase meat production and to eradicate petit bourgeois attitudes. Many slaughtered their animals instead. Cooperatives were in fact quite unprepared and ill-equipped for large-scale herding. Even more seriously, the regime's obsession with self-sufficiency in wheat meant that far too much of the country's pasture land had been given over to grain cultivation. There was thus a disastrous shortfall of animal fodder. One consequence of this campaign was the shortage thereafter of dairy and meat products, and the introduction of meat rationing.

The combination in the 1980s of severe droughts (1983-1985, 1987-1988), the end of foreign aid, the clampdown on private plots and confiscation of privately owned animals, led to rationing, undisguised discontent – 'they pretend to pay us, we pretend to work' – and finally, crisis. Cooperative labour in the fields had effectively been an unpaid workforce. In areas of poor land the daily wage was three leks, the price of a small loaf of bread or a packet of cigarettes. In fertile areas the wage was ten leks. The cooperative sector had in practice acted as an employment buffer for a political system which prided itself on providing full employment. With an annual increase in the workforce of 40-50,000 people in the 1980s (Sandström and Sjoberg 1991: 935) and a very weak economy, creation of sufficient new jobs was a problem. The yearly increase of 4.5 percent of cooperative members reflects the absorption of this surplus into the agricultural sector. What appeared as decreasing labour productivity was in reality disguised unemployment.

In 1987 a food production crisis, and the patent inability of Albania to feed its population, led to a reversal, albeit gradual and covert, of orthodox ideology with respect to household plots. By 1988 peasants with plots (Sjoberg 1991: 128-129) had been exhorted to produce their own vegetables, and a new statute was introduced to provide landless cooperative households with plots. Farmers were given progressively more land to cultivate privately, until by 1990 they had received a fifth of a hectare per family. By this time the demotivated and demoralised work brigades were only going to work in the cooperative's fields if there was some special motivation such as the wheat harvest. Theft of animals, materials and tools from the cooperatives by members over these final years occurred on a large scale.

When the regime finally came to an end in 1991, there followed an extraordinary orgy of destruction and vandalism. As if the world had come to an end and there would be no future needs, vineyards and orchards were destroyed, cooperative buildings razed to the ground; school windows, furniture and books demolished; machinery broken, and the entire rural telephone system ripped out.

Decollectivisation

In July 1991, the democratically elected coalition government introduced land reforms to cope with the economic crisis, starting with the decollectivisation of cooperative land. The basic principle for redistribution was as follows: an elected village land commission re-established the original village boundaries. The resulting quantity of land was divided by the number of people (including newborn babies) resident in the village. Thus the larger the family, the more land it received. State employees such as teachers, resident in the village officially received less, though individual villages could exercise a certain amount of discretion. Allocation of land parcels was by lottery; parcels were dispersed to ensure fair distribution of differentially fertile land. All previous ownership was nullified. The land thus distributed might not be sold, but would devolve to the individual holder's heirs. Sale of rural land is still illegal. By contrast, livestock allocated in the same way could be sold. Any cooperative property which had withstood the vandalism, such as the shop and the house of culture, was sold off very cheaply.

During the three months which I spent in the south of Albania in the autumn of 1992, this programme appeared to have been satisfactorily carried out. That is, the evenness and perceived justice of the distribution have led to minimal friction. Certain factors prevalent in the south have contributed to this positive process. One is the southern settlement pattern whereby village houses are clustered, while fields are outside the village. The earlier date of collectivisation in these areas (1950s) means that fewer villagers are old enough to have strong attachments to former holdings. Moreover, in much of the south, land belonged to larger landlords and not to the majority of the villagers at all. Finally, and critically, the southern countryside has sufficient grazing land to provide families with an income from flocks.[2] This is particularly significant in areas such as Laberia in the south-west, where families are large and land holdings modest. Laberia, which before 1945 was an area of small owner-cultivators, has an average holding size today of between 0.6 and 1 hectare, while the number of children per family averages six to seven. (The average landholding in Albania is 1.4 hectares. [Wyzan and Sjoberg 1992: 17])

This positive conclusion with respect to decollectivisation in the south is not to suggest that the regeneration of agriculture does not face formidable obstacles. Lack of suitable small-scale machinery, lack of cash for inputs, absence of a developed marketing infrastructure, and often, difficulty of access to markets, pose serious problems. However, proximity to Greece facilitates migration (usually illegal) as a means at least to 'overcoming the imperfections of the rural credit market' (see Griffin 1976). An estimated 80 percent of families in the southern areas have one or more members working in Greece for at least a few months at a time (before being deported by the police). Foreign earnings are not necessarily only invested in agricultural improvements or flocks. Better-

2. A very common complaint by teachers is that children graze the flocks rather than attending school. However, a child may be more usefully employed increasing the family income than sitting in classes where the current material and ideological crises have resulted in demoralisation and demotivisation of both staff and pupils. There is now a serious and growing lack of qualified teachers as a result of emigration or urban migration. In most cases there are no books or equipment, often no glass in the windows, and no heating for classrooms in winter. Discipline for these reasons is often a problem. Under Communism discipline was rigorous, and although much of the learning was rote as well as imbued with Communist propaganda, the school system produced a high level of literacy, numeracy and articulacy, both in rural and in urban areas. There is now a real danger that children in certain age groups will grow up virtually uneducated even if they attend school.

off families, such as those who had *privilegjia*, (e.g., loyal Party members in cooperative administration who had access to scarce goods, or were in a position to embezzle state funds or to steal state goods) under the Communist regime, are also likely to invest in an urban building plot and/or a car. The majority first invest in house improvements and clothes, and then in agriculture and animals.

What is positive is the acceptance of the land division, and the possibility for most southern dwellers, through a combination of land, flocks, and migrants' cash, to make a living despite high local unemployment and an underdeveloped rural infrastructure.

Collectivisation in Less Productive Areas

A favourite slogan of Enver Hoxha's in the 1960s was: 'Let us take to the hills and mountains, and make them as beautiful and fertile as the plains'. This was part of the regime's twin campaigns to promote, at least in theory, regional equality and to extend the arable land area as much as possible. In time the phrase was reduced to 'in the lowlands, but also in the hills and mountains' with a concomitant reduction in attention to hill and mountain areas. Lowland cooperative workers earned more than those in upland areas where yields were lower, 'norms' rarely reached and pay consequently less. North Albanian areas such as Puke, Tropoje, Mirdita, were amongst the last to be collectivised. The terrain for the most part in these areas is extremely steep and rocky, and certainly not suited to economies of scale. Ideology took precedence over economics, however, and despite strong resistance on the part of the locals, the land holdings in the mountainous north were cooperativised by 1966.

At the same time, fortunately for the inhabitants' economic survival, the hitherto unexploited mineral resources (chrome and copper), as well as forestry and hydro-electric resources, were opened up in the northern districts. Extractive enterprises, often in remote rural areas, were usually small scale and labour intensive. However, their great advantage over agriculture, apart from increasing employment opportunities, was the higher pay and the access they gave their employees to state benefits such as social insurance and pensions – benefits which were not available to cooperative workers.

One consequence of local industrial employment opportunities for men, chiefly in mining, was that the feminisation of agriculture became even more marked in these areas than elsewhere. (In Puke, for example, women made up 70.7 percent of cooperative labour in 1981, as compared with the national average of 52.4 percent[Sjoberg 1991: 117, 137]). The poorer the district agriculturally, the larger the number of families with members employed in industry; in Mirdita, for example, a copper mining district, three quarters of Mirditan families had members employed outside agriculture.

This then is the background to the central theme of this chapter – the effects of democratisation and decollectivisation on an agriculturally poor area in a very poor country. What is happening to Albania's poorer areas now that Communism's policy of full employment is being replaced by one of economic rationalisation geared to profit? Overmanning of 100 percent was standard in industry and agriculture in Albania (Aslund and Sjoberg 1992: 145) under Communism. What is happening after half a century of pro-natalist policies, retention of rural population, and urban underdevelopment, in a country where emigration abroad is very severely restricted and unemployment runs at 50 percent at least?

Mirdita

Mirdita, an area of 867 square kilometres, has a population of 54,000.[3] A hilly mountainous district much of which is 400 m. above sea level, it includes the whole of the Fan River Basin, into which empty the Big Fan and the Little Fan rivers. There is a state farm in the Fan Valley. The three towns, Rreshen (pop. 4,100), Kurbnesh (pop. 1,100), and Rubik (pop. 2,800), were only established in the 1960s. During the Communist period mining and copper processing in Mirdita constituted 17 percent of Albania's mining and metallurgical industry. Industry accounted for four-fifths of the area's total production.

The most accessible town, Rubik, a mining and copper refining centre, is an hour and a half by bus from Tirana. Few of Mirdita's regions today are at a great distance from passable roads, but many of the regions, particularly the highland ones, known as the *thellsi* (the depths), are still remote in terms of social and cultural distance. This is partly because the area was without a developed road network until the late 1970s. Former inaccessibility likewise accounts in part for its history of independence from any central government, as well as for its strong

---

3. I am grateful to the Nuffield Foundation for a fieldwork grant for research in this area in 1993.

sense of distinctive cultural identity. At the same time, in the nineteenth century and earlier, one factor contributing to the region's independence under the Ottomans was its control over the route between Shkoder and Prizren, much of which runs through Mirdita. The largest of the northern tribes, Mirdita paid no taxes to the Porte throughout the five centuries of Ottoman occupation, and resisted conversion from Roman Catholicism to Islam.[4]

In common with all the northern Albanian peoples (Ghegs), Muslim and Catholic, Mirditans had self-governing tribal organisation. A tribe consisted of a group of exogamous clans usually, but not always, geographically separated. From Ottoman times these were called *bajraks* (Turkish 'standard-bearing group') recalling their military function in the empire. The *bajraktar* was the clan headman. The tribal system was abolished under Communism. Today each village again has a headman, usually a descendant of the village's pre-Communist *bajraktar*, known as the *krye plak*, 'chief old man', and a council of elders with a representative from each clan. Tribal law was based on the canon of Lek Dukagjin, a fifteenth-century chieftain credited with the reform of the body of customary law which up until 1945 was the sole repository of legal knowledge in the tribal north. The canon provides a complete moral and legal framework for social interaction. Its key elements are the inviolate nature of private property, and a dispute settlement system by the people for the people. The canon's rules cover every area of life including establishment of property boundaries, division of property, blood feud, marriage, dispute settlement procedure, rights of way, compensation for theft, watering rights. A central feature of tribal life up until 1945 was the blood feud.

'Total scarcity'

In common with most northern districts, there was greater resistance in Mirdita to Communism in the 1940s and to cooperativisation in the 1960s, than there had been in the south. The nature of the terrain, steep and rocky, meant that there had never been a landed class, and this

---

4. The northern tribes were originally all Roman Catholic, possibly from as early as the fourth century. The Ottomans targeted the Catholic Albanian population for conversion leading to a decline of Catholics in the seventeenth century, and many forced converts were resettled in Kosova. Catholic numbers were increased in the eighteenth century through the influence of the Venetians and Hapsburgs, rivals to Ottoman power (Jelavich 1983).

posed an ideological problem for the Communists' class war (*lufta e klaseve*) campaign, though they tried to portray the *bajraktars* as exploitative landowners (see e.g., *Almanak Mirdita* 1968, 1969, 1975). It is clear from the ethnographies that the *bajraktars* were in fact closely controlled by the tribe, with little freedom of political or judicial action; a point which is confirmed by older Mirditans today. Edith Durham observed early this century 'Of old the bairaktar is said to have been important. In my time he had lost ground and was often quite cut out in council by abler men' (1928: 16). In the 1930s Margaret Hasluck notes 'In all areas the jurisdiction of the bajraktar was subject to certain limitations. If the commoners did not like one of his decisions, even if made in concert with the headmen and elders, they were not bound to abide by it and could compel him to re-examine the case. Neither he nor a headman could, singly or in combination, fine a tribesman without first securing authority from the tribe' (1954: 121-122).

Control of economic resources, where these were so inadequate, could hardly provide the basis for a powerful hierarchy. Material poverty was matched by institutional poverty. Albania figures importantly as an example of a sedentary feuding society in Black-Michaud's study of feud in the Mediterranean and the Middle East. Black-Michaud argues that the principal concomitants of feud are 'material poverty which inhibits the spontaneous development of an internal power hierarchy based on the control of economic resources', and 'lack of an adequate system of communications'. A chronic inadequacy of the means of production, and the precarious nature of an existence on the margins of subsistence, give rise to a folk model which Black-Michaud terms 'total scarcity'. 'Total scarcity may be summarised as the moral, institutional and material premise of a certain type of society in which everything felt by the people themselves to be relevant to human life is regarded by these people as existing in absolutely inadequate quantities. ... a permanently felt inadequacy of all existing resources and political structure to meet the minimal conscious requirements of the whole population' (1975: 160). It is the result 'of a set of ecological, technological and historical circumstances which cause an endemic insufficiency of material goods and resources and prevent the acquisition and long-term accumulation of wealth by individuals or groups. This in turn inhibits the development of social stratification and an attendant power structure based on economic differentiation' (Ibid.: 122).

The anthropologists, Durham and Hasluck, were frequently told by tribesmen that what the area really needed to prosper economically was a strong government with an efficient army to compel them to abandon the feud. There existed no logical alternative to feud in the absence of government, Mirditans maintained, other than anarchy. The totalitarian Communist government with its powerful Sigurimi was well equipped to supply this perceived need. From the mid-1940s until 1991, blood feud was eradicated.

Collectivisation in Mirdita

Complete cooperativisation of the area was achieved in 1966 despite extreme reluctance on the part of Mirditans. There was no overt coercion; giving one's land to the cooperative was 'voluntary' in the same spirit as the referendum which approved the abolition of religion in 1967. It was found expedient ultimately to avoid the *sy keq*, evil eye, of the Party.

There were good reasons for resisting cooperativisation. The terrain dictates the settlement pattern, which in contrast to the southern type, means that houses are surrounded by their land, with often half a kilometre or more between houses and only scattered parcels suitable for cultivation. The steepness of the terrain and the poor quality of the soil preclude economies of scale and profitable grain production. Up until the 1950s, the population which, as noted above, was extremely poor, was a third of its present size (with a high rate of mortality). Families kept a small flock of goats or sheep, and grew subsistence crops of maize and beans. Had cooperativisation policy been limited to small-scale collectivisation of flocks, and increasing orchard cultivation, the results would have been better for agricultural productivity. As usual however, priority was given to wheat cultivation.

Industrialisation in Mirdita

In the 1960s and early 1970s, Mirdita's mineral resources were opened up. Copper mining and processing were developed in three centres, Rubik, Kurbnesh and later (1976) Spac, and became the main source of income for the region. This certainly contributed to the reduction of material scarcity in the area, the more so that with a policy of total employment, no family was without a wage. Indeed, three-quarters of Mirdita families had one or more members, mostly male, who worked outside agriculture. The majority worked in the copper industry; a smaller number were employed in forestry or in a hydro-electric plant. One consequence was the predominance of women in the agricultural workforce, 70-75 percent. Another was the aspiration to educate one's children beyond middle school so as to qualify them for non-agricultural employment where wages were higher. Local vocational schools established by the government enabled children to learn technical skills, qualifying them for jobs in metallurgy, copper refineries and mines, as well as agriculture. Some schools offered general courses enabling pupils to go on to teacher training, accounting, interpreting, etc. However, strong Party loyalty was a pre-requisite for a career in such fields. No able candidate could enter a form of higher education other than technical, unless he or she came from a family manifestly and actively supportive of the regime. Children of families who had opposed Communism initially were automatically disqualified.

Without this industrial development in Mirdita it would have been quite impossible for the region to have sustained its population which, thanks to the rigorously enforced pro-natalist policy and rural population retention, had tripled by 1989.

Decollectivisation and the canon of Lek Dukagjin

Already before the fall of the Communist government in 1991, Mirditans had started to reclaim and cultivate their patrimonial land. (Landholders had surrendered title to their land when they joined cooperatives.) This was easier than in the south as it surrounded their houses. In June 1991, Mirditan village land commissions decided to ignore the new government's decree on land distribution. Instead they restored the pre-1966 landholdings to the hereditary heads of each family. Mirditans agree that a per soul distribution would have been more equitable. More equitable, for example, because families differ in size, and properties differ in quality of land. But they maintain that it would have been unworkable. The proximity of the landholdings to the owners' houses, and the intense feeling of jealous ownership up until 1966, where scarcity had imbued land with such value, ruled out such a solution.

In restoring the pre-1966 landholdings to the original owners, local land commissions followed the code of Lek Dukagjin which provides exhaustive guidelines on boundary recognition and marking. A majority of the men on the land commission were older men familiar with the former boundaries. The fact that decollectivisation in the area took place according to the fifteenth century canon, *sipas kanunit*, rather than according to the government's law, *sipas ligjit*, is characteristic of Mirdita's independent response to democratisation. It indicates a lack of confidence in central government as well as remarkable continuity in customary law. (In view of the fact that the Communist government suppressed the canon, it is noteworthy that those in their teens and twenties today are familiar with the canon's rules.)

The reinstitution of Lek's Law is not limited to the redistribution of land. Today it provides the guidelines for community activities and dispute settlement as it did up until the 1940s. Thus the village council of elders, the lowest tier in local government, observes traditional law in electing representatives from each clan *(fis)* to the council. The prevalent view in Mirditan villages, while it is not unanimous, is that as long as the state law lacks force, it is essential to have some alternative legal framework. This is all the more essential as a return to total scarcity following democratisation and rationalisation of the area's industry, looks imminent.

Economic deterioration and survival strategies

A severe blow to the area's economy has been the partial, sometimes complete, closing down of local industrial concerns connected with copper, hydro-electric power and forestry. The official claim (by the Democrat regional governor in Rreshen), is that local industrial production, following the initial collapse, has reached 50 percent of its previous optimal level. This is probably an over-estimate as there are frequent stoppages due to lack of materials and breakdown of antiquated equipment. Unemployment in Mirdita following the industrial crisis and the end to administrative employment on cooperatives, is probably at least 70 percent. (Local government officials in the administrative centre of Rreshen say no accurate estimate can be made since it is not known how many former employees now work in agriculture or abroad. My suggestion that the number drawing the year's unemployment pay following dismissal could provide some guide, was for this reason not accepted.)

Although former state employees receive unemployment pay (about US$15 a month in 1993) for a year following dismissal, their prospects for finding a new job are remote. Social welfare thereafter is about US$5 a month (1993). Moreover, wages are so low (US$20 a month on average in rural areas, US$30 in Tirana in 1993) in proportion to newly liberalised prices (1 kg of bread costs fifty cents), that it makes far more sense to try to work illegally in Greece, even though illegal workers risk deportation within a few months, or sooner, of arrival. An Albanian migrant working in Greece can earn US$500 a month. It is much more

difficult for northern Albanians to migrate to Greece than for southern-
ers, who are both closer to the border and more familiar – through Greek
television channels not received in the north – with Greek language and
culture. Nevertheless, a surprisingly large number of families in Mirdita,
around 30 percent, has, or has had, at least one son in Greece, and the
number of emigrants is increasing.

On migrants' return, their earnings are handed over to the head of the
family who decides together with the rest of the family, how it should be
spent. As in the south an initial sum is usually spent on house improvements. In Mirdita this often includes a television and a sewing machine.
(One indicator of the area's relative poverty is the far lower number of
households with televisions as compared with southern Albania.) The
rest is likely to be spent on agricultural inputs such as fertiliser which is
very expensive at US$2 a kilo; wages for an itinerant plains ploughman;
and acquisition of animals. A few families with sons who are particularly
enterprising and have been able to work longer in Greece, have invested
foreign earnings in a second-hand bus or truck. A truck or bus would
probably cost a million leks, that is about twenty months work in Greece
or US$10,000. With the profits from haulage or transport, some hope
eventually to acquire property in the plain. A few of the better off (such
as a village school head teacher, or a former cooperative agronomist)
have bought houses in Lezhe or Lac, two plains towns. (It is now legal to
buy urban property under certain conditions.) Capital can also be raised
by taking out a state loan. Some families have used a state loan to buy a
visa for Italy where wages are higher than in Greece, or to invest in a
truck for haulage. The financial risk is significant; a visa for Italy is not a
guarantee that one will find work once there; the truck may suddenly
need a new engine or expensive spare parts.

For the most part foreign earnings are used simply to improve the
means for subsistence from farming. Those families who have no member
available for emigration must resort to more modest cash raising activities
such as seasonal gathering. For example, itinerant merchants buy bilber-
ries for pharmaceutical use (5 kg fresh = 1 kg dried sold for US$9), herbs
such as thyme (1 kg after sorting and drying sells for US$4 per kg). Tra-
ditional professions still practised today include playing the *cifteli* (a local
two-stringed instrument) at weddings and the making and selling of bur-
ial costumes (*veshje e vdekjes*). Rituals connected with life crises ensure a
continuing demand despite the very difficult economic conditions.

Conditions for the new family farmers are very difficult indeed. As
well as having insufficient and often poor quality land, farmers must

contend with the decay of the material rural infrastructure; always minimally developed, this is now collapsing following years of neglect. Maintenance has been minimal for at least a decade. Thus many bridges are very dangerous or have actually fallen into the river below. This is very serious in an area dominated by two rivers, Fan i vogel, Fan i madhe, especially in winter when rivers are much too high to wade across. In addition, neglect of (the often misguidedly) terraced mountain sides is leading to erosion.

Landholdings range from 200 square metres to, exceptionally, one hectare. Where a household has one hectare it is usually because one or more brothers now lives elsewhere. Prior to Communism each village owned forest and grazing land which was common land. Today former common land and forest belong to the state. Lack of pasturage is a major obstacle to the accumulation of animals.

To convey the nature of conditions confronting small farmers, there follow two case histories.

Case 1

This family in the Mirditan mountain district of Fan has 500 square metres of land, and eight surviving children (aged one to eighteen, five girls, three boys). The family grows maize and beans. They produce beans which cover three months of their annual consumption needs, and maize enough for only three weeks. (The cooperative in this village was only able to produce maize to cover three months of the village's consumption needs, despite abundant fertiliser use.) The family rotates beans with rye which is grown for animal fodder. In addition they grow vegetables: garlic, cabbage, and in summer tomatoes and peppers. They have fruit trees (cherries, plums, quince, pears), a walnut tree, and some grape vines. Water for cultivation is inadequate; their only access to irrigation water is through a rota of a few hours at ten day intervals in summer. They own a cow which the eleven and nine-year-old children take to graze daily, a pig and some hens. For part of the year the cow provides them with a small quantity of kos, sour milk, (which they dilute with water), and a small quantity of cheese.

The father used to work as an electrician in the mining village of Spac, a two hour walk across the mountains. He is in his early forties, has had a serious kidney operation, and now has no job. Occasionally, a villager needs some electrical work done; a two day job of this kind brings the father 100 lek, about one dollar. The mother used to work on the cooperative. Together with her husband she now works on the family's land. The eldest son, aged fifteen, has won a scholarship to the School of Foreign Languages in Tirana where he learns German. It is hoped that he will become a teacher. The eldest daughter, aged eighteen, looks after the children, cooks, washes, gets water (helped by the younger children) from a source 150 metres from the house, and when necessary helps her parents with the crops or with gathering.

The family's two biggest problems are getting enough to eat, particularly in winter, and clothing themselves. Owing to a quarrel over inheritance, the family lives in one room of the patrimonial house independently of the grandparents who occupy the other three. As a result of too little to eat, the children look much younger than their real age; the fifteen-year-old looks nine or ten years old. The father who is intelligent and articulate, recently solved the clothes problem for the time being by writing to the Catholic organisation, Caritas, requesting a parcel of old clothes. Getting enough to eat is more difficult because there is no available family member to make the journey to Greece. Whenever seasonally possible the family gathers and sells various local herbs. Three adults and a child can gather and sort 20 kg of thyme in three days. Unfortunately, more and more villagers are now turning to gathering, diminishing local supplies and making it necessary to go further and further afield. Thirty out of seventy families in this village have built up small flocks of goats, but the village has almost no pasturage nearby, so that anyone with a larger flock must take the animals to a distance of several kilometres up the mountain. Social relations are bad in this village and none of the disputes over land of the type discussed below has as yet been resolved.

Case 2

This family lives in the mountain district of Oroshi. They own 0.55 hectares. Their fields are very steep which makes cultivation more difficult, but they are lucky to own one of the few holdings in this area with an abundant supply of water. The landholding is larger than the village average partly because the grandfather, an army officer under King Zog, made quite a lot of money in the army, and partly because he invested some of this money in a property in the plains where one of his two sons settled.

The head of the family is in his sixties. His eight surviving children are grown up. The three sons live with their parents. Under Communism the father worked for the forestry commission, while his wife worked on the cooperative. The eldest son, aged thirty-two, married with no children, worked in the mine at Spac as a foreman. He is now jobless. Last June the family made the decision to take out a state loan to buy him a visa for Italy. The second son, aged twenty-six, learnt welding at high school, and is also a self-taught and skilled stone mason and carpenter. Until 1991, he worked on the cooperative. Last year he worked in Greece, picking olives and oranges, and doing some carpentry. After six months, he was arrested for having no visa and returned to Oroshi. Some of the money he had earned was spent on tools, seeds and fertiliser. Some was set aside for necessities like sugar and coffee, dental treatment and bus fares. The family's biggest problem is not so much shortage of food, though they almost never eat meat, as shortage of cash. This son will return illegally to Greece as soon as the autumn agricultural work has eased.

The third son, aged twenty-one, learnt agronomy at school. He is a very keen horticulturist and agriculturist, both systematic and experimental. The mother and father see to all the irrigating work, most of the grazing (they have one cow and a calf), and care of the animals, which include a pig and hens. The young wife helps in the fields with sowing, hoeing and harvesting, as well as doing all the household cooking, washing and cleaning. Until she married last summer, a daughter who worked at the copper refinery at Reps, five kilometres away, contributed cash to the household. After her marriage regular income came from the father's pension and the eldest son's year's unemployment pay, now ceased. The family's monthly income is now about US$20.

Since reclaiming their land, the family has cultivated chiefly maize and beans. Beans are every family's staple. They have planted new fruit trees in addition to the cherry, plum, walnut, apple and pear trees which they already had. They have also planted vines. Thanks to their abundant water supply, they are able to provide vegetables adequate for the family's needs (cabbage, garlic, peppers, tomatoes and some potatoes).

One obstacle to grain cultivation is the absence of draught animals or small-scale machines, such as a rotovator, which could be used on small steep fields. In the cooperative period, an enormous amount of fertiliser was used on what is mostly fairly infertile, stony land. The priority given to wheat production meant that crop rotation was neglected to the detriment of the soil quality. Today, acquisition of fertiliser is one of the biggest problems facing these cash starved farmers. Without flocks for manure, and with artificial fertiliser at prohibitive cost, it is impossible to maximise productivity. This family plans to gradually reduce the area devoted to maize and beans, labour-intensive crops requiring hours of tedious weeding. They reason that it makes more financial sense to reduce labour input so as to release two brothers for work abroad. Foreign earnings will provide cash for these staples, and for the accumulation of animals, while in place of maize and beans they will concentrate on forage crops such as clover, and plant more vines and fruit trees. The married brother plans to move down to the plain eventually, leaving the patrimonial house and property to his younger brothers.

Migration to the plain

Before 1945, one solution to land scarcity (and also to vendetta) was to move down to the coastal plain, despite the prevalence of malaria there. Today makeshift tents and huts set up in the plain since 1991, testify to the same trend following the end of the population retention policy. The plain is no longer malarial but much of it is state farm land, and future ownership is still quite unclear. Nevertheless, a great many Mirditans, especially the younger ones, hope to move down to the plains. The scarcity of land in higher areas, the tripled population, and the unsuitableness of the mountain terrain for extensive agriculture, urgently necessitate organised outmigration.

Disputes following decollectivisation

Disputes were plentiful pre-1945. But whereas some quarrels, allegations of misuse of irrigation rights, and accusations of theft are common to both periods, one phenomenon directly consequent to Communist policies stands out today. This is the extreme nature of the concept of privatisation which tends to reject any notion of community rights or common good. This is in contrast to notions of community rights as dictated by the canon up until the 1940s. Although private ownership of house and land was absolute prior to the Communist period, public good overrode private loss. A man could emigrate with his family temporarily or for good without losing the title to his house or land. Even if he sold his property, 'the piece constituting the site of the house remained his in spite of the sale, and so long as one stone stood on another, no-one might use the site' (Hasluck 1954: 23). But if a public road was diverted to higher ground because it became too muddy in winter, the men whose land was taken for the diversion received no compensation (Ibid.: 89). The same principles apply today, but because the new problems have arisen from a discredited order outside the canon's aegis, it is more difficult for the elders to assert their authority.

During the collective period, fields and access roads had to be altered to increase the size of areas to be cultivated cooperatively, and to permit machinery and trucks to reach the fields. Numerous instances have arisen, for example, where restored properties include a portion of an access road for wheeled vehicles. Owners have barricaded the access points. Quite often it is not simply a question of access to another part of the village, but a question of an access road between distant villages. There are cases of wheeled access to a village several kilometres away being blocked by a few hundred meters of barricaded field, so that the only access to the further village is by foot. In one case, the track formerly used by traffic between two villages has been closed off, forcing people to follow the river bed which in winter is impassable, and in summer only possible on foot.

Where a villager's reclaimed property includes a graveyard established during the Communist period, owners have refused villagers access. This is quite a common occurrence as it was Communist policy to replace more distant graveyards with new ones within a village's borders. This was part of the campaign to 'smash the fetters of faith, the Canon of Lek, and old reactionary norms and customs which, like a black spider, have paralysed the Mirditans' moral world. Religious prejudice still prevents each village from having a systematised and beautified graveyard nearby' (Tusha, *Almanak Mirdita* No. 3, 1975: 99).

Another problem arising from the collective period concerns houses which were built on what was then cooperative land, but is now private land. It was Communist policy to build new houses in the centre of villages in an effort to replace the scattered homestead pattern, characteristic of northern villages, with the southern clustered pattern. The immediate object was simply to house a married son where his father's house was becoming overcrowded. In many such cases today the pre-Communist property owner refuses to allow the house owner to remain, and is unwilling to consider any kind of compensation or exchange of land.

These problems have arisen as a result of the decision to distribute cooperative land to the hereditary owners. At the same time, given the nature of the terrain, it would have been extremely difficult, as discussed above, to have effected the official decollectivisation plan. The question today is how to resolve these conflicts fairly and effectively where central government's powers are weak, and its interest in the affairs of poor, largely rural provinces limited; where provincial government is without funds and virtually powerless, and where the scale and blatancy of political corruption has left state administration generally, with very little credibility.

Success or failure in the resolution of village disputes depends to a large extent on the nature of social relations within a village, which in turn appears to correlate strongly with a village's resources. Where these are poorer than average, interpersonal relations tend to be correspondingly more difficult and acrimonious. Where social cohesion is greater, the council of elders has often been successful in defusing tensions and resolving the kinds of problems described above. For example, some villages (such as Xhuxhe discussed below), have solved the graveyard problem by villagers clubbing together and buying (unofficially, as rural land sale is illegal) a new piece of land in a suitably accessible place. In several villages in the districts of Fan and Orosh, a landowner obstructing a road has been prevailed upon by the elders to cooperate. A brief sketch of one village where disputes have been successfully resolved indicates the kinds of factors which contribute to social cohesion.

Xhuxhe (pronounced Jooge) is a highland village in the Thellsi (Depths) of the district of Fan. Before the Communist period, village income came from keeping flocks. The terrain is very steep with a mixture of forest and open pasture land. Today the average landholding is 200 square metres. As the holdings are so small, village families have reverted since privatisation of land to herding for their chief source of income. The forest plays a subsidiary but significant role in the village's economy. The stone houses have wooden floors and ceilings, roof tiles are wooden, wall insulation is made from pine cones. The state owns the forest, and woodcutting and hauling businesses operated by the villagers of Thirra across the valley from Xhuxhe are taxed, but wood for domestic use is not paid for.

During the Communist period thirty villagers from Xhuxhe (out of 1,400 inhabitants and 200 households) were members of the communist party. There was initially massive resistance to communism, and throughout the Communist period the village remained more politically united than most.

Asked to explain their comparative freedom from disputes today, villagers usually replied 'Because our main occupation is with flocks, we have much more work than villagers who just cultivate the land. We don't have time for quarrelling'. A crucial factor is of course that they have sufficient pasturage for their flocks. Moreover, since agricultural land is not the main source of income, there is both less cause for boundary disputes and less friction over land inheritance. Grown sons tend to remain in their father's household, thus providing labour for herding, cultivation, carpentry, and temporary migration to Greece. An additional factor may be contributing to village solidarity: in contrast to most villages in northern Albania, Xhuxhe has within the village some unrelated tribes (who settled in the village at a much later date than the founders); this makes marriage within the village possible. Interrelatedness, added to the village's remoteness from any administrative centre, probably increases cohesion.

Disputes over division of property

A second phenomenon which stands out today is partly a consequence of Communist pro-natalist and population retention policies. It concerns the current escalation of property disputes between members of the same family. The restoration of pre-Communist landholdings to their hereditary owners was achieved successfully despite considerable initial friction. Today the boundaries are no longer in question thanks to the authority of the land commissions and the memories of older villagers. Division of family property, by contrast, is not controlled by village elders, but by the head of the family. The tripling of the population over the last fifty years has resulted in more heirs contending for less land. Inheritance is partible, only male heirs inherit. The canon stipulates that each son must receive an equal part of the father's land, regardless of economic situation or the number of children each may have. An old local saying says 'separation ruins a family'. Many families still live in joint households with several married sons now farming their reclaimed land together. The jointly held land provides for a common family budget. It also enables at least one family member to be released periodically to earn, usually in Greece. Difficulties arise where sons were older at the time of land distribution and already living in independent households. In such cases disputes over division of family land have been frequent and often violent. A son with numerous children may feel bitter that his landholding is no larger than that of a brother with only two children. A brother whose property is further away from a water source, or whose property is cut through by a road, may feel that he has got an unfair deal. Often there has been injustice. The frequency of press reports of murders and violent assaults between heirs and their families in Mirdita and the coastal plain area of Lezhe, (a part of Mirdita until the Communist government altered the boundaries), is striking. That the reports do not exaggerate was continually confirmed by my own direct experience of disputes during fieldwork, of which the following is an example.

This quarrel occurred in Fang, a riverside village in the foothills of Mirdita, an hour and a half's bus ride from Tirana. At the time of decollectivisation two brothers, in their sixties, each took a half (0.4 hectares) of the patrimonial land. The younger brother has two unmarried sons. The older brother has three sons, two unmarried in their mid-thirties, and five daughters (three of whom are married, one widowed). All three sons are employed outside agriculture, though two of them regularly help on the holding. Two work in Rubik, five kilometres away, in jobs connected with the copper refinery. The third son is an army officer. In May 1993, the younger brother's two sons, having ascertained that their cousins were out, entered their uncle's house and beat their uncle and aunt senseless, leaving them for dead. After a six week hospital stay the elderly couple recovered and returned home. One of their nephews has never been caught by the police, the other is in prison. The latter's defence was as follows: neither my brother nor I have jobs outside agriculture; my cousins all have non-agricultural incomes – what kind of justice allows their family to have the same amount of land as we have?

Conclusion

The causes of disputes are land and water shortage, and decreasing employment outside agriculture. The increase in poverty in the 1990s recalls the situation in the 1930s when Hasluck observed that boundary disputes were endless, not because there was usually real doubt as to the exact position of the boundaries, but as a result of land hunger (1954: 98). Commenting on dispute settlement, Hasluck wrote:

> Settlement in private disputes might be effected by the parties themselves, by elders or by the government. The first method was the quickest, the second tried when the first failed, and the third when the second failed. In practice recourse to the authorities was rare and seldom as effective as action by elders.

The situation today is less straightforward. Since Hasluck wrote, more roads have been built (in the 1970s) making much of Mirdita accessible by wheeled vehicles and bringing government centres closer. At the same time, as noted earlier, central government functions patchily. This places the burden of dispute settlement on the council of elders and their ability to enforce the Canon of Lek. The problem is not the lack of legal framework or precedent for settling disputes, but rather the coexistence of state law and local law where state mechanisms have gained to some degree in authority and proximity, while the canon, following half a century of Communist opprobrium and disuse, has lost some of its authority. Differential access to rewards and benefits under Communism had already led in many villages to political divisiveness before democratisation and overt economic crisis. Loss of community cohesion and autonomy have weakened the force of moral sanctions and public opinion on which ultimately the elders' authority rests. Quite often neither the state law nor the canon are enforced, and falling between these stools can be very convenient for law breakers.

Furthermore, current unemployment, land scarcity, and insecurity are not improving social relations. An incident in the district of Fan illustrates the implications such conditions may have for the future. A man stole his neighbour's cow but denied the theft at a village council where he took an oath following customary law, swearing his innocence. His neighbour then killed both the thief and the thief's son. The murderer is now in prison while his family has fled to the plain for fear of retribution. It has emerged that in the 1940s the two families were in blood-feud. Deteriorating social relations and the end to a police state are leading to a revival of old grievances and ensuing feud.

With very high unemployment, overpopulation, water and land shortage, minimal social welfare, and no official emigration or outmigration policies, the situation looks set for a return to total scarcity. The question today is are we going to see anarchy predominate, or will there be a full scale return to feud?

REFERENCES

Almanak Mirdita. Tirana, 1968, 1969, 1975.

Aslund, A. and Sjoberg, O. 'Privatisation and Transition to a Market Economy in Albania', *Communist Economies and Economic Transformation*, Vol. 4, No. 1, (1992): 135-50.

Black-Michaud, J. *Cohesive Force.* Oxford, 1975.

Durham, E. *High Albania.* London, 1909.

_____, *Some Tribal Origins, Laws and Customs of the Balkans.* London. 1928

Economic Intelligence Unit *Albania (Country Report)*, 2nd Quarter, 1993.

Clarissa de Waal

Griffin, K. 'On the Emigration of the Peasantry', *World Development*, Vol. 4, No. 5, (1976): 353-361.

Hasluck, M. *The Unwritten Law in Albania*. Cambridge, 1954.

Jelavich, B. *History of the Balkans*, Vol. 1, Cambridge, 1983.

Sandström, P. and Sjoberg, O. 'Albanian Economic Performance: Stagnation in the 1980s', *Soviet Studies*, Vol. 43, No. 5. (1991): 931-947.

Schnytzer, A. 'Albania: the Purge of Stalinist Economic Ideology', in *Industrial Reform in Socialist Countries*, ed. I. Jeffries, Aldershot, 1992.

Sjoberg, O. 'The Agrarian Sector in Albania during the 1980s' in *Studies in International Economics and Geography*. Research Report No. 4, Stockholm, 1989.

_____, *Rural Change and Development in Albania*. Boulder, 1991.

Tusha N. 'Afirmimi i normave dhe zakoneve te reja ne jeten familjare e shoqerore behet ne lufte kunder koncepteve e zakoneve prapanike' in *Almanak Mirdita*, Tirana, 1975.

Vjetari Statistikor. Tirana, 1990.

Wyzan M. and Sjoberg O. 'Agricultural Privatization in Bulgaria and Albania', *Working Paper No.61*, Stockholm Institute of East European Economics, Stockholm, 1992.

8. GETTING LAND IN CENTRAL EUROPE

Nigel Swain

Introduction

*I*n this paper I shall consider ways in which people are gaining, or regaining, property rights over land in the four countries of Central Europe in which I am currently working – the Czech Republic, Hungary, Poland and Slovakia.[1] I shall first introduce some analytical distinctions and then present a case study from each country. My knowledge and experience of Hungary is greater than the other countries and this is reflected in the more extensive consideration of the Hungarian case.

1. Research for this chapter has been conducted through projects funded by the Economic and Social Research Council under its East-West Programme and the European Commission under its COST programme. These are respectively 'Transitions to Family Farming in post-Socialist Central Europe' (Y309253037) and 'Rural Employment and Rural Regeneration on post-Socialist Central Europe (CIPA-CT93-3022). The author gratefully acknowledges the assistance of all collaborators on these projects, and especially Beba Bodnarova, Michal Lostak, Cyrila Markova, Wanda Wrobel and Grzegorz Zablocki who interpreted. Thanks are also due to Yohanan Stryjan who gave me the benefit of his expertise on Czech and Slovak cooperative transformation and, of course, to Pisti and his family for putting up with me.

'Getting land' in Central Europe is a complex process, and under-standing it is not helped by the fact that both observers and participants tend to use words imprecisely and assume a degree of familiarity with the context which it is difficult for outsiders to share. Analytically two processes can be seen to be at work. On the one hand there is *restitution* in respect of unacceptable (illegal or legal but unfair and retrospectively deemed unconstitutional) expropriations in the past. On the other there is the creation of an acceptable new basis for the ownership of agricul-tural assets formerly held in common by agricultural cooperatives – the *transformation* process. Procedures for the restitution of land are gener-ally the same as restitution of other forms of property and covered by the same legislation. Similarly, procedures for privatising state farms are not dissimilar from those for privatisating state owned property generally. But complications arise in the cooperative sector, for collective farms were cooperatives. Their assets were neither state owned nor (wholly) privately owned and, as a consequence, neither privatisation nor restitu-tion legislation are entirely appropriate. In the cooperative sector, the issue is not so much one of selling to new owners as creating 'genuine owners' out of purely nominal ones.

The concrete forms taken by the restitution and transformation processes in the agricultural sector in Central Europe are not identical and have been influenced by two factors. The first of these is a funda-mental policy decision of the new post-socialist governments concern-ing the nature of restitution: should it be partial or full, direct (that is to say returning, wherever possible, the actual property lost) or indirect (offering some sort of monetary instrument as compensation)? Most of Eastern Europe opted for full and direct compensation. In the former Czechoslovakia this was unambiguous. In Poland, where restitution was not considered a major issue, final legislation had not been passed by parliament by the spring of 1995, but the general principle seemed to be full and direct compensation, with the proviso that no private farmer who benefited from land nationalisations in the post-war restructuring and resettlements would lose land. In such cases, restitu-tion would be indirect.

Hungary's politicians, on the other hand, opted for partial and indirect compensation. All restitution claims are scaled down and then converted into vouchers which can be used in a number of ways – to buy agricul-tural land, to buy a flat owned by local authorities, to obtain a pension supplement, to participate in the 'pre-privatisation' of shops and restau-rants, to buy shares in the privatisation of certain state companies, to participate in 'decentralised privatisation', to use as security for certain government credits, to purchase shares in Employee Share Ownership Programmes, and to invest in certain state investment funds. The first three uses for the vouchers are restricted to individuals personally entitled to restitution. Anyone who obtains vouchers, by whatever means, such as purchase on the secondary market, can use them for the other six purposes. Those eligible for vouchers are able to use them to purchase formerly cooperative or state land at auction, irrespective of the basis on which eligibility for the restitution voucher was granted, be it loss of property or loss of liberty as the victim of political trials or incarceration as a prisoner of war. Moreover, they are eligible to exercise their right in a number of places – where the confiscated land was located, where claimants now live, or where they were cooperative members on 1 January 1992. In addition, because cooperative farms had land in many villages, the right is not simply limited to the village where the claimant lived, had his land, and so on, but to land in any of the villages where land is farmed by the cooperative that also farms land where the claimants lived, had their confiscated land located, or were a cooperative member. In Hungarian restitution, then, cooperative farms do not return directly plots that former owners actually lost, but hand over for auction consolidated 'land funds' of land of equivalent quality to that specified in restitution claims in each of the villages in which the farm operated, under the supervision of a publicly appointed land administration committee.

The second factor influencing the restitution and transformation processes was not something the post-socialist governments could influence, because it was part of their socialist inheritance: the pattern of ownership of cooperative assets. The creation of 'genuine owners' for cooperatively farmed assets requires two things. First, property-related rights, such as rights of disposal, should be returned in respect of property that had always been privately owned on paper. Second, shares in communal cooperative assets should be allocated to all cooperative members. It follows from this that a distinction has to be made between situations where the land and property brought into the cooperative upon its formation legally remained the private property of those who contributed them and situations where the cooperative itself gained legal title to those assets (in addition to its common ownership of new assets). Here again the Hungarian experience differs from most of the other countries in Eastern Europe. In the former Czechoslovakia, and in the small cooperative sector in Poland, those who contributed property to a cooperative farm always retained legal title to that property. Administrative restrictions meant that they could not in fact withdraw it from the cooperative (or, in the Polish case, could only withdraw it with difficulty) and, in the Czechoslovak case, they received no rent for it; yet legal title remained. In the legalistic climate of Hungary at the time of its New Economic Mechanism on the other hand, collective farms rejected administrative solutions and were encouraged to buy up their members' land, albeit at excessively depressed prices. By the end of the 1980s only roughly a third of cooperatively farmed land in Hungary was privately owned. Since these sales were considered to have been made under duress, they were included amongst the historical injustices covered by restitution legislation.[2]

Some consequences of these different approaches to restitution and contexts for transformation as they affect the mechanisms for 'getting land' in Hungary and the more typical former Czechoslovakia should be spelled out. In the Czech Republic and Slovakia restitution legislation as such, in relation to cooperatively farmed land, only comes into play in political cases where peasants had been branded a *kulak* and their land actually seized. For the majority, land and associated property had always been theirs and getting the land returned is, in theory, merely a matter of asserting the reality of existing paper rights. In Hungary, only a third of cooperatively farmed land can be returned in this way, and those who sold to the cooperative can only get back land (not the same land) by pursuing a restitution claim.

The fact that title to land remained with the cooperative member in Czechoslovakia also had an impact on the cooperative transformation legislation. In the Czechoslovak case, the process of allocating assets to new owners did not include land, because land already had its (former) private owners. As a consequence, those who had joined landless, as many had over the course of their thirty-year history, remained landless. In Hungary, however, because land was part of the communal property, it was included in the division of the spoils. Under Hungary's cooperative transformation legislation all members, including those who had contributed no land to the farm, received a 'proportionate share' of cooperative land.

Four Case Studies

In the four case studies that follow we shall see how these different contexts influenced the process of getting back land in Central Europe.

2. For more detail see Swain (1994), Fiser (1994), Tomczak (1994), G. Blaas *et al.* (1994), and Stryjan (1992).

Poland

Poland, as is generally known, abandoned mass collectivisation after 1956 and hence restitution and cooperative transformation are relatively minor, although not uncontentious, issues there. But the fate of state farms and their land is not. The socialist sector in Poland was represented by the state sector, roughly a quarter of all agriculture, farming nationally owned land, much of it confiscated from German landowners at the end of the Second World War. As the bulk of Polish agricultural land is already in private hands, 'getting land' in Poland is more a question of getting additional land than regaining land that had been lost, and, because the larger share of socialist land was owned by an anonymous state, the state farm is an obvious source of additional land. In Jurek's case, getting additional land was a question of getting some land since he was a landless state employee.

Jurek is a young man, in his late thirties, who comes from a family which claims 'nobility' in the distant past but which, at the end of the Second World War, had only a small farm in the village in the remote far east of Poland where he still lives. With the advent of socialism, his father joined the state farm and was given a job as a foreman. His mother worked as a dressmaker. Jurek graduated from an economics 'high school' (a college of higher vocational education) and went to work on the local state farm, progressing up its ranks to become a deputy director. Before the fall of the Berlin Wall and the 'change of system', neither he nor his wife had a background in family farming. She was a nurse and he was an administrator, despite working on a farm.

This was to change for two reasons. First, as a politically untainted deputy director, Jurek was given the job of privatising the state farm where he worked. Second, it became obvious that he would have to find a new job. By his calculations (figures borne out by the scale of subsequent redundancies) there was two-thirds overemployment on the state farm, and the scale of the farm's debts meant that break-up of the farm was inevitable. His chances of finding a job for which he was qualified would disappear with the farm, and his chances of finding work of any kind were very low given redundancies on this scale. His only possibility was to seize the moment and become a private farmer.

Privatising a Polish state farm is not easy. The standard procedure is for the old director to be replaced and new people, like Jurek, to be brought in. The new guard is then sent to Warsaw to attend a course explaining principles and practices before returning to put this knowledge to use and draw up plans for their own institutions. The centre dictates the principles, but the actual solutions are left up to the local responsible person, in this case Jurek, in consultation with the regional (*wojwodstwo*) agency. The privatisation plan is then sent to Warsaw for final approval. Jurek was pleased with the speed with which he accomplished his task. The whole process was completed within a year, from November 1992 to November 1993. The planning took about six months, and the sales a further six. There was no obligation on Jurek to break up the farm, of course. Privatisation could have taken the form of selling the farm as a 'going concern'. However, in this case, as with most state farms, it was deeply in debt and this could only be recouped by selling all machinery and animals. Luckily there were plenty of takers for the agricultural machinery. Polish farmers are hungry for tractors and machinery, especially the larger tractors that they were prevented from buying under socialism.

A particular problem with Polish state farms derives from the fact that for most of the socialist period they were under an obligation to buy land. They became the medium for the socialisation of land after collectivisation had failed. They inherited land for which there was no owner and, from the 1970s onwards, were obliged to take over the offerings of peasants who opted to swap their land for a state pension. A unique feature of agriculture in socialist Poland, then, was that the dispersal of holdings so typical of the private sector was true for the socialist (state and cooperative) sectors as well. In no sector was there the sort of consolidation of land holdings that accompanied collectivisation elsewhere. Even state farms, although they did farm consolidated parcels, were the owners of a patchwork of tiny plots. Jurek's problem was to split such a mixture into saleable units. His solution was to divide the 1,500 hectare farm three ways. Five large farms of 100-150 hectares were created out of consolidated land, located, where possible, adjacent to existing farm buildings; some 700 hectares were split into small plots of between one and fifteen hectares; and 200 hectares of forest was returned to the State Forestry Commission. In accordance with government regulation, the sale of state land of over 50 hectares was carried out at auctions which had to be advertised in advance in two national papers (a requirement similar to the Hungarian regulations for land auctions). For the sales of smaller plots, the approval of the regional (*wojwodstwo*) office and the local village headman (*soltys*) was all that was required.

Jurek decided that if he was to farm successfully he should go after one of the bigger units, but he realised that, on his own, he could neither afford one nor did he have the requisite knowledge. He therefore went into partnership with two slightly younger colleagues who had qualifications from agricultural mechanical schools. He is the 'brains' behind the organisation, supplying an understanding of economics and, more important, the contacts with banks and marketing companies he has made over his career in socialist agriculture; they supply the technical know-how and practical experience. Indeed, unlike his partners and their families, he and his wife do not even live in the village where the farm which they eventually bought is located. The day-to-day running of the farm is in the hands of the partners and their wives, aided by two full-time employees and some seasonal staff.

We must assume that the fact that Jurek was responsible for privatising the state farm played no role in his successful bid for one of its successor farms. Like any other new purchaser Jurek and his partners benefited from relatively generous conditions for the purchase of state farm machinery: a 20 percent down payment with repayment of the remainder over seven years. But the conditions for getting land are not at all advantageous. As restitution issues have not been resolved, state land cannot be bought outright. Rather, it must be held on a ten-year lease in the expectation that it will be bought at a later date when restitution issues are resolved. In addition, because restitution has not been resolved and the possibility of successful restitution by a private owner remains, the lease must contain a clause allowing for its abrupt curtailment. Indeed, in Jurek's case, a former owner is endeavouring to prevent the sale of the land. Jurek has therefore staked a lot of money, money he obtained by exploiting the opportunities (on the fringes of legality) offered by the newly opened eastern border, for land which he may never own and may very well be obliged to relinquish at very short notice. In reality this is unlikely. As in Hungary and the former Czechoslovakia, most of those with forty-year-old claims to land are part of the urban middle class and have little interest in farming. If the worst comes to the worst Jurek is likely to be able to rent the land from its former owner. But the continuing delays in finalising restitution legislation mean that he has gambled a great deal against considerable uncertainty.

There is a further restitution issue, or rather restitution-type issue. As already noted, restitution is likely to be resolved either directly or indirectly depending on whether the beneficiary of the post-war land reform was the state or a private peasant. But there were other injustices associated with the formation of state farms. In the 1950s enormous pressure was put on peasants to sell their land to state farms. The sale was always 'legal', but the price paid was derisory. It was legalised expropriation. Current legislation makes no attempt to redress this wrong. In his work, Jurek constantly encounters villagers who complain at having to buy back, at current market prices, land that was effectively (but of course not legally) confiscated from them four decades ago. Polish legislators appear to prefer to ignore this question, although *mutatis mutandis* this is the very wrong that Hungarian restitution legislation sets out to redress. The sale of land to Hungarian cooperative farms from 1967 onwards was never illegal but, in the minds of post-socialist legislators, the relevant legislation would have been ruled unconstitutional, had there been an independent constitutional court to rule against it. Polish legislators appear to have shied away from this level of refinement. The sales to state farms in the 1950s were legal and anyone wanting to get land from the former state sector has to pay the market price for it.

Czech Republic and Slovakia

In the former Czechoslovakia, as noted above, when peasants were persuaded to join cooperative farms they did not lose legal title to the land or property they contributed. With the 'velvet revolution', former owners did not need to demand the return of land, but simply the return of rights that normally accompany ownership. Restitution, as distinct from regaining full ownership rights in this way or reclaiming property as part of cooperative transformation, was only necessary in the case of *kulaks* whose land had been seized for political reasons. Either way, in the former Czechoslovakia the re-claiming of land and property is a more individualised process than in Hungary. Whether individuals attempt to re-establish ownership rights and take their land out of the cooperative or reclaim under restitution legislation property that was formerly theirs, they must do so in direct negotiation with the leadership of the collective farm that appropriated the property. It is a recipe for acrimony and obstructionism as cooperative farm leaders selectively interpret the regulations in their own interests. Cooperative farms are under severe economic pressures at the present. The last thing they want to be bothered with is giving away possibly strategic plots of land, buildings or machinery to those claiming restitution for the past. However, whereas a Hungarian cooperative president who tries to put only land of poor quality into the restitution land fund has to face the wrath of the land administration committee, often headed by local politicians from parties hostile to collective farming, his (for it is nearly always a he)

Czech equivalent confronts individual claimants, or their informal associations, in the context of a legal system that until the passing in early 1993 of the 'sanctions law' made no provision for sanctions against cooperatives which deliberately ignored the law. If the cooperative farm president is unhelpful, the claimant must personally complain to the Land Office (the local arm of the Ministry of Agriculture) or, as a final resort, to the courts. In Hungary, if legal redress is necessary, the dispute is between publicly constituted institutions, the land administration committee and the agricultural cooperative.

Problems of acrimony and obstructionism were encountered by Jiri and his family. Jiri married into a family that had farmed 30 hectares in south-western Bohemia between the wars. It had been branded *kulak* in 1953 and prosecuted and found guilty of 'threatening the economic plan'. For this 'crime' both husband and wife were deprived of their civic rights for three years, the husband was also imprisoned for eighteen months, the wife for eight. They were further forbidden from ever visiting the district again. The husband never did go back to the village, although, following the Prague Spring, permission was given for him to be buried in the local cemetery. This family was not alone. The four richest farmers in the village were all expelled and their houses were occupied by the cooperative farm leadership. A possible explanation for this harsh treatment (much harsher than in surrounding villages) was the fact that the district secretary of the Communist Party lived in the village and felt that it would not look good for him if there were seen to be *kulaks* in his village.

Getting this former *kulak* land back was not easy. Jiri, formerly a deputy theatre director, and his wife, a nuclear engineer and granddaughter of the *kulak* couple, decided to become farmers and set in motion restitution proceedings. But as the old couple's daughter complains, 'It took an hour to evict us in the 1950s, it is taking years to get the land back.' The story is complicated because it also depends on the outcome of the restitution claims of another former *kulak* family from whom Jiri plans to rent land. For Jiri knows that times have changed and that 30 hectares no longer makes one a wealthy farmer. He plans long term to increase the farm to 250 hectares, and even then does not see the venture as being viable unless they secure additional income by running a shop and taking in paying guests in the tourist season.

As a consequence of their restitution claim they received, intact but in a very run-down condition, a courtyard surrounded by farm buildings, and a house. Because the original farm house owned by Jiri's wife's family had been knocked down by the cooperative, they received in its place a former school building, part of which they have converted into a general store. But this was the extent of the cooperative's generosity. Its opening gambit in respect of the land was that it would be returned, but only on the condition that Jiri and his family agree to rent it back to the cooperative. Jiri and his family had to complain to the Land Office. The cooperative then accepted that it would have to return the land, but only agreed to give back two thirds of it on the pretext that one of the sisters involved in the claim had not filled in her form correctly. The family had to apply to the regional court. A piquancy was added to the legal procedures by the rumour that the lawyer acting for the cooperative was the very man responsible for sending the old couple to prison in the 1950s. The cooperative was still reluctant to return one field conveniently situated immediately behind the courtyard that they had already received, although it eventually relented. A scruffy, semi-circular piece of tarmac – a road to nowhere – had been built on the land. The cooperative claimed that this constituted 'improvement', for which alternative land would be offered because only 'unimproved' land could be returned under restitution. The cooperative was no more generous in its return of machinery. It returned a tractor which it valued at roughly £1,500. It is at least twenty years old and needs to be filled with water every time it is used. As noted, Jiri's plan only made sense if he could rent land from another neighbouring former *kulak* family. But the cooperative tried the same tactics with them. It first said that they could have their land back, but only if it was rented back to the cooperative. It then argued that the original land could not be returned because it too had been 'improved'. The farm's petrol pumps had been located on it, which had caused environmental devastation which cost £50,000 to clear up. This dispute too had to go to court, which found for the claimants.

The delays and procrastinations on the part of cooperative farm management experienced by Jiri and similarly placed individuals led them to organise. They – the 'radicals', descendants of former *kulaks* – began to mobilise all claimants and, gradually, but not without hostility from some other private farmers, they took over the leadership of the private farmers in such bodies as the newly created Chamber of Agriculture, a body which had initially been dominated by representatives from the cooperative farms. The 'radicals' even took on the Land Office which they suspected too of dragging its feet and being soft on the cooperative farms. As a result of the radicals' pressure on the Land Office, Jiri himself was made its director. With his appointment its role has changed. It is now committed to facilitating and accelerating restitution and supporting the development of private farming.

Hassling with collective farm management and local agencies as Jiri had to was too much for Stanislav, as indeed it was for most citizens of both the Czech and Slovak Republics. Stanislav too had come from a *kulak* family, although in the poor area of eastern Slovakia where he lives, *kulak* meant that the family had farmed six hectares of land against a norm of between two and five. But six hectares was enough for the opprobrium of the Communist authorities and Stanislav was a déclassé for the rest of his life, although his land was not confiscated. One of socialist Slovakia's achievements (positive in terms of job creation within a centrally planned economy, negative in terms of the environment and employment prospects within a market economy) was the industrialisation of the countryside. Industrial plants are scattered all over the Slovakian countryside, especially its mountainous and agriculturally marginal regions. One such chemical works (now owned by a French company) opened just down the valley from the village where Stanislav lives, and most of his working life was spent in this factory. Condemned to manual employment, he passed the time teaching himself Romany so that he could communicate with the gypsies who made up the majority of his fellow workers. He is still a welcome guest in the squalid gypsy settlement located just outside his village. His wife, on the other hand, joined the agricultural cooperative and continued to work on it until she retired. She is a shareholder in the new post-socialist cooperative.

After the 'velvet revolution', when it became possible to reclaim his land from the cooperative, Stanislav had little use for six hectares. Both he and his wife were retired. One daughter was an academic living in Bratislava, the other a teacher in the regional centre. His son lives and works locally, but is busy using the expertise he had gained as a middle manager with a state-owned glass company to become one of the village's entrepreneurs and major employers. His small factory, located in a former kindergarten now returned to church ownership, currently employs thirty-five and he is intending to increase this to around one hundred. The family clearly saw no future in farming. Stanislav did reclaim land, but only 0.5 hectares of it. This small plot, just beyond the inner village boundary, provides potatoes and other vegetables for his and his wife's needs, and for those of the teacher daughter's family which spends most weekends in the parental village escaping the environmental pollution of the regional centre, and putting the finishing touches to the house they are building there.

It should be noted that it is pure chance that in our examples of two former *kulak* families in the former Czechoslovakia it is the Czech case which illustrates the desire to return to commercial farming, whilst in the Slovak case the family is satisfied with a small plot on which to grow vegetables. It might be tempting to think that the former is more typical of the more 'westernised' Czechs and the latter of the more 'nationalist socialist' Slovaks, but all the evidence I have available suggests that this would be wrong. The reality of agriculture in both countries is very similar, and the reality is that the desire to move into full-time commercial farming is as weak in the Czech Republic as it is in Slovakia or, indeed, in Hungary or Poland.

Hungary

The norm for getting land in Central Europe is that the land obtained is the land that had been lost, and the motivation for getting land is to farm it, although only rarely on a commercial basis. In Hungary the situation is different. Restitution is indirect, all who qualify for compensation vouchers can use them to buy land, and land is a good investment. All sorts of people are interested in getting land therefore, although few are interested in farming it. Pisti, a university teacher whose father's bakery was nationalised in 1952, certainly never envisaged himself tilling the soil of the plot that I helped him buy at an auction in the Spring of 1993.

The auction takes place in the local concert hall and is scheduled to last from eight in the morning to midnight, to be continued on the following Monday if all land is not sold. It is almost ten when we set off. But there was no need to hurry. When we arrive there is a melee of people surrounding some tables outside the hall, and another group poring intently over a map pinned rather precariously to the stage curtain. We spend the first quarter of an hour or so just taking it in. Some of the others present are clearly as much novices as we. But others have a very professional air, armed with the official gazette announcing which parcels of land are to be sold and maps identifying their location.

The first step is to register. After half an hour at the end of a queue which does not move, we join another one which does. The purpose of registration is two-fold. First, it acts as an additional check on eligibility. (The official has to confirm with his superior that Pisti is indeed able to bid even though his family had lost no land.) Second, more important, participants lodge the restitution vouchers that they intend to use in this particular auction (together with all the other documents pertaining to the claim and including a 20 percent caution non-returnable in cases of malfeasance) in a large white envelope. This is stored away in a temporary filing system made up of the sorts of coloured plastic baskets parents encourage their children to keep toys in. Participants can only bid to the value of the vouchers lodged in their envelopes, irrespective of whether they might have additional vouchers elsewhere. (This causes problems later on when a curmudgeonly old peasant bids with vouchers he has neglected to lodge in his envelope.) In return, bidders are given a small numbered yellow auction paddle. In the bidding process, it is paddles and not hands that shoot up in the air. For the remainder of the auction Pisti is paddle number 352.

The auction proper does not start until the bulk of those present have registered, which is almost midday. (Registration remains possible throughout the auction, although those who register after the bidding has begun deprive themselves of the possibility of bidding for the first plots which are, by common consent, the most attractive on offer). The auctioneer's first announcement is that not all the advertised land will actually be sold. For one thing, they have simply not had enough time to prepare the necessary documentation for all the land; for another, it turns out that some land has been wrongly described as arable when it is actually grassland. An expert from the land office then describes the parcel of land on offer in the first round of bidding. Maps have been available all morning and most interested parties have already studied them. Nevertheless the official stands up at the front of the stage before an audience of some six hundred people and diligently indicates with a pencil the plots concerned – on a faintly drawn map just over a metre square, visible to perhaps the middle section of the front two rows of the audience.

Pisti arrived with no firm intention to bid, indeed he was under 'orders' from his wife not to. But he has always had a hankering after land in the area where the first plots are on offer and becomes carried away by the atmosphere of the occasion. Before I know it, we are not merely observing the process as disinterested bystanders, we are bidding for land. To say that the bidding process is complex is an understatement. The starting point is the 'Gold Crown value'. The Gold Crown value is a measure of land quality introduced in 1875 under the Austro-Hungarian monarchy and still in use. All land in Hungary has a Gold Crown value per hectare (originally per cadastral yoke) which is periodically related to the real unit of currency, the forint. For the purpose of the restitution process, the forint equivalent of one Gold Crown value of land was set at one thousand forints, and entitlement to vouchers was calculated on this basis. The first thing to know about the land auctions is that bidding is not a question of how much people will pay for the land itself, but of how much they are prepared to pay for each Gold Crown value of the parcel of land up for sale.

When the auctioneer finally calls the meeting to order, his first question is: 'Has there been an agreement?' In order to speed up the restitution process the law makes provision for prospective bidders to come to a prior arrangement privately to buy all of a given parcel of land on offer at the official rate of one thousand forints per Gold Crown value. But the auctioneer's second question is: 'Is anyone against an agreement?' If anyone at all is against an agreement, then it is not valid and the auction must take place, even if, as happens in one round of bidding, the person who opposed the agreement does not subsequently bid for land. In the case of the first land on offer many people object to a prior agreement. The first plot is in a prime site and competition for it is high.

The principle behind the bidding is simple enough. The auctioneer starts at 3,000 forints per Gold Crown value and, if necessary, moves down in units of one hundred forints until there are takers. Bidding then goes up in hundred forint units until a price is found at which the land can be sold. If there are no takers when the auctioneer reaches 500 forints per Gold Crown value, the sale is abandoned. But the reality is much more complicated. The phrase 'until a price is found at which the land can be sold' is not as straightforward as it sounds, and it reveals the second peculiarity of Hungarian land auctions – that there are normally multiple winners.

In the case of the first parcel of land on auction there are immediate takers at three thousand forints. Hundreds of little yellow numbered paddles shoot into the air. The next surprise in the bidding procedure is that it does not continue until only one buyer remains. As the bidding goes higher and paddles drop away, the auctioneer fixes on 3,800 and calls, in the time-honoured fashion, 'going once at three thousand eight hundred, going twice, going three times'. No higher bid is made from the floor and the auctioneer sets about trying to sell the land at 3,800 forints per Gold Crown value – with well over fifty people still in the race. The process is laborious. First the auctioneer copies down the numbers of all the paddles still in the air. In theory no new paddles should be raised once the third call has been made, but a number slip up surreptitiously as their owners decide they can afford it after all. Once the paddle numbers have been copied down, the auctioneer reads them back in case any one has been left out. He then goes around the room asking the bidders in turn how much, in thousands of forints, they want to spend on the land. Figures of all types emerge, from the minimum one thousand forints (which would buy a few square yards) to over a million forints from a character who already has the air of a gentleman farmer and, it soon emerges, is bidding for as much of the land as he can get in order to establish a farm. (He uses the English rather than the Hungarian word.) Once all fifty or more bidders have called out their forint values, the mathematics begins. One of the auctioneer's assistants first adds together the sums bid; he then calculates how much money is necessary to buy the eighteen hectares on offer at 3,800 per Gold Crown value and compares the total amount bid with the sum necessary to buy some or all of the land at this price per Gold Crown value. Needless to say, with over fifty bidders, the land could have been sold many times over at this price. This attempt to sell the land has therefore failed, and bidding must begin again. In theory it should start again at three thousand forints, but all agree to rush quickly through to 3,900. The sum of 4,500 is also called three times, with the same result, although the number of bidders has fallen to around thirty.

Bidding restarts and goes up to 4,700 before stopping again. This time one of the bidders asks the auctioneer for a few minutes' break. The purpose of this is to call together all those still in the running to see if they can agree privately on how to split up the land between themselves. But agreement proves impossible. The gentleman farmer-to-be needs to have as much land as possible in a single unit, and he is willing to pay for it. At 5,100 forints per Gold Crown value, however, a purchase can be made. The actual amounts that individuals are willing to spend (which remain remarkably consistent through each round of the bidding) add up to less than the cost of the land at 5,100 forints price per Gold Crown value. There are fifteen buyers.

The next stage is to allocate plots. Here, in contrast to the fiasco with the map at the beginning, high technology is introduced to great effect. When the unfortunate agronomist was describing to the audience the area for sale, he had made a point of saying that plots would be numbered parallel with the road going north. The significance of this now becomes clear. First the order of allocation is determined. This is either done informally by those who remain in the bidding, or lots are drawn. In this case lots are drawn, from a hat, and assigned to paddle numbers. Then the personal computer comes into its own. It calculates how much land the paddle holder with the first lot drawn gets for the money s/he

wants to spend at the agreed price per Gold Crown value and maps it
onto its screen, moving north from the road. It then does the same for
the paddle holder who drew the second lot, measuring north from the
northern perimeter of the first person's plot. And so on.

There is, however, yet another complication. Before lots are drawn,
bidders can opt for their plots to go jointly into the hat so that they
come out with adjacent plots. (This makes sense for couples who have
separately gained restitution rights but wish to hold their land jointly.)
Furthermore, if, in the auctioneer's view, the plot that any individual
receives is so small as to be unviable (because it comes out as two metres
wide by one hundred metres long for example), he can insist that it too
be merged with another person's plot. The rapid computer allocation of
plots reveals that a substantial 'remainder' area of the original parcel is
left unsold at 5,100 forints per Gold Crown value. It is given a new
number and the whole process begins again; and it is repeated again, and
again, until the whole parcel is sold. As the 'remainder' gets smaller, the
auctioneer is keener to exercise his discretion and insist that only viable
plots emerge. Multiple winners means remainder areas and multiple
sales of land from each parcel on offer.

It is at the 'remainder' stage of the second half of the first parcel of
land up for sale that Pisti is finally carried away. In the first stage, bidding
went up incredibly quickly to a figure over six thousand forints and, as
a result, the unsold 'remainder area' is quite large. The first number to be
called three times in its sale is only 3,500, with some ninety people still
in the bidding. It seems clear from the outset that it will be fruitless even
to begin the calculations to see if the land can be sold at this price; but
the auctioneer sticks to the rules. Ninety numbers are read out; ninety
paddle holders call out the amount of money they are willing to spend;
the calculation is made; and the parcel is bought many times over. The
process begins again; 4,100 is called three times, and an attempt is made
to sell the land to some fifty bidders who remain. This too fails. But
when 4,800 is called three times, there is a call for a break to see if an
agreement can be reached between the fourteen, including Pisti, who
remain in the bidding.

We troop out of the hall and take up position in the corridor outside.
Somebody better informed than Pisti takes control. He essentially per-
forms the auctioneer's task for him. We collectively have to lower the
amounts we want to spend by a few hundred thousand forints in order
to jig the figures so that we end up buying all the land between us at
4,800 forints per Gold Crown value. The question is: 'Who is willing to

reduce their offer'. The bidders fall into two groups: prospective farmers and others. The prospective farmers are two men in their early middle age who act in tandem and each control two paddles apiece. They want to spend 300,000 forints per paddle – over a million forints in all. The remainder, except for one man who wants to spend 100,000, only want to spend token amounts of 20-30,000 forints. The smaller prospective purchasers expect the bigger ones to come down further because proportionately it is less of a sacrifice. The big purchasers are reluctant to give way too much because they need sizeable plots for farming. In the end, everyone gives way a little, with the exception of Mr Awkward who insists that 30,000 forints is his absolute minimum. Pisti goes down from thirty to twenty thousand. Then we realise we have got our the sums wrong. There is still a 14,000 forint overbid. 'We'll all make a further thousand forint reduction.' But Mr Awkward sticks to his 30,000. Pisti's neighbour in the auction room, a middle-aged woman who is as much a novice as we are, volunteers to go down by two thousand forints and agreement is reached.

We move back into the hall. The auctioneer asks us how much we want to spend and we read out the figures we have agreed on. But something is wrong. It is still too much. With tension mounting, and the rest of the audience increasingly impatient because our 'few minutes' break' has lasted at least half an hour, it emerges that the auctioneer has misheard a figure. The land is sold after all. But Pisti has not got very much. After a moment of euphoria when the computer operator makes a mistake in his calculations and declares that his plot might be 18 metres wide, it turns out that all bids in the 20,000 forint bracket must be merged in order to make viable plots. Some bidders have friends or neighbours with whom to form a single indissoluble plot. Pisti has noone – except his middle-aged neighbour, whom he does not know from Adam. But there is no choice. They become joint owners of a 0.4 hectares of land (0.2 hectares each). There is no need to draw lots for the plots. Those who have strong views come to an agreement, and the others, like Pisti, do not care precisely where on the parcel of land their tenths of hectares are located.

We have done it! Pisti has become a landowner, although he does not have a very clear idea what he is going to do with it. By now it is four o'clock and we were expected for lunch. A quick phone call home reveals that perhaps we had better call it a day, for now at least. We join a queue to register our purchase and reclaim the unused vouchers from the white envelope. By the time we reach the front of the queue, the envelope contains most of the necessary documentation concerning the sale. All that is necessary is a signature. At some future date Pisti will be informed formally by the Land Office that the land is his. One thing is missing, however: the map identifying his plot. This will be ready at about ten 'o clock in the evening.

We lunch and then drive out to see the newly acquired land. We still do not know exactly where on the parcel our plot is, but Pisti has lived in the area all his life and knows pretty much where it must be. It is just a ploughed field, sown with barley. But he seems genuinely pleased that it is his.

Coming back to the auction at about nine o'clock in the evening to collect the map (a clever computer-produced affair of the whole parcel with a criss-cross pattern shading in Pisti's plot), it is rather a different scene. The packed auditorium has dwindled to a few dozen people. Admittedly the land now on offer is not so attractive as earlier, but the prices are correspondingly lower. Prior agreements are common, and if an auction is necessary, bidding rarely goes beyond the three thousand band. On one occasion the auctioneer uses his authority to force an auction when the bidders had hoped to come to an agreement. After watching thirty people squabble for over half an hour about how the land might be distributed, he states the obvious: 'You are unable to come to an agreement, let's have an auction.' Only half a dozen of the original thirty remain in the bidding at the end. Needless to say, all the land cannot be auctioned before midnight, and we leave as arrangements are being made to continue on the Monday.

I return to Pisti's home some months later and things have changed. First, most surprising, his wife, who disapproved of the whole process earlier, now encourages Pisti in his claims. Indeed, a second plot has already been purchased in my absence, and neighbours are acting on his behalf in an auction at which Pisti is hoping to buy a third plot as I visit. The reason for this change of attitude is not hard to understand. The restitution process might be economically irrational and morally unjustifiable, benefiting the victims of one historical injustice at the expense of the victims of another, but it is happening; and land is a good investment. Moral rectitude is one thing, bringing up three children on declining incomes is another. Why should they miss out if the accidents of history have given them a windfall?

Second, there is an increased reliance on proxy bids. Pisti's neighbours, for example, now regularly act on his behalf. They have more time than Pisti, now that the husband is unemployed, and they have

become regular faces at the local auctions. Because land can be claimed
in so many places, and because in general three auctions are scheduled
per village, there are plenty of auctions to chose from. But it is not just
friends who help their neighbours out. Some lawyers have spotted a
business opportunity and, for a fee, will represent clients at auctions.
Lawyers attending every auction with scores of paddles in their hands
have become figures of hate for the other (often equally regular) participants. The basis for this antipathy is not so much that they are profit-
ing excessively from the fees that they charge for attending the auction
as the suspicion that some of the paddles that they wave so conspicu-
ously are their own which they have bought cheaply for speculative
purposes from unsuspecting elderly villagers who do not realise the
value of their vouchers.

The third and most interesting change concerns the auction process
itself. The procedures for selling land by agreement rather than auction
have become more sophisticated. In many parts of Hungary sale by
agreement, or sale by a 'rigged' auction so that the price can be pushed
down to 500 forints per Gold Crown (rather than the fixed 1,000 forints
for agreements) has always been the norm because there is so little interest in obtaining land. Indeed, in areas where interest in land is slight, *de
facto* direct restitution is possible. It is not uncommon for there to be an
informal agreement between bidders that plots that once belonged to
elderly villagers who want to regain their patrimony should be uncon-
tested. But Pisti lives near Lake Balaton where the interest in land is
intense. Whilst the attendance at inland auctions might be sixty to seventy people, and in regional centres perhaps one hundred, when the
land for sale is near Lake Balaton 700-1,000 people attend (in spa towns
like Balatonfured 2,000 are likely), and the majority of those in attendance are outsiders. Pisti's neighbours estimate that when prime plots
near Lake Balaton are up for sale the outsiders outnumber the locals,
those who actually live in the village where the land is located, by six or
seven to one. What is more, because the vast majority of the peasants in
the region were poor in the past, the majority of the locals have at their
disposal vouchers equivalent to only a rather small sum of money.

In this situation community pressures have emerged to further the
interests of the locals by making use of the opportunities for sale by
agreement inherent in the auction regulations. In Pisti's region too, sale
by agreement has become the norm, and the main beneficiaries are the
locals. Procedures here are less formal than in other areas where local
mayors arrange 'agreement meetings' prior to the auction and even

211

advertise them in local papers, but they are no less effective. The order of events is as follows. Prior to the auction somebody – a local figure, the chairman of the land administration committee, the mayor, even the chairman of the local cooperative – agrees with the villagers that they will insist on locals receiving a percentage (usually in the range 50-60 percent) of the land that is up for auction. As soon as the auction is formally opened the locals' representative addresses the audience and tells them that the locals will be claiming this agreed share of the land. This statement is simply accepted by all present, and the participants turn to reaching agreement on the sale of the rest. Spokespersons from among the outsiders, usually members of the select group of people who attend almost every auction and know each other well (for the process has been going on for a year), announce that they will take on the job of trying to reach an agreement for all those interested in a particular plot. Lists of interested parties are drawn up and a bartering process ensues. It is in the interest of outsiders too, to come to an agreement if they want to get any land at all. Even at 1,000 forints per Gold Crown most claimants will have to share part of an indissoluble plot. If the sale goes to auction, not only would the small local claimants soon be outbid, so too would many of the outsiders.

This whole procedure is informal. The legislation makes it possible, but it did not anticipate it and does not regulate it. There are no sanctions. Anyone present could insist that the sale be by auction proper and the auctioneer would be obliged to commence the bidding. But people adhere to the popular will. Perhaps there is a tacit admission of bad faith by the outsiders, a recognition that their claim is weaker than that of the people who actually live in a village and make use of the land, that there is something immoral about indulging in land speculation; or perhaps it is a common recognition of the rights of everyone to a little piece of the pie, however small. Whatever its basis, moral pressure suffices. There was one case locally of the forcible ejection from the auction of someone who did not abide by the popular will, but it was not repeated. Moral pressure, perhaps with the underlying threat of violence and social ostracism in the background, is enough.

By the time Pisti buys his third plot, this informal system is well in place. The 'auction', which his neighbour proxies attend on his behalf, lasts a whole weekend (until midnight on both days). But there is no bidding. Much of the first day is lost because of delays with registration, as at the previous auction. The remainder of the day is devoted to the process of reaching agreements. This is complicated because, once the locals' share has been set aside and account has been taken of the fact that far more people are interested in the plots in the area between the village and Lake Balaton than elsewhere, the reality of the auction is that two-thirds of the 700-800 people in attendance are interested in only a third of the land. Reaching agreements proceeds slowly and claimants are inevitably lumped together into indissoluble plots. Once again Pisti is obliged to buy land jointly with a complete stranger. The 'auction' proper only begins on the Sunday, although, of course, it is not an auction at all because there is no bidding. All sales go through 'by agreement', as thrashed out on the previous day. But because there is some swapping between and removal from lists, a consequence of the decision that the same paddle should not figure in more than one agreement, the smooth process of formally agreeing the previous day's work once more drags on until midnight.

Conclusions

This account has revealed a number of features of the restitution and transformation processes which are common to the four countries of Central Europe studied. First, the result of restitution or land return, in either Hungary, the former Czechoslovakia, or indeed Poland, is not the creation of a rational structure of land ownership for future commercial family farming. In Hungary, what emerges from restitution is not large, privately owned, economically viable holdings, but a myriad of small plots. Communal pressures for sale by agreement and the provisions within the land-auction procedures which permit multiple buyers at a given price for a given parcel of land promote equity rather than efficiency, in the classic formulation of the dilemmas of restitution and privatisation. As Pisti's first auction revealed, those who want to establish a viable farm must outbid the rest and pay over the odds. In the former Czechoslovakia and all countries where the emphasis is on return to the pre-socialist status quo, farms are of necessity undercapitalised and inviably small because they are forty years out of date. Jiri is well aware that he must add to the family patrimony if he is to survive. Stanislav is content with supplementary income only from his land and reduces his claim to meet this modest need. Again equity wins out over efficiency, but it is an equity of the past rather than the present. Even in Poland, as Jurek's case illustrates, where private ownership has been the norm, decisions to develop holdings of an economically viable size through the purchase of former state land face problems because of uncertain property rights.

Similarly, the procedure is time consuming and expensive in all countries. In Hungary the original deadline for completing land auctions was 31 March 1993. This was moved back to the end of December 1993, but auctions were still under way in spring 1995. In the Czech Republic, restitution is progressing no more rapidly. In November 1993 officials in Jiri's region reported that restitution was only a third complete, a proportion repeated elsewhere. In Poland, even the principles of restitution had not been passed by parliament by spring 1995. Restitution has also proved a bonanza for lawyers. In Poland and the former Czech Republic there are conflicting claims for the same land which only the courts can resolve. In Hungary courtroom battles are less common, but lawyers are benefiting indirectly by acting as proxies in land auctions. Claimants can save themselves the frustration of whole weekends lost in auction halls by paying lawyers to act as agents.

However, there are important ways in which the restitution and transformation processes differ. Owing to its adoption of partial and indirect restitution and its socialist inheritance of cooperatively owned land, the process of regaining land in Hungary is altogether more public. More people are affected, more people participate, and there is a greater involvement of publicly appointed bodies. The Hungarian process is also somewhat more orientated to the present and the future than the past. All restitution procedures are ultimately motivated by righting the wrongs of history, but the tone that has emerged from mass public participation in Hungary's auction halls, whether sale is by bidding or agreement, is one of 'everyone should get something' rather than 'I should get mine back'. And, unlike Poland, there is an explicit attempt to redress the 'legalised expropriation' of sales of land made under duress. Similarly, in Hungary's cooperative transformation, even the landless have gained some land which, in theory, they can use for some future venture of their own.

There are two very general lessons to be learned from these accounts, one concerning restitution, the other democracy. First, our four cases suggest that, in the end, there is not such a big difference between direct and indirect restitution. Hungarian partial and indirect restitution avoided the expense and uncertainties of private litigation but incurred massive public expense in establishing a network of auctions, and created no greater certainty concerning the ultimate pattern of land ownership; and the process became equally protracted. The delays and uncertainties had different causes, but their impact was very much the same. Second, Hungary's more public procedures have potentially profound political implications. Hungarian political scientists are greatly concerned about the growth of the politics of unreason in Eastern Europe and the political immaturity of its population.[3] The spontaneous manifestations of the popular will of Hungary's rural population, as revealed in the land auctions described above, seem to be the very opposite of unreason. Ordinary men and women are working together to develop reasonable, equitable and mutually acceptable solutions to very complex problems.

REFERENCES

Blaas, G. *et al.*, *The Economic, Legislative, Political and Social Policy Context of Slovak Agriculture.* Centre for Central and Eastern European Studies, Rural Transition Series Working Paper 23, Spring 1994.

Csepeli, G. and Orkeny, A., *Ideology and Political Beliefs in Hungary.* London, New York, 1992.

Fiser, Z., *The Legislative Framework for Agricultural Transition in the Czech Republic.* Centre for Central and Eastern European Studies, Rural Transition Series Working Paper 15, Spring 1994.

Stryjan, Y., 'Czechoslovak agriculture: institutional change and cooperative solutions', *Journal of Rural Cooperation*, Vol. XX, No. 2 (1992): 139-165.

Swain, N., *The Legislative Framework for Agricultural Transition in Hungary.* Centre for Central and Eastern European Studies, Rural Transition Series Working Paper 25, Winter 1994.

Tomczak, F., *The Legislative Framework for Agricultural Transition in Poland.* Centre for Central and Eastern European Studies, Rural Transition Series Working Paper 16, Spring 1994.

3. See for example Csepeli and Orkeny (1992).

CONTRIBUTORS

Ray Abrahams is a University Lecturer in Social Anthropology and a Fellow of Churchill College, Cambridge. He has carried out research in Tanzania and Uganda and more recently in Finland and Estonia. He has published several books and many articles based on these studies, and he has a special interest in relations between local communities and the state.

Chris Hann is Professor of Social Anthropology at the University of Kent, having previously taught for many years in Cambridge. He was one of the first Western anthropologists to carry out research in eastern Europe. He has published several books and many papers based on his research in rural Hungary and Poland, and on eastern European society and socialism more generally.

Deema Kaneff is a post-doctoral Research Associate in the Department of Social Anthropology, University of Cambridge. She has carried out extended fieldwork in rural Bulgaria in both the socialist and post-socialist periods. Her work has focused on the rewriting of history and the political uses of the past as part of the contemporary processes of transformation, and she has recently examined ethnic issues stemming from these processes.

Lucjan Kocik is Professor of Sociology at the Jagiellonian University in Krakow, Poland and is well known among western rural sociologists. He has conducted research on rural society in Poland and he has also studied Polish farmers in the United States. He has published several books and many articles based on these studies, and he was recently a visiting Professor of Sociology at Utica College in the University of Syracuse.

Katalin Kovács is trained in both Ethnography and Sociology and is currently a Research Sociologist with the Centre for Regional Studies of the Hungarian Academy of Sciences. She has a wide range of experience of research in rural Hungary and is well known internationally as an expert in this field. She has published a number of books and several articles based on this research.

Arvo Kuddo is currently at the World Bank, following a period of research at the W.I.D.E.R. Institute in Helsinki on 'The Social Determinants and Consequences of Transition in Central and Eastern Europe'. He has been Head of the Department of Social Policy and Demography in the Estonian Academy of Sciences, Estonian Minister of Labour and Social Affairs, and a Senior Specialist in the Bank of Estonia. He is the author of a book and many other publications.

Frances Pine is a Research Associate of the Department of Social Anthropology in Cambridge. She has conducted fieldwork in the Polish Carpathians and, as an Economic and Social Research Council Research Fellow, in industrialised central Poland. She has published many articles based on this work. She has a special interest in gender issues in eastern Europe.

Nigel Swain is Deputy Director of the Centre for Central and Eastern European Studies at the University of Liverpool. He has worked extensively on the social and economic history of Hungary during the socialist period, and he now heads an international team investigating rural transformations in central and eastern Europe. He has published a number of books and many papers on these issues.

Clarissa de Waal is a Research Associate of the Department of Social Anthropology, University of Cambridge. The subject of her doctoral dissertation was rural development and urban aspirations in southern Greece. More recently she has been carrying out research on social and economic changes in contemporary Albania with support from the Nuffield Foundation and the Wenner-Gren Foundation.

INDEX

Index

HD 1333. E3 AFT